William Gibson is Professor of Ecclesiastical History at Oxford Brookes University specialising in the history of Britain in the seventeenth and eighteenth centuries. He has written widely on the eighteenth-century Church. He is the author of *James II and the Trial of the Seven Bishops* (2009) and a biography of Bishop Benjamin Hoadly. He is also Director of the Oxford Centre for Methodism and Church History.

Highlights from the series

A BRIEF HISTORY OF

BRITAIN 1660–1851

WILLIAM GIBSON

ROBINSON

In memory of Eileen Gibson 1929–2010

Constable & Robinson Ltd
3 The Lanchesters
162 Fulham Palace Road
London W6 9ER
www.constablerobinson.com

First published in the UK by Robinson,
an imprint of Constable & Robinson Ltd, 2010

A copy of the British Library Cataloguing in Publication
data is available from the British Library

ISBN: 978-1-84529-715-2

Printed and bound in the EU

1 3 5 7 9 10 8 6 4 2

CONTENTS

ACKNOWLEDGEMENTS

I am grateful to the many people who have helped me while I was writing this book. Professor Jeremy Black has been characteristically generous and supportive, and I am very grateful to him for inviting me to contribute this volume to the series. Leo Hollis has combined the helpfulness and encouragement of an editor with the steady eye of a fellow early modern scholar. Graham and Amina Hughes, Mary Sweeney, Byron Young and Laura Cairns read and commented on this book to my great benefit. Each of them took considerable time and trouble to help improve it and I owe them a debt of gratitude. I alone am responsible for the errors and shortcomings it retains. I have included dates for some but not all of the individuals in this book; I have not done so for better-known figures, whose dates will be familiar, or for those who role is only incidental.

William Gibson
January 2010

INTRODUCTION

In 1839 the sixty-eight-year-old Reverend Sydney Smith marvelled at the changes he had seen during his lifetime. He thought of gas lighting, without which he had 'groped about the streets of London'; of railways, which saved him from the '10,000 contusions' he suffered in stage coaches; umbrellas and waterproof hats; braces, which enabled him 'to keep my small clothes in their proper place'; banks 'to receive the savings of the poor'; posts to whisk letters 'to the remotest corners of the empire' for a penny. He wrote: 'I am ashamed that I was not more discontented, and utterly surprised that all these changes and inventions did not occur two centuries ago.' Unimaginable products were available, such as whale oil for lamps, first extracted in 1748, and by Smith's day it had become a staple commodity, with a million gallons of oil exported to Europe from North America.

But Sydney Smith was only skimming the surface of the unprecedented changes that happened in Britain between 1660 and 1850. As a nation, Britain in this period underwent dramatic alterations. In 1660 Britain was still a geographical term for three separate kingdoms: England (united with Wales), Scotland and Ireland. During our period these kingdoms became a single United Kingdom. In 1660 Britain's global possessions were modest in comparison with the Dutch and Spanish empires. Within two hundred years Britain's empire was truly global and provided strategic interests in every corner of the world.

The monarchy changed radically. In 1660 kings were warriors who led their troops in battle; they chose their ministers and determined their policies. Charles II ruled as well as reigned. He appointed ministers at will, declared war and signed a treaty with France without his ministers' knowledge. Charles even maintained the fictional claim to be king of France. Much of his reign was preoccupied by who would succeed him. The reigns of Charles' brother and nieces were to be consumed by rumours of invasions, plots and revolts. By 1850 the sovereign's role was becoming largely ceremonial and in politics that of a constitutional monarch. Queen Victoria was obliged to choose her prime minister from the party with the majority in the House of Commons, and was expected to follow her prime minister's advice. In the Bedchamber Crisis of 1839–41, she was even forced to concede that the prime minister was responsible for appointing her household staff. Her uncle, William IV, had already conceded the primacy of the Commons over the Lords. He agreed that a prime minister with a majority in the Commons could insist on making enough peers to swamp opposing votes in the House of Lords.

The economy had also seen unimaginable changes. In 1660 Britain's economy was that of a pre-industrial society; there was no large-scale manufacturing. The national debt and effective taxation were yet to be devised. By 1850 not only had Britain become the first industrial nation, but manufactured goods marked 'Birmingham', 'Sheffield' or 'London' could be found on every continent. In consequence, Britain had developed an industrial working class, the professional and middle classes, and the structures of finance, transport, urbanization and education to support the industrial economy.

Social conditions in Britain were transformed in this period. In 1660 Britain was profoundly hierarchical, with the king, aristocrats and landowners ruling society. It was a society framed by the divine sanction of the Church and a society in which most people saw themselves as subjects not citizens. Social relations were governed by faith, deference and duty. By 1850 people lived under a Bill of Rights that guaranteed the rule of law, and increasing numbers had the right to vote. The government recognized that it had the duty to intervene to legislate in many areas of society, something that was unthinkable in 1660. Merit, rather than kinship or patronage, was becoming more important, and people had increasing expectations that talent and education counted for more than family relationship or a patron's influence in appointments to many jobs.

Britain in this period would appear and sound strange to someone from the twenty-first century. In reading this book you will have to step into a past that is different from modern Britain in many ways. For example, the English that people spoke in 1700 would sound very odd to us today and it was also spelled erratically. Lord Peterborough pronounced his title 'Peterbrow' and the Duke of Marlborough's title was often pronounced 'Marlborrow' and sometimes 'Marlbroo'. Alexander Pope rhymed 'tea' with 'obey'. Milton had rhymed 'end' with 'fiend' and 'sea' was often pronounced 'say'. The way Americans today pronounce clerk, Derby, Berkeley and leisure are the way they were said in England in the seventeenth and eighteenth centuries. The separation of the letter W from V was still underway in 1660, so some late seventeenth-century guides to London referred to 'VVestmynster'.

The lack of standard pronunciation led to the publication of a number of pronouncing dictionaries during the eighteenth century, the most popular of which was written by Thomas Spence. Spence addressed his *Grand Repository of the English*

Language (1775) to the working people of the country. He told people that 'strut' rhymed with 'foot' and 'put'. Some people pronounced 'lord' as 'laard'. 'Cucumber' and 'asparagus' were pronounced 'cowcumber' and 'sparrow grass'. In the mid-eighteenth century there were furious discussions between Lord Chesterfield and Sir William Yonge whether 'great' should be pronounced to rhyme with 'state' or 'seat'. Words such as 'hostile' and 'servile' would have been pronounced with a short 'ill' sound at the end. In fact, there were many differences in pronunciation, and eighteenth-century English would sound very peculiar, perhaps incomprehensible, to us. Even at the time, the differences were noted. Sheridan's *Course of Lectures on Elocution* of 1762 noted that cockney and 'court end' (West End) accents had created a linguistic divide in London.

Words are as fashion-prone as clothes, and many came and went in this period. We no longer use 'shrammed' (meaning cold) or 'gradely' (for thorough) or 'fettle' (meaning 'make' – though it remains in the phrase 'fine fettle'). Today we might use 'hew' (to quarry or dig), which was first recorded in 1708 (although of Old English origin), or 'clout' (which was brought to England by Irish navvies), and 'dunny' for a lavatory was exported to Australia from eighteenth-century England. By the end of this period, Liverpool was beginning to receive the large influx of Irish immigrants who gave the city's dialect its distinctive Liverpudlian twang.

The years 1660–1851, stretching from the Restoration of Charles II to the middle of the Victorian period, lend themselves to two big interpretations: those of the optimist and of the pessimist. The optimistic 'Whig' interpretation of this period would suggest that it was one of progress and advancement. Led by the development of the constitution from a divine right monarchy into a parliamentary monarchy, this optimistic account of the period would emphasize the development of the economy, the growth of towns, roads, canals and, in the nineteenth century, railways. It would also see the development of empire as a cause and reflection of material wealth and political liberty and would argue that this was the era of great scientific and cultural achievement, from Isaac Newton and Robert Boyle to Nicholas Hawksmoor and George Gilbert Scott, from Alexander Pope to the Brontës. It was also the time of the British Enlightenment.

In contrast, the pessimists would suggest it was a period in which people were locked out of government by an unrepresentative electoral system. People were treated appallingly by brutal aristocratic, legal and prison systems. Jacobites, Scots, Catholics, Irish, women and the poor were among the groups who could claim that they were oppressed by society. Most people's lives were marked by illness, grinding labour and a lack of pleasure, leisure and recreation. Personal liberty was limited by economic enslavement. Working conditions were grindingly hard and life expectancy declined in ghastly urban slums. Britain's empire and economic advance were built on the backs of slavery and misery. Cultural achievements rarely touched the lives of the poor, who, for the most part, were kept in pitiable conditions by the illusion of a regime which enjoyed some external sanction. Such is the pessimist viewpoint.

Neither of these perspectives is entirely correct; in most cases both are. In much of this book, differing views of the events and trends are presented, although I have tended to avoid the deep thickets of academic historical debates and controversies. You will need to make up your own mind about which views you agree with. But, whereas this book will not present a solely optimistic or pessimistic view of the past, it will present a wholly subjunctive or conditional view of the past: a view of the past that incorporates the contingent nature of the changes and developments that happened. Nothing was bound to happen; nothing was inevitable. Few of the events or processes in this book happened without some human action, which could have been directed in other ways. All of the people mentioned in this book could have made different choices and Britain could therefore have been different.

Dividing history into periods such as 1660–1850 assumes that no one lived from one age to the next – or that the weight of history did not bear on people as heavily as it had before. It is important to remember that, for men and women in 1660, the reign of Elizabeth I was only two generations earlier. We should also bear in mind that they had the same high hopes for the future as people today have.

Britain in 1660 had many similarities with Britain in 1603, when James I succeeded Queen Elizabeth I. In both cases expectations were high. A new king was entering his kingdom; in both cases religious issues were to the fore. And in both cases the throne was to pass to heirs who would not normally have succeeded and who lacked the subtlety and agility of their predecessors.

Britain in this period was very different from continental Europe. It was much smaller than, for example, France, so that many places were more accessible. It might take over a week to get to Scotland from London, but this was a third of the time it took to get from Paris to Marseilles. Even by the end of the eighteenth century, the majority of Britons had a much more acute sense and knowledge of the world beyond their own horizons, compared to French peasants – most of whom did not have any notion of the outside world.

The English language, despite its quirks, dialects and variations, was a unifying force in Britain in a way no other language was in Europe. In Cornwall the last Cornish-only speaker died in 1676 and the last to speak it bilingually in 1777. Welsh was alive and well and Gaelic still important in Ireland and the Highlands. But most speakers also spoke English. In contrast, in France, Abbé Grégoire's study on the eve of the Revolution showed that French was not a single national language. In some parts of France even small areas had their own unique dialect, which was unintelligible to outsiders. By 1790, such was the linguistic diversity of France that six million French men and women could not speak French and a further six million could only conduct a faltering conversation in it. In total about 40 per cent of the population did not know the national language well. In Britain, the English language was much stronger.

Unlike the British climate, the continental climate was so bad that in some countries people were almost completely hibernational. People stored food in the summer and confined themselves to dwellings, and sometimes caves, in the winter. They did not venture out into the potentially lethal cold. Even in the nineteenth century there were accounts of Burgundian peasant farmers spending the winters packed together in beds to conserve energy and warmth.

While Britain was different from other European countries, we should not slip into a jingoistic sort of history. Britain may have developed as the first industrial nation in this period, and expanded across the world into a global power. But this did not make Britain 'better' than other countries; in some ways it created contemporary problems, and stored up more for the future. It certainly meant that the lives of people in this period were subject to greater pressure, stresses, anxiety and misery in industrial and imperial processes.

In writing this book I have been struck by contemporary parallels, so I have not been shy about indicating these, although I have tried to avoid anachronism or contrived comparisons. I have also sought to balance the need to provide coverage of political events with chapters that consider economic, imperial, cultural and social issues. I hope I have also sufficiently enlivened the broad sweeps of events and trends with vignettes of the details of people's lives and attitudes. It is, after all, the stock in trade of the historian to employ a healthy interest in other people.

A book covering nearly two hundred years of complex and interwoven historical events needs a guide to how the ground will be covered. Chapter 1 surveys Britain in 1660. It was a time closer to the Middle Ages than it is to today. So, in many ways, Britain was a very different society and country from that of the twenty-first century. Most important, Britain was not a single nation. England and Wales, Scotland and Ireland each had their own governments and parliaments in London, Edinburgh and Dublin. Britain in 1660 was also recovering from the crisis of the execution of Charles I in 1649 and Oliver Cromwell's Commonwealth regime. So Chapter 1 focuses on how much Britain was changing and how much it remained much as it had been in the past.

Chapter 2 gives an account of the principal political events between 1660 and the Hanoverian succession in 1714. In 1660 Charles II returned to Britain after eleven years of exile. He was succeeded by his brother James II in 1685. But James' absolutist Catholic policies led to the Glorious Revolution of 1688, which saw James' Protestant nephew and daughter, William and Mary of Orange, force him from the throne. They became King William III and Queen Mary II, and were succeeded in 1702 by Mary's sister Anne. It was in Queen Anne's reign that England and Scotland united in 1707. Under both William and Mary and Anne Britain engaged in a series of wars with France that laid the foundations of its empire. Since Parliament would not permit another Catholic monarch, and Anne had no surviving children, she was succeeded by a distant cousin, George, the Elector of Hanover in Germany. The period was one of political instability and latent violence. It was only in this age that the unresolved constitutional problems of the earlier seventeenth century were finally settled.

Chapter 3 considers the 'Enlightenment' in Britain – the idea that the period 1660–1800 was one of progress and the advancement of knowledge. In science, economics, literature, religion, the role of women and other aspects of society, knowledge and reason replaced superstition and ignorance. Many of these ideas emerged slowly, over the late seventeenth and eighteenth centuries, so they were often imperceptible to people at the time. But viewed from some distance, this period was one in which reason and science played an increasingly important role in the way people thought.

Chapter 4 turns to Britain's connections with the outside world. These connections grew from trade and commerce, as well as from wars with other European countries. Britain also needed to protect and defend her colonies and trade routes, which involved it in overseas wars. Distant trading stations and emigrant agricultural communities evolved into colonies. In the space of less than a century Britain developed into a worldwide power. Britain's empire quickly eclipsed the overseas possessions of Holland, Spain and France. Even the loss of America in 1776 did not significantly inhibit the growth of empire. Britain's imperial exploits and conquests helped to form a national identity. They also made Britain rich. But they sometimes did so by shamefully exploiting slaves and at the expense of the poor.

Chapter 5 covers the main political events from George I's succession in 1714 to the end of the Napoleonic wars in 1815. It was a century in which the government of Britain went through periods of relative stability. This was particularly the case under strong political leaders, such as Robert Walpole and William Pitt. But there were also periods of instability. Politicians had to face problems familiar today: how to raise taxes and control government expenditure; how to respond to the demands of sectional interests, attacks from the media and overseas entanglements. They also had to face situations that are not recognizable today. These included the intervention of monarchs, whose political views had to be accommodated, the interests of a narrow electorate and threats to overthrow the ruling dynasty.

Chapter 6 surveys the way in which Britain's economy changed in this period. The economy saw astonishing and dramatic changes, certainly more than in any other period of British history. Farming, transport, manufacturing, finance, consumption, towns and the countryside were all unrecognizable by the end of our period. Productivity rocketed and Britain became the first nation to experience the process of industrialization. This had a dramatic effect on people's lives.

Chapter 7 considers the ways in which Britons between 1660 and 1851 challenged the established order in Church and State. They did this by supporting those who wanted to claim the throne for the son and grandsons of James II. They also did so by demanding the reform of Parliament and reforms to the religious laws of the country. Crime and the treatment of criminals show how people viewed authority. Sex too could often present a challenge to the established order, as did the fairly frequent outbreaks of riot and disorder. In local communities people could express their views of those who broke neighbourhood 'norms', and sometimes did so violently. Finally, this chapter also considers Romanticism, which challenged the established intellectual and political order.

Chapter 8 turns to the events of 1815–51. In this period, unlike most other European countries, Britain did not experience a revolution, but did experience serious unrest and social strains. These were dangerous enough to force a number of governments to change policy and concede reforms to religion and the constitution. Reform became a focus of governments in the 1830s and 1840s as voters and their concerns weighed more heavily with governments.

Chapter 9 takes stock of Britain in 1851 and considers why we think of the Victorian period as one of supreme confidence and self-assurance. That confidence can be seen in popular attitudes to the monarchy, religion, land, the economy, education, empire and foreign policy. The confidence and strength of Britain in 1851 can be illustrated by the Great Exhibition of 1851. In each of these areas, the mid-Victorian period might be viewed as one in which national pride, resilience and assurance was dominant.

I

BRITAIN IN 1660:
CONTINUITY OR CHANGE?

The King Returns to his Own

On the bright sunny morning of Friday 25 May 1660, the English fleet anchored off Dover. Among the ships was the flagship, *Royal Charles*. Its name had been hastily changed from *Naseby*, which commemorated the defeat of King Charles I in 1645. The ships carried an important cargo. On board were the new King, Charles II, and his brothers, the Dukes of York and Gloucester. They were returning from a dozen years in exile on the continent after their father's execution. Oliver Cromwell had died two years earlier and the Commonwealth he established had collapsed. The brothers lunched on boiled beef and peas, and then used the admiral's barge to land on Dover beach.

As soon as he reached English soil, Charles knelt and gave thanks for the restoration of his throne. From the beach he walked the short distance into Dover, where he was greeted by the mayor and corporation. He travelled on, via Canterbury, Rochester and Chatham, to London, his progress only impeded by the many people who wanted to greet him. Charles was overcome by the reception he received. From Canterbury, he wrote to his sister, Henrietta-Anne, on 26 May, 'my head is so prodigiously dazed by the acclamation and by the quantities of business that I know not whether I am writing sense or no'.

Four days after his arrival at Dover, on his birthday, the King entered London amid much pomp and ceremony. It took more than ten hours for the huge procession to travel the four miles through the city and on to Westminster. The army that led the pageant had been joined by city-trained bands of volunteers, local county militias and 1,600 pikemen. The pikemen had all served under the new King's father, Charles I, in the Civil War.

Eventually, at seven o'clock in the evening, the two houses of Parliament made an address to the King. He had been on the move for fourteen hours, and his exhaustion meant that a public service of thanksgiving was postponed, in favour of a short private service. After this the King retired. He joked that it was obvious that it was his own fault for staying away so long as everyone he met in England said they had long wished for his return.

The diarist John Evelyn (1620–1706), witnessed the procession, in providential mood. He recorded in his journal:

> I stood in the Strand and beheld it and blessed God: and all this without a drop of blood and by that very army which [had] rebell'd against him … it was the Lord's doing.

General George Monck (1608–70), who had commanded the army and engineered the Restoration, had the same thought. Monck was so overcome at the end of the evening that he burst into tears. He told his chaplain 'it was not I that did this … it was God alone who did it. To him be the glory.' Already, in Dublin, at Monck's request, Charles' supporters had seized the castle. There were celebrations in London for three more days; 29 May would be celebrated annually in the calendar of the

Church as Oak Apple Day – the oak being the symbol of Charles' salvation during the Civil War at Boscobel. For almost two centuries bells rang from many steeples on this anniversary.

A medallion was struck to celebrate the return of the King. It depicted the landing at Dover, with figures representing England, Ireland and Scotland greeting him. In Cambridge, two weeks later, the proclamation of the new King got completely out of hand. There were announcements in eleven places over three days, culminating in a proclamation from King's College, accompanied by the firing of a volley by a troop of soldiers.

For the moment it seemed as if everything had changed, but the joy was short-lived. The first official act of the King, on 30 May, was to issue a stern proclamation denouncing those who expressed their joy at the Restoration by spending their time in taverns and whose only evidence of loyalty to Charles was drinking his health. Mayors and magistrates were ordered to be vigilant and to punish dissolute and profane behaviour. A few days after his arrival, the King held an elaborate entertainment in the Mulberry Garden – on the site of what is today the garden of Buckingham Palace – some believed it violated his own proclamation. It was all a sharp contrast to the Puritan leadership of Cromwell.

The new King was declared to have succeeded his father on his execution in 1649 and therefore 1660 was regarded as the eleventh year of his reign. This gives rise to the main question that haunts the Restoration of Charles II in 1660. Did things change, or did they stay the same? Was it one of those real break points in British history, which justifies school and university syllabuses ending the Tudor and Stuart era in 1660, and starting the 'long eighteenth century' in 1660? Was it a true turning point?

There were some visible changes that cannot be ignored. Parliament passed a law that reversed many of the acts of the preceding Commonwealth regime. Initially Parliament sought to settle disputes and pacify the country. The Act of Indemnity and Oblivion of August 1660 gave a widespread pardon to those who had cooperated with the Commonwealth. In fact, the pardon was so broad as to infuriate some royalists, who felt that many of their former enemies had been included. However, the regicides who had tried Charles I and signed his execution warrant in 1649 were punished. Cromwell's corpse was dug up and exhibited as a symbolic punishment. Of those regicides still living, ten were executed and nineteen were imprisoned for life. Others implicated in the Civil War fled to Europe or New England.

The execution of the regicide Thomas Harrison on 19 October showed the desire of the crowd for bloody revenge for the errors of the Civil War and the execution of Charles I. Harrison's death was gruesome. After hanging, he was cut down still conscious, and even after disembowelling and castration was sufficiently alive to punch his tormentors. The scene was so appalling that Charles pardoned the remaining offenders.

Those who had opposed Charles I during the Civil War and the Commonwealth were pardoned if they swore an oath of loyalty within forty days. Land sales during the Commonwealth were accepted if the sellers had consented to them, but compulsory sales were reversed. Church and Crown lands were restored to their former owners where possible, though in time the government was forced to legitimize the sale of confiscated land in all but a few cases. In this, the Restoration Parliament was obliged to compromise because it could not simply turn the clock back to 1649. Some people decided that it would even be better to change their names. The Puritanically named If-Jesus-Had-Not-Died-For-Thee-Thou-Wouldst-Be-Damned Barbon sensibly renamed himself Nicholas Barbon (d. 1698).

One event that represented the conscious desire of the King to show continuity with the past was his coronation, on 23 April 1661. The same coronation oath that his father had sworn was found and copes were made for the canons of Westminster Abbey from ancient patterns. The crown jewels had been broken up and sold by Cromwell, but drawings of Charles I in his crown and regalia were carefully studied to recreate them.

The St Edward's Crown, the Imperial State Crown, the sceptre with the dove, the orb and most of what we know today as the Crown Jewels were made for this coronation. Money was so tight that the gems for the St Edward's Crown – which is only used at the crowning of the sovereign – were hired for the ceremony. The gems for the Imperial State Crown – worn regularly by the King – were bought. Altogether the regalia cost £12,000 and robes of state a further £5,000, more than £2 million in modern values.

Charles II also insisted on copying his father's coronation by having a great processional entry to London. The night before the ceremony he left Whitehall for the Tower of London by royal barge. This enabled him to process formally from the Tower to Westminster. The route of the procession passed through four huge triumphal arches, specially built for the event. Along the route, twenty-eight groups of musicians provided music, accompanied by two choirs. After the procession, free cakes and wine were distributed to the crowd. There was also a morality play featuring actors embodying 'Rebellion' and 'Confusion' who showed the dangers of flouting royal authority.

Before the coronation, there were also symbolic ceremonies that were copied from the past. The Order of the Bath was revived and the King created sixty-eight new knights, as well as six earls and six barons. A coronation medal was struck with 100 gold and 800 silver versions to be distributed. Uniquely, the coronation ceremony included the reading of a pardon for Parliamentary rebels. Following the crowning, the King went to the coronation feast in Westminster Hall. He was greeted by the spectacle of 1,400 platters laden with sweet and savoury foods. The ancient ritual of challenge by the King's Champion throwing down a gauntlet for any who disputed the new King's right to the throne was enacted, and the evening ended with fireworks on the Thames.

The feast was momentarily marred by a fight between the King's footmen and the barons of the Cinque Ports, with both groups claiming the right to take the royal canopy after the ceremony. The brawl broke out during the feast and the King ordered the arrest of the footmen. It was not the only event that descended into violence. Later that year a royal procession through London also witnessed a violent battle between the carriages of the ambassadors of France and Spain, both of whom claimed the right of precedence over the other.

Across the country, church bells, sermons, feasts and pageants celebrated the coronation. In Cambridge, the whole town was decorated with herbs and tapestries, while in Bath there was a procession of 400 virgins. Charles' hasty coronation as King of Scotland in 1650 was felt sufficient, so there was no Scottish ceremony. The news of Charles' Restoration took some months to reach all his dominions, the last of which, Jamaica, only received the news when a ship arrived in August 1660.

All this suggested that Charles II was returning to his father's throne on the same terms. But, before Charles had set foot on British soil, Parliament had formally declared that 'according to the ancient and fundamental laws of this kingdom, the government is, and ought to be, by King, Lords and Commons'. This phrase gave an impression of what the situation had been before the Commonwealth, but did not clarify what had been 'restored'. What exactly were the powers of the king? Was he a ruler by divine right, as Charles I had claimed, or were his powers limited by Parliament? In Scotland, in the weeks before the Restoration there had also been proposals to separate the thrones of England and Scotland.

Charles accepted that he had no right to raise taxes without Parliament's agreement or to establish royal prerogative courts; in other areas it was unclear what had been restored. In some cases the clock was clearly turned back to 1643. For example, the restoration of the powers of sheriffs, lords lieutenant and magistrates, and the removal of Cromwellian restraints on magistrates undid the legislation of the Commonwealth. But, in other respects, practices and laws that had been passed during the Commonwealth were continued. One example was the use of Secret Service money to pay informers to report information to the government, which by 1675 cost £4,000 a year. In other spheres, such as in military and foreign policy, the King made it clear that he regarded his prerogatives unaffected by the Civil War.

The appearance of old structures masked a remarkable new inclusivity. At his first Privy Council meeting, on 31 May 1660, Charles II brought together royalists, Puritans and even some who had served under the Commonwealth, including Lord Sandwich, who had been a Parliamentary army commander during the Civil War. The Privy Council under Charles gradually expanded its role. Scotland was largely administered by the Privy Council in London, as were colonial matters. From 1666, Charles established a third secretary of state, for war. In Ireland, the government structures of a separate Privy Council and judiciary were restored under a lord lieutenant, to which post the King appointed General Monck, newly created Duke of Albemarle.

One of Charles II's innovations was to establish the modern form of the British army. In 1661 the Militia Act granted responsibility for national defence and control of the armed forces exclusively to the king. The abolition of feudal military tenure of land in 1660 ended the monopoly of the aristocracy on armed service. This opened the way to a new class of professional soldier. Charles established a new ceremonial bodyguard formed of four elements: the Life Guards, the Royal Horse Guards, two companies of Foot Guards and the Coldstream Guards. On to this structure other regiments were later grafted, such as garrison troops for Tangiers and Bombay.

Charles also set up the Board of Ordnance, which controlled the guns and cannon for both the army and navy.

Although the navy had been strengthened under Cromwell, Charles II rebuilt it in the 1660s and 1670s. The navy was ably led by the King's brother James as Lord High Admiral. Trade and the Navigation Acts gave the navy a new importance: Britain's colonies in North America and the West Indies were a growing source of trade, and the Navigation Acts laid down that all trade with them had to be carried in British ships. This excluded the Dutch, French and Spanish from profiting from British colonies; it also meant that the navy had to enforce these laws. In 1665 the navy's 'fighting instructions', its tactical rules of battle, were updated and reissued. From 1677, it was compulsory in the Royal Navy for all officers to have served onboard ship, and slowly the ranks of naval officers became more professionalized. Some people were clear-sighted in seeing that the navy was the basis of British power. Thomas Sprat (1635–1713), later Bishop of Rochester, said that British greatness would never be increased, except through maritime wars.

Religion

One of the most important changes brought in by the Restoration was the religious settlement of the country. During the Commonwealth, the Puritans had rooted out Anglicanism and had replaced it with Presbyterian and independent congregations, based on Puritan articles of faith. Bishops had been removed and cathedrals had been neglected, or abandoned altogether as a place of worship. Part of St Paul's Cathedral became a stable for horses. In April 1660, while still in exile in Breda in Holland, Charles had issued a declaration that promised a degree of religious freedom to those of 'tender consciences' who would not conform to the Church of England.

The Church of England was restored as the official or 'established' Church in England and Wales. The clergy who had been thrown out during the Commonwealth were restored to their parishes. The same happened in Ireland, where in 1660 two archbishops and ten bishops were consecrated in Dublin to lead the restored Church of Ireland. Only six of the new Irish bishops were Irish, the rest were from England and Scotland. Yet religious toleration did not follow in the three kingdoms. While the King sought to heal the rift between the Anglicans and Presbyterians (though he said Presbyterianism was 'not a religion for a gentleman') by offering English bishoprics to four of the leading Presbyterians, only Edward Reynolds accepted one.

Tensions over religion came to a head almost immediately. In April 1661, Bishop Gilbert Sheldon of London (1598–1677) convened a conference at the Savoy Palace. It brought together twelve bishops and twelve Presbyterians, with a view to revising the prayer book so that both Puritans and Anglicans could be accommodated within a single broad church. The conference lasted ten weeks, but it was clear that the two sides would not reach an agreement. The Church of England therefore pursued its own revision of the prayer book which, in 1662, was enshrined in the Act of Uniformity. This law required all clergy to conform to and use the liturgy of the Church of England. It offered little room for Nonconformists. Presbyterian ministers were given until St Bartholomew's Day (24 August 1662) to conform to the Church of England or be ejected from their parishes.

In the long hot summer of 1662 (the hottest for half a century) about 1,000 ministers, 15 per cent of the total, were ejected from their parishes for not conforming (and thereby becoming 'Nonconformist' to the Church of England). Among them was Adam Martindale of Rostherne in Cheshire. After ejection from his church, Martindale invited his former parishioners to his house for dinner, where they criticized his successor's sermons – demonstrating that ejection did not always mean that a congregation abandoned its minister. The ejection of these ministers created an alternative to the Church

of England in the form of organized Nonconformity (sometimes called 'Dissent'). At a stroke, worship outside the established Church grew dramatically. This was a factor for political
instability in Britain for more than a century.

The King renewed his Breda declaration at Christmas 1662,
but the House of Commons refused to permit widespread
toleration of Nonconformists. Parliament was determined to
enforce the Act of Uniformity and followed it with the
Conventicle Act in 1664, forbidding those who refused to
conform to the Church of England from holding meetings –
'conventicles' – for worship. The Five Mile Act of the
following year banned Nonconformist clergy from living
within 5 miles (8 km) of their old congregations. Altogether
these laws were called the Clarendon Code, after Lord
Clarendon (1609–74), who proposed them. Under these laws,
about 8,000 Nonconformists, including many Quakers, were
imprisoned. Among the prisoners was John Bunyan (1628–88),
the author of *The Pilgrim's Progress*, who spent twelve years in
jail. In this respect, Restoration England became a persecuting
state in which the Church and State tried to force all men and
women into membership of a single national Church, and
punished those who would not comply.

Restoration Anglicanism did bend a little. Sabbath observance, the more Puritan plain style of preaching and the dominance of the pulpit were absorbed into the Church's liturgy. In
addition, folk religion, which was beyond official control,
returned to Britain very swiftly. In Wales the Christmas traditions of 'Plygain' – greeting the Christmas dawn – and carols
written by Huw Morys and Edward Morris were in use within
a year of the Restoration. Nonconformists also found their
views changing: in particular, Nonconformity gradually lost its
focus on the 'godly community' in favour of individual
salvation. It also adopted a greater rational approach to faith.
There was, too, a fear of religious 'enthusiasm' – in its original
sense of an unreasoning possession by a spirit. It was felt that
religious enthusiasm had given rise to the violence and wars of

the 1640s. Concern about 'enthusiasm' also made public suspicion of sects such as the Quakers widespread.

Religion and the Church continued to have a strong hold over the everyday lives of the English. For example, religion controlled the calendar. Britain, unlike most of Europe, stuck to the Julian calendar, eleven days behind the European Gregorian calendar, which was viewed as a popish innovation. In addition to the liturgical cycles of Christmas, Candlemas, Easter, Lady Day (25 March, the feast of the Annunciation of the Virgin Mary) and Michaelmas, there were popular commemorations that the Church adopted. These included Twelfth Night, St Valentine's Day, the anniversary of the martyrdom of Charles I, Oak Apple Day, All Souls' Day and the anniversaries of such events as the accession of Elizabeth I, the defeat of the Spanish Armada, and the foiling of the gunpowder plot on 5 November. All these were observed by parish churches. Together with local fairs, festivals and market days, the passage of time – and the heritage of the country – were primarily in the possession of the Church.

The hold that religion and moral laws had on the behaviour of men and women can be seen in the decline in the rate of illegitimate births as Church courts returned to regulate moral behaviour. In the first decade of the Restoration, illegitimate births declined from 3.4 per cent earlier in the century to 1.5 per cent.

For all Christians, Britain remained a strongly providential society in which God was thought to intervene directly in worldly matters. The Plague and the Fire of London in 1665 and 1666 were both occasions for national prayer. A London clergyman, Thomas Vincent, preached a sermon entitled *God's Terrible Voice in the City*, which claimed to explain the 'cause and design' in visiting the plague and fire on London. Other sermons also warned people that such events were divine punishments for sin. In 1692, called 'the trembling year', an earthquake sparked fears of a national punishment inflicted by God. The deaths of public figures such as Queen Mary and

Archbishop John Tillotson of Canterbury (1630–94) in 1694 were regarded by some as divine punishment. When Bishop Richard Kidder (1633–1703) was killed by a falling chimney in the great storm of 1703 some said it was a divine judgement. Comets and eclipses were also thought to be portents of punishment.

Witches were widely believed to exist. In 1664 a senior judge, Sir Matthew Hale (1609–76), said that he had no doubt that they existed, and the 1660 Act of Pardon excluded those who had practised witchcraft. The last witch convicted in England was Jane Wenham, in 1712 at Hertford, whose execution was commuted. The last witch executed in Scotland was in 1722 at Dornoch. But fear of witches and spells remained a major element in folk lore and folk practices. Joseph Addison (1672–1719), editor of the *Spectator*, wrote in 1711 that he believed in witchcraft, 'but at the same time can give credit to no particular instance of it'.

Nevertheless, the Restoration period also saw the emerging elements of new rational principles. These underpinned the Enlightenment – the flowering of reason and science in place of superstition and ignorance. Scientific explanations for all manner of things, such as gravity, seemed to question the idea of a God-made world. Although thinkers and scientists such as Isaac Newton (1642–1727), John Locke (1632–1704), Robert Boyle (1627–91) and Robert Hooke (1635–1703) were committed Christians who conceived their ideas within a religious framework; their ideas replaced a world in which the earth was the centre of the universe, with the ceiling of heaven above it, with an infinite universe governed by laws of nature.

In Ireland, in contrast, religious persecution was much less prevalent than in England. Catholics made up 800,000 of a total population of 1,200,000. At the Restoration, Catholic clergy were able to return from the continent because, while the government did not officially tolerate Catholicism, it concentrated on re-establishing the Anglican Church. Charles II made an effort to conciliate Irish Catholics with some compensation and land grants, but most Catholics were disappointed that Cromwellian land confiscations were not reversed. On the other hand, tension arose because Protestants felt that Irish Catholics had been treated too leniently. Some thought that they deserved to be punished for their massacres of Protestants during the Civil Wars. There were occasional acts of persecution of Catholics, such as the imprisonment of Bishop Peter Talbot (1620–80) and the execution of Archbishop Oliver Plunkett of Armagh (1629–81), but the breathing space from 1660 to 1690 enabled Catholicism to re-establish itself.

Scotland's religious establishment was similarly neglected. Charles concentrated on consolidating his rule in England, and permitted considerable latitude to the Duke of Lauderdale (1618–82), his secretary of state and high commissioner to the Scottish Parliament. Despite his own Presbyterianism, Lauderdale supported Charles' policy of trying to establish episcopalianism in the Scottish Church. He suppressed conventicles and rooted out Puritanical Covenanters, who were stern Scottish Presbyterians. Though not entirely unpopular, in 1679 the policy provoked a Presbyterian rebellion in southern Scotland. Charles' illegitimate son, James, Duke of Monmouth (1649–85), put down the rebellion at the Battle of Bothwell Bridge and brutally suppressed the Covenanters in the period known as the 'Killing Time'. Covenanters were routinely tortured and Highlanders, with government agreement, displaced Lowland Covenanters from their own land. In 1684, two Covenanters, 18-year-old Margaret Wilson and 68-year-old Margaret McLauchlan, were punished by being tied to stakes on a beach and drowned as the tide slowly rose. In 1682, James, Duke of York, set up the Commission for Pacifying the Highlands, which cooperated with clan chiefs and sought to build up goodwill in Scotland.

People, Towns and Disease
Other features of the changing nature of Restoration Britain were the result of longer-term causes. London exerted an

increasing pull on England's population of 5 million. By 1660, London had a population of about 400,000, and was to grow to nearly 675,000 in the following ninety years, overtaking Paris and Constantinople as the biggest city in Europe. In the century before 1660, England's population had doubled, while London's population had grown ten-fold. Sir John Reresby (1634–89), the MP for York from 1682 to 1689, wrote that London drained people from all over England, attracting them to the city by work and other opportunities. Such people had to be housed and urban sprawl began. By 1768 Arthur Young (1741–1820) coined the term 'outskirts' for the way Gravesend had been connected with London.

London was not alone in being a magnet for rural people. The numbers of people living in towns tripled in the years leading up to 1660. Norwich, Plymouth and Newcastle-upon-Tyne were boom towns, built on weaving, dockyards and coal respectively. Other towns were soon to grow too: Birmingham was to develop the metal working that boosted its population to 8,000 inhabitants by 1700; Manchester was also standing on the brink of a boom, based on textiles. There were periods of population crisis, such as the plague outbreaks of the 1660s, but these did not prevent long-term growth.

Nor was urban growth just an English phenomenon. In Scotland, with a population of around 1 million, the number of people who lived in towns rose to 50,000, two-thirds of these in Edinburgh. Ireland's population was also growing, adding 100,000 people during Charles II's reign. Urban settlements were becoming more prominent in Ireland too, with new towns at Charleville, Portarlington and Lanesborough, and Dublin's population rose to 32,000. The failure of the parliaments in Edinburgh and Dublin to cooperate with each other led to almost unrestricted emigration of Scots to Ireland in this period. Cromwell accelerated the policy – begun under Charles I – of settling Protestants in Ireland, and it continued under Charles II. By 1690, 320,000 men, women and children arrived from England, Wales and Scotland – half were from Scotland.

While the populations of the three kingdoms were growing and being drawn to towns, they were also affected by a very different feature: emigration. In the decade before the Restoration of Charles II, Oliver Cromwell's brutal repression in Ireland took effect. From 1650, 100,000 Irish Catholics, as well as the desperately poor from England and Scotland, were transported across the Atlantic, chained below decks. They were bound for the Caribbean, where they formed a cheap workforce for the tobacco and sugar plantations on islands such as Montserrat. These indentured labourers had agreed to act as servants to their masters for years at a time, which made them virtual slaves. It was this process that pump-primed the transatlantic slave trade. It taught the plantation owners that they could be highly successful if they obtained large enough supplies of cheap labour. Within a few years the slave trade from Africa supplied that need.

Forced emigration from Ireland was not the only reason for people leaving Britain. During the seventeenth century about 300,000 people had emigrated from Britain to North America. Most left seeking religious toleration; Puritans went to New England, Catholics to Maryland. There were more than a few, however, who left England in the 1640s seeking religious freedom and returned during the Commonwealth. There were also some economic migrants, both to New England and to continental Europe. One of the most important destinations for Scottish emigrants was Poland, which in the mid-seventeenth century received many thousands of migrants – more than either Ulster or North America. But gradually emigration to America became most popular. In 1720 the writer and journalist Daniel Defoe (?1661–1731) said that if Scottish emigration to Virginia continued at the same rate, in a few years the colony would be Scottish rather than English.

We should not overlook some of the minorities that made up the population of Britain. In 1656, Cromwell legalized the return of Jews to England and by 1662 there was a synagogue with a congregation of a hundred men in Creechurch Lane in

London. Within fifteen years of 1662 the Jewish population of London had doubled, with new synagogues opening in Aldgate and Bevis Marks – the latter with roof beams donated by Queen Anne. In 1753 a law permitted the naturalization of Jews, but was repealed a year later after widespread opposition, and petitions from the Lord Mayor and Corporation of London.

The years of Charles II's reign also witnessed the arrival of Protestant refugees from France. Louis XIV initially persecuted and then, in 1685, banned Protestants altogether, requiring their forcible conversion. Many chose to leave France rather than convert to Catholicism. By 1700 these Huguenots numbered 23,000 in London, and there were also Huguenot communities in Bristol, Canterbury, Southampton, Edinburgh and Dublin.

Popular prejudice against immigrants was common. They arrived at a time when the British population was growing naturally. There were common complaints, familiar today, that foreigners worked more cheaply than Britons and brought new ideas and technology with them. They also ate strange new, and smelly, foods, including garlic, oxtail soup, pickles and caraway seeds. In London in 1675 there were riots directed against the Huguenots, who were using new looms and thereby affecting the livelihoods of silk weavers. Of course, foreigners arriving in Britain often brought economic benefits and innovations. Spitalfields, on the eastern outskirts of London, developed a damask and brocade industry based on imported techniques. Gold and silversmithing were also boosted by foreign skills, as was paper making.

Arriving in Restoration London must have been a frightening sensation for the 8,000 men and women who came seeking work and fortune each year. If they entered from the south they would pass over London Bridge, on whose southern turrets the heads of the executed were displayed. The scale of the bridge must have been daunting: it had eighteen arches and was lined on both sides with houses and shops, some rising to six storeys. Once inside the city they would also be struck by an almost constant pealing of church bells, especially the slow tolling of the 'passing bell', which told of the death of a parishioner. The bell tolled nine times for a man, six for a woman and three for a child, followed by a brief pause and then a chime for each year of the person's age. Some parishes paid large amounts to the bell-ringers, who were important people in the city.

One of the dominant experiences of London inhabitants was the smell of the city. Piles of sewage and other waste were dumped on roads and routes into the city by night-soil men, who were responsible for carrying away the sewage. Streets and ditches were deep with human excrement and urine; and animal excrement marked the drovers' routes to the markets. These attracted flocks of kites, which bothered people more than pigeons and gulls do today. Mayor Richard Whittington's fifteenth-century public lavatory, which had 128 seats, had not been maintained and had fallen into disuse. Consequently the streets were often the only place for people to defecate and urinate. A law of 1662 made each parish responsible for employing scavengers to ensure that refuse did not obstruct the streets, but it was not always possible to enforce.

The horses used to draw wagons and carriages left their own marks. To feed the many draught animals, the Haymarket, in today's West End, was used to store and supply foodstuffs. A proclamation in November 1660 required all carriages, carts and their horses to be stabled overnight rather than left standing in the streets to avoid traffic congestion. Two years later, the Privy Council limited the number of hackney carriage licences to 400 – the forerunners of the modern taxi. In addition to animal nuisances, tanners and weavers used urine in their work and carried it through the streets. Soapmakers and gluemakers boiled the carcasses of animals to make their products, adding to the smells. With thoroughfares often congested, many used the Thames as an alternative means of transport. Most major organizations had their own barges, boats or ferries – the archbishops of Canterbury used barges as their main means of transport until the middle of the next century. But the river could also menace the city, as it did in 1663, when high tides flooded Whitehall.

In most areas of London, two or three families were crammed into single houses, and sewage vaults sometimes overflowed into cellars. The diarist Samuel Pepys (1633–1703) recorded on one occasion that he was ankle deep in turds from next door. Water supplies from rivers, springs and wells were badly contaminated by this effluent. People sometimes talked of 'thick water' because it was so cloudy. Wealthy areas were supplied with water from reservoirs in Islington and other suburbs, carried by elm pipes. In 1667 the New River Company raised £8,000 to supply clean water to west London. The inhabitants of Piccadilly and Pall Mall were probably better off than others since they drew their water from springs. One of the first major water supplies organized outside London was that designed by the Revd Stephen Hales of Teddington (1677–1761) in the 1750s, which provided fresh water for the area.

There were modest attempts at urban improvement. In 1660 the residents of Charing Cross petitioned for the place of execution to be moved, and the King agreed that Tyburn, near the modern Marble Arch, was a better location. Here libellers were punished by nose-slitting or ear-lopping. The pillory was also erected, at which serious offenders could often die at the hands of an angry crowd, and hangings were conducted there.

With the population of London and other towns growing, churchyards overflowed and sometimes the bodies of the poor were left in the streets. At times of famine or epidemic, large burial pits were dug for paupers, such as the one in Tottenham Court in 1665, and left open until they were full. In some ways modern London is literally a city built on its ancestors.

Coal smoke poured from thousands of domestic chimneys and from furnaces. By 1680 dyers began to move out of London because they could not dry their cloth in the open air for fear of staining from the pollution. Later, William III, who suffered from asthma, had to move to Kensington to avoid it; the poor simply wheezed.

In such an environment there was constant coughing and spitting, both of which spread disease. The phlegm of a consumptive's cough would carry airborne bacilli far and wide. Tuberculosis, or consumption, was one of the biggest causes of death in London. The environment also led to low standards of hygiene, resulting in endemic fleas and lice. The poor had nowhere to wash their hands after they defecated and urinated. Equally, John Evelyn noted that the royal palaces were stinking and filthy because there were no lavatories so courtiers sometimes defecated in corridors, as did the King's spaniels. Dirt led to contamination of food and drinking water, causing stomach complaints. In a hot summer the population suffered from gastric infections often described as griping, twisting or flux in the bowels. Dysentery could be easily contracted and was a major killer; chronic and acute diarrhoea could lead to convulsions. Many who survived the disease died for lack of replenishment of liquid and salts after diarrhoea.

Intestinal parasites were especially common, often caught from undercooked pork. Pepys reported that meat from the many cook-shops was often rare. Tapeworms sometimes passed to the brain and might be responsible for fits, known as the 'falling sickness'. Tooth decay was also a common problem and dental infections could be so serious as to be fatal, as well as agonizingly painful. Sometimes people who had lost their teeth could not eat vegetables and fruit, which then led to scurvy, which was called 'the disease of London'.

Children housed in London's slum rooms and surrounded by pollution might only rarely see the sun. Consequently, they suffered from rickets, caused by a lack of vitamin D – from sunlight or fruit and vegetables – which is essential for the absorption of calcium. Girls with rickets might have malformed pelvises and would often later die in childbirth, but death in childbirth was high for all classes. There were 23.5

maternal deaths per 1,000 baptisms. Women had a 6–7 per cent chance of dying in childbirth, and there are no records of a woman surviving a caesarian section until the mid-eighteenth century. Midwifery was something of a mystery; the Chamberlen family, which had invented forceps for birth delivery, kept them as a lucrative professional secret throughout the seventeenth century. Annual pregnancies were typical, especially among upper-class women, who did not breast feed and enjoyed a good diet. Queen Anne, for instance, had seventeen pregnancies in as many years. London remained a city of the young: in 1700 a third of its population were children.

The mid-seventeenth century also saw a dip in the birth rate, probably as a result of lower levels of marriage and better contraception. There were drops in the birth rate in the 1670s and 1690s, during which emigration also lowered the population. Childhood diseases such as measles, mumps, whooping cough, scarlet fever, diphtheria and meningitis were killers. Other illnesses were the cause of deformity and weakness. Thousands of workers who moved from the countryside, and who had never been exposed to them when younger, succumbed to these diseases.

Once past childhood, more illnesses lurked. A diagnosis of ague or fever usually meant malaria, which was one of the most common causes of death. Meningitis, called 'spotted fever', typhoid and typhus were also common in crowded conditions. Newgate Gaol had an outdoor courtroom because of the fear of these 'gaol' fevers, and judges kept posies of flowers on the bench to keep contagion at bay. Smallpox – called *small*pox to distinguish it from the pox, or syphilis – was inhaled from people incubating it. It affected the great as well as the lowly: Charles II's younger brother, the Duke of Gloucester, died of it four months after the Restoration. William III lost both his parents, and also his wife, Queen Mary II, to it in 1694. There were few whose complexions were not marked by the scarring of smallpox. Occasional minor epidemics could affect a town or village dramatically. In 1734 the village of Llanfechell in Anglesey lost half its population to disease. There were also periods in which the death rate rose dramatically, for no apparent reason. From 1727 to 1730 the ague, probably an influx of influenza from overseas, affected the country. In both the 1730s and 1770s this happened, and people were concerned about its causes and effects. Some felt that it led to a rise in religious fervour.

There were very few medical treatments of any use. Londoners could buy drugs from apothecaries, and cannabis, for example, was freely available. Physicians were only for the rich; for everyone else there were about 1,000 apothecaries in London, all seeking to make a living from the sick, and few with any great skill at it. Medicine was as much a matter of superstition as of science. Charms and spells were used for aches, and quacks would diagnose illness on the basis of an examination of stools or urine. The idea of 'humours' – blood, phlegm, black and yellow bile – still dominated medical thinking and therefore bleeding, laxatives and enemas remained popular treatments. Quinine, derived from tree bark, was used to varying effect – although this was not known, it had a mildly antibiotic effect.

Surgery was limited to superficial operations, while most penetrating wounds were fatal. A broken arm or leg needed to be amputated to prevent gangrene. It was possible to operate for kidney stones: Samuel Pepys had such an operation and showed his friends a stone as big as a tennis ball to prove it. But successful appendectomy could not be achieved as the surgery was too deep. Carrying out an operation on a table in the patient's home, and relying on alcohol to render the patient senseless, the best surgeon was a speedy worker. Gradually diagnosis grew to be a more precise art, but treatments remained rudimentary. It took until 1811 before there was a well-documented case of a mastectomy, without any anaesthetic, that of Fanny Burney (1752–1840), who survived another thirty years.

The sick tended to stay at home, since most treatments meant frequent vomiting and purging. Healthcare paid for by the parish was limited to the elderly. The two London hospitals, St Bartholomew's and St Thomas', served the needs of paupers and provided them with beds to recover or die in rather than treatment. Bethlehem Hospital in Bishopsgate, known as 'Bedlam', was for the 'distracted and lunatick'. Attitudes to the mentally ill were cruel: a visit to Bedlam to view the antics of the insane was regarded as an entertainment. In 1675 Bedlam moved to better buildings, designed by Robert Hooke, at Moorfields, outside the City boundary.

The Plague and the Fire
The conditions in London were ideal for the spread of disease. In 1665 the last great outbreak of the plague swept through the city. The disease had been spreading across the continent for two years; Charles II even imposed an embargo on travelling to and from Holland, where there was a serious outbreak. But the long hot summer of 1665 enabled the fleas by which the plague was spread to thrive. The first serious outbreak was in April 1665, in the parish of St Giles in the Fields, on the site of modern Tottenham Court Road and Oxford Street. The symptoms – fever, swollen lymph glands, spots, bleeding from the nose and mouth, vomiting and delirium – led to coma and death. Plague nurses were recruited from the poor and unemployed to take bodies to burial pits and to isolate houses where the infection had been. They also painted red crosses on the doors of the houses infected by the disease. Plague burial pits were dug, but soon filled as deaths reached over 8,000 a month. The numbers of dead overwhelmed London churches. The bell at Cripplegate broke from frequent ringing for the dead, and the bells of the city fell silent.

By June 1665, the rich, including most physicians, fled London and a permit was required to enter the city. The royal family and court moved first to Hampton Court Palace, then to Salisbury and finally to Oxford. Among those who remained to administer London were the Duke of Albemarle, Lord Craven (1606–97), Archbishop Sheldon and the mayor, Sir William Lawrence. Bishop Humphrey Henchman of London (1592–1675) warned his clergy that if they left their parishes during the emergency he would eject and replace them. Nevertheless, the Dean of St Paul's, William Sancroft (1617–93), fled to Tunbridge. In all, eleven London clergy died during the outbreak. Shops and public places were closed and the government banned sports and imposed a 9 p.m. curfew. To prevent any opportunistic republicanism from taking hold, old Cromwellian supporters were rounded up and imprisoned.

The poor resorted to living on boats on the Thames or turned to quack remedies, such as lighting fires to 'cleanse' the air with smoke. Deaths reached a peak in August and September 1665, and only fell away with the frosts in November. The lists of the London dead, known as the Bills of Mortality, calculated that there were 68,596 plague victims in 1665, but this was an underestimate, and probably more than 100,000 – approaching a quarter of the population – had died. The King did not return to London until February 1666.

Although the disease was concentrated in London, it seeped out into other areas of the country. At Cambridge University students (among them the young Isaac Newton) were sent home. Mercantile towns such as Southampton, Dover, Leicester, Ipswich, Yarmouth, Gloucester and Bristol were badly affected. In 1666, an outbreak took place in the village of Eyam in Derbyshire, arriving with a merchant carrying cloth from London. Eyam was quarantined to stop the spread of the disease beyond the village and saw the death of around three-quarters of its inhabitants.

Most people knew that when they were crowded together illness was rife. 'Army fever' had been common during the Civil War, as soldiers were housed in barracks. People were also accustomed to illnesses that came in the wake of poor harvests, such as influenza and smallpox, when the population's poor nutrition resulted in susceptibility to illness. It was also clear that towns which were not crammed were generally healthier. During the 1650s Gloucester was free of epidemics, partly because the population declined with the departure of the garrison and refugees, and food stocks were replenished.

London was only just recovering from the ravages of the plague when the Great Fire broke out. It came at the end of a second long dry summer; it was exactly what was needed to end the plague, but the houses were tinder dry. The weather was so dry that, in some parishes, there were prayers for rain. On 2 September 1666 Thomas Farriner, the baker of tack biscuits for the Royal Navy, failed to extinguish an oven properly and between 1 a.m. and 2 a.m. the fire caught hold. Hay in the yard of the nearby Star Inn turned a small fire into an inferno. The fire destroyed 300 homes during the night. At first there was little alarm and the Lord Mayor, Sir Thomas Bludworth, famously said 'a woman might piss it out!' It was a phrase that was to haunt Bludworth, who later fainted – like a woman, it was said – when he saw the extent of the fire. The next morning, Samuel Pepys, viewing the fire from the Tower of London, realized that it was out of control and took a boat along the Thames to tell the King.

The failure to create firebreaks by pulling down houses, or to appreciate that the strong easterly wind would spread the flames, led to serious destruction. Chains of firefighters carrying buckets from the Thames had no effect, nor did the efforts of a team of Westminster School scholars marshalled by their headmaster. And when the *forcier*, a waterwheel that fed the city, burnt down there was no means of pumping large quantities of water on to the flames. The only concerted action came when James, Duke of York, took control of the efforts to stop the fire. It was finally checked at the Temple and London Bridge – though not before St Magnus Martyr Church and a number of houses on the bridge's northern end had been destroyed. A sixth of London was destroyed: about 13,200 houses, 400 streets and courts and 87 churches. All the city company houses were lost, with 44 livery halls and some of the wharves. The lead on the roof of St Paul's Cathedral had melted, run down into the crypt and destroyed the stores of books and paper there – worth £2 million. At wharves along the Thames £1.5 million worth of wine, tobacco and sugar was also lost. In all, over 400 acres of London lay in ruins, and as far west as Kensington ash covered gardens, and was even seen in Windsor. In Cambridge, Alderman Newton recorded the 'heavens ... seemed many times to burne and bee all of a redd fire'. For days afterwards the London pavements were still hot from the fire and for two months coals in some cellars continued to smoulder. Incredibly, only five people died in the fire.

The poet and playwright John Dryden (1631–1700) summed up the fears of many that the twin disasters were expressions of some divine punishment. In 'Annus Mirabilis' (1667) he wrote:

> We all have sinn'd, and thou hast laid us low,
> As humble earth from whence at first we came:
> Like flying shades before the clouds we show,
> And shrink like parchment in consuming flame.
>
> O let it be enough what thou hast done;
> When spotted Deaths ran arm'd through every street,
> With poison'd darts which not the good could shun,
> The speedy could out-fly, or valiant meet.
>
> The living few, and frequent funerals then,
> Proclaim'd thy wrath on this forsaken place;
> And now those few who are return'd again,
> Thy searching judgments to their dwellings trace.
>
> O pass not, Lord, an absolute decree,
> Or bind thy sentence unconditional!
> But in thy sentence our remorse foresee,
> And in that foresight this thy doom recall.

The rebuilding of London took more than a decade. In the short term, many organizations had to find temporary accommodation. The Exchequer moved to Nonsuch Palace in

Sutton, the shopkeepers of the Royal Exchange moved into Gresham College, the wealthy goldsmith Sir Robert Viner (1631–88) and his business managed to move to Windsor, and the City Post Office was set up in Bloomsbury. For a few weeks the business of government came to a standstill. Aphra Behn (1640–89), the playwright who was a secret agent for the government in Antwerp, wrote repeatedly for funds in the days after the fire but got no reply. Eventually she had to go into debt to fund her return to London.

One hundred thousand homeless London citizens had to camp in fields in Islington, Highgate and Moorfields. In the days after the fire the King rode out to calm the refugees, who were fearful of food shortages. There were widespread rumours that foreigners had started the fire, and many innocent strangers were attacked. Robert Hubert, a French simpleton, was hanged for confessing to starting the fire and his body was torn to pieces by the mob.

With the loss of so many houses, rents rocketed from £40 to £150 a year. The rebuilding of London required special Fire Courts to be set up to adjudicate on competing claims to plots of land. Despite the impetus to remove rubble from the burnt sites, the authorities found it almost impossible to conduct a swift survey of the burnt area. Consequently, the King had to order the site of St Paul's to be cleared. A Rebuilding Act in 1667 laid down building rules for the size and construction of houses, prices of bricks and timber were controlled and local taxes were suspended. So much timber was required for rebuilding London that a new wharf was built to land it at Puddle Dock. A second Rebuilding Act in 1670 ordered that fifty-one churches would replace the eighty-seven destroyed, and only seventeen of these would be on the site of the original churches.

By 1671, 8,000 houses had been built, and, although 1,000 plots were still empty, many citizens decided to move permanently to the suburbs where they had temporarily squatted. Church briefs, permitting parish churches across England and

Wales to raise money for the homeless in London, were issued and raised almost £1,500 in Devon alone.

In 1677, a monument to the fire was erected. Characteristically, given their wide scientific interests, the architect Sir Christopher Wren (1632–1723) and the scientist Robert Hooke designed it for use as an instrument. The column had an underground laboratory and a central shaft to be used as a telescope and for gravity and pendulum experiments.

The Economy

Perhaps the biggest transformations that occurred after the Restoration were economic. These happened gradually after 1660, and therefore were probably barely perceptible to people at the time. The rhythmic 'heartbeat' of the economy, the harvest, remained vulnerable. Up to the middle of the eighteenth century about one in four harvests was deficient and one in five seriously failed, leading to famines; only two in five produced surplus food. The weather, then as now, caused problems. Wet years, such as 1695–6, produced epidemics of animal diseases such as sheep-rot and 'murrain' – an infection that affected sheep and cattle. In 1739 the 'great frost' killed thousands in Ireland, and the following harvest failure led to mass starvation.

Climate change – not the monopoly of the twenty-first century – also affected the economy. The 'little ice age' of the late seventeenth century (roughly 1650–90) meant that the Thames froze over on several occasions. The great freeze of 1683–4 was the longest in London's history. Fairs held on the frozen river Thames became common in this period. John Evelyn recorded that 'Streetes of Boothes were set upon the Thames ... all sorts of Trades and shops furnished, & full of Commodities ...' A Cambridge alderman recorded that in 1675–6 there was a single frost that lasted from 28 November to 5 February, and the sea at Deal was frozen as far as 2 miles (3 km) from the shore. Poor nutrition made people susceptible to ill-health, including fevers that were prevalent between 1677 and 1682; coinciding with bad weather, this naturally affected productivity.

Other factors beyond the control of ordinary people affected the economy, such as war. In the 300 years to 1763, Europe enjoyed fewer than fifty years without a war. Even when Britain was not a combatant, foreign wars could disrupt trade and cause problems for exporters. Sometimes, though, they also created new markets and new demand.

Despite the growth of towns, three-quarters of people still lived in the countryside in 1660 and were dependent on the rural economy – although this figure was declining. There were important changes in the rural economy at this time: farm yields were steadily rising. In the 1630s prime beef cattle weighed 4 hundredweight (200 kg), whereas by 1683 the navy could stipulate a standard weight of 5.5 hundredweight (274 kg), and this grew to 6.7 hundredweight (335 kg) in 1780. Milk yields also grew by about a quarter in the two centuries after 1600. In the century and a half after 1660 there was also a 43 per cent rise in cereal production. Much of this growth was due to an increase in productivity of land: in 1700 an acre (0.4 hectare) produced 20 bushels (728 litres) of wheat, compared with just 12 (437 litres) in medieval times. Wheat production was supported by a government bounty, in the form of incentive payments, to cereal growers after 1675.

Some of the growth in agricultural productivity was the result of land drainage, which expanded the total acreage under cultivation. The middle of the seventeenth century saw the drainage of the Bedford Levels around Ely in Cambridgeshire, using Dutch expertise. The success of the project was such that in 1663 a General Drainage Act promoted other land drainage plans. In the Lincolnshire fens drainage took longer, but in Norfolk the drainage of land was quickly successful. By 1680 oats, wheat, onions and root vegetables were grown on land in Norfolk that had previously been unusable.

Much of this drained land was immediately enclosed with hedges into the fields we recognize today, rather than farmed on the strip-farm basis of the medieval period. Enclosure of land into fields had begun in the sixteenth century, but remained at a low level in the Midlands, whereas most land in counties such as Kent, Cumberland, Cornwall, Cheshire, Hertfordshire and Suffolk had been enclosed by 1660. This, in part, explained higher agricultural yields.

The higher agricultural output supported the growth of towns. Farming districts close to London – and also areas near large regional towns such as Bristol, Norwich and Newcastle – became important sources of food. Transport was a problem for distribution, because coach travel was limited to 40 miles (64 km) a day and laden wagons were even slower. Consequently Kent and the Thames valley became the market garden for London.

The droving of animals brought fresh meat from further afield. About 30,000 Scottish cattle were driven to London each year, while some Welsh drovers met in Stockbridge, Hampshire (where there remains Welsh drovers' graffiti on some houses), before bringing their cattle and sheep to London. Geese and turkeys, some wearing leather boots, others with feet dipped in tar, were driven from East Anglia. The great London beef, fish and poultry markets of Smithfield and Billingsgate grew up to handle these great influxes of food. They enabled Samuel Pepys, for example, to eat a huge meal of fresh veal and bacon with two capons and sausages and fritters. Tanners were able to use the pelts to good effect in supplying leather.

London also promoted the hop and malt production in Kent and East Anglia to provide beer and ale for the city. There was also growth of wholesale baking, which reduced the price of bread. In a number of towns, including London, salmon and eels were raised in ponds called vivariums for food. The production of food was protected by the government, especially from Irish competition. The Cattle Acts of 1663 and 1666 outlawed the import of foreign cattle to England for fattening, for fear that they would undermine English livestock sales.

The sale of land declined after 1660. This was because large landowners were buying smaller estates, marriage alliances focused on consolidating estates, and legal agreements called 'entails' meant that estates were inherited intact and could rarely be broken up. Estate consolidation was undoubtedly a reflection of the belief that land ownership was the best financial security. There were also relatively low taxes on land, the government preferring indirect taxes on imports and goods. The growth of larger estates tended to promote better productivity, but it also reduced opportunities for investment in land. This released money for investment in commerce and trade.

Large landed estates were also exploiting their mineral rights in the seventeenth century. The Willoughby, Beaumont, Wentworth, Saville and Spencer estates were extracting coal, iron, lead and salt. Iron smelting was underway by the Scudamore, Paget, Dudley and Talbot families on their land. The London Lead Company was relatively rare as a company in extracting lead from the Pennines. Iron ore was also imported from Sweden, Spain, Poland and Russia to boost iron output. Coal was mined and shipped to Newcastle and Bristol, and coastal shipping brought the coal to London.

Commerce was becoming increasingly important. In 1660 the Duke of Newcastle told the King that only merchants brought 'honey to the hive', and urged him to 'keep up the merchant'. The authors Samuel Fortrey (in *England's Interest and Improvement*, 1673) and Roger Coke (in *A Discourse on Trade*, 1670) also argued that the State had an obligation to promote trade, peace and prosperity. Commerce, of course, needed ships, and between 1660 and 1750 the capacity of British shipping doubled to more than 400,000 tons. Coastal trade, linked to London, boosted small eastern ports such as Yarmouth, King's Lynn and Ipswich. The large transoceanic shipping needed deeper ports such as Southampton, Bristol, Hull and the new ports of Liverpool and Whitehaven. To cope with such large ships, the first London dock, the Howland Dock, was begun in 1660 near Deptford and was extended into the Great Wet Dock as part of the Surrey Commercial Docks in 1698.

These ports and docks were needed to handle a range of new trade ventures. Cromwell's seizure of Jamaica in 1655 led to the establishment of the island as a colony, with the appointment of an English governor in 1662. Within a dozen years the population of Jamaica had quadrupled and formed the base for expansion of the British sugar and tobacco trade in the Caribbean. Between 1660 and 1700 imports of North American and Asiatic dyestuffs grew four-fold.

In 1662, Bombay was given to England by Portugal as part of Catherine of Braganza's dowry on her marriage to Charles II. The English East India Company, chartered in 1600, acquired Bombay on lease from the Crown in 1668 and used it as a base to develop the trade in calico – rough woven cotton. The trade was so large that by 1700 an Act banned the import of calico because it was damaging the domestic textile trade. The East India Company quickly developed about fifty factories in India producing textiles and other products. Its monopoly on trade with India gave it almost governmental status within the subcontinent.

Trade was also boosted by three overseas companies. The Hudson Bay Company was chartered in 1670 to exploit the interior of the Hudson basin in North America, and to capture the fur trade from the French. The Royal African Company was set up in 1672 to develop trade with Africa, including the slave trade. And in a series of Acts in 1670 the East India Company was permitted to make territorial acquisitions, mint money, command fortresses and troops, form alliances, make war and peace, and to exercise civil and criminal jurisdiction over its territory. These three companies became the power-houses of British trade in the years after the Restoration. They also provided an outlet for the talents of some of the 16,000 younger brothers and sons of gentlemen who were born during Charles II's reign, and those who had lost their inheritances during the Civil Wars.

Shipping was also boosted by what was called the 'mercantilist system' (though this phrase was not used at the time). Mercantilism, begun under the Commonwealth, assumed that the total volume of trade was limited and that the government should help domestic traders to obtain the largest volume of it. By 1663, the Navigation and Staple Acts sought to ensure that English shipping controlled as much trade as possible. The Navigation Act of 1660, as we have seen, excluded any foreign nation from shipping items from English colonies. The Staple Act (1663) laid down that all colonial staple products had to be landed at English or Welsh ports, and tax paid on them, before they could be exported.

By 1674 these measures ensured that the Dutch were excluded from trade with America. European imports of colonial produce via England grew, especially in textiles, rice, sugar, tobacco, coffee and hard woods. In addition, exports of domestic English produce to Europe also increased, including paper, glass, soap, textiles and metal wares. Welsh traders were as closely linked to Brittany and Bordeaux as to England. Slaves were also subject to the Navigation Acts and by 1677 a legal ruling permitted them to be treated as property in cases of their owners' debt. In Ireland, the mercantilist system had the effect of discriminating against domestic industry. The Irish wool trade was badly affected by restrictions placed on the export of cloth to prevent it from competing with the English trade.

In England there was a period of unprecedented growth in spending. From 1660 to 1750 the price of meat, wool, coal, sugar and tobacco fell and at the same time there was a real-value rise in wages of 20 per cent. This increase in spending brought more people into the consumer market. It made London the centre of a growing market in luxury items such as cloth finishing, furs, gold and silver.

Inventories made of the goods people had when they died showed that even the poor owned a wide range of products. Food made up a declining percentage of most people's spending. The average person spent 45 per cent of their income on food, and even the poor spent only 70 per cent of their money on food. This left money to spend on other things. Annual sugar consumption – always an indicator of affluence – reached 4 lb (1.8 kg) per head in 1740, and by 1775 had grown twenty-fold over 1660 levels. The rent paid on land increased but, by 1680, wages were at least keeping pace.

When, in 1688, Gregory King (1642–1712) made a calculation of the income of the country, he estimated that 43.5 per cent of the people lived in 'middle-income' households, with earnings between £38 and £69 a year. This compared with less than 20 per cent of people in households with incomes over £200 and the rest with incomes below £37 a year. The savings of the 'middling sort' earned less in banks – where the interest rates fell from 10 per cent in 1650 to 4 per cent in 1750 – than if they invested in commodity trades, and this provided a supply of investment for new companies.

Government finances were by no means healthy in the early years of the Restoration. The King's income was voted – as today – by a Civil List payment by Parliament. But this was too small for Charles II. In 1662 he got round his inability to levy taxes without parliamentary approval by raising a 'free and voluntary gift', in which counties vied to show their loyalty by giving money to the King. Such gimmicks could not be repeated, however. In order to finance government and household spending, the King had to borrow money from continental bankers as well as wealthy merchants such as Sir Robert Viner. They lent the King £500,000, but this quickly got out of control. In 1667, during the Second Anglo-Dutch War, some naval ships were seized by the Dutch and sold to enforce repayment of a royal debt. Five years later Charles II had to impose a 'stop of the Exchequer' – a halt on payments of interest on loans – which staved off bankruptcy but damaged confidence in the security of public borrowing. Ten thousand investors were damaged by the decision.

The three main sources of government income were customs, excise and direct taxation. In 1671 the King abandoned the system of 'farming' customs – whereby an individual paid a sum of money for the right to collect customs in a particular area. Instead, Charles established a Board of Commissioners to collect customs on behalf of the government. From the 1680s this increased money from customs to 20 per cent of government income. Excise, a form of sales tax, grew as the economy developed. By 1688 it also brought in 20 per cent of government income, although it was affected by corruption. Direct taxation was a problem for the government, because of widespread attempts, often successful, to evade payment. Successive governments experimented with new taxes on, among other things, hearths (1662), windows (1696), a poll tax (1660), a tax on bachelors (1694), and a 'burial in woollen' tax (1667), which required everyone to be buried in a taxed woollen shroud.

Attempts to evade window taxes led people to brick up their windows so as to reduce the tax they paid: these bricked-up windows can still sometimes be seen on older houses. Other taxes, such as that on bachelors, required the collection of information, and the 'burial in woollen' tax was largely unenforceable. Land tax was perhaps the least easily evaded, and was also the least popular tax among the landed classes, who elected the Commons and sat in the Lords. Consequently, the land tax remained at its 1690 rate for two centuries.

There were also significant problems with the coinage. In 1672, Charles II agreed to issue small copper coins. Previously the Crown had minted gold coins and silver crowns, shillings and pennies, and had only allowed small copper coins to be issued as local trading tokens. The new copper coins were the first to have an intrinsic value less than their face value, so they were only legal tender in amounts of sixpence or less. Initially these coins had to be made using imported copper. Hoping to assist the domestic tin industry, as well as increase the minting profit, Charles introduced tin farthings. Tin was cheaper than copper, so that the intrinsic value of these coins was even lower, and a large number of counterfeit halfpennies appeared in circulation.

By 1692, there were serious worries about tin coinage. Although the Crown's minting profits were much higher, the move had not helped the tin industry and the public disliked coins with a low intrinsic value. Moreover, counterfeits hurt the poor if they were left with worthless coins. In 1693 and 1694 copper farthings and halfpennies were brought back, and tin coins abandoned and exchanged for copper. In the following year, the coinage was again reformed to reduce the clipping that took place as people clipped the edges off silver and gold coins, reducing their weight and value. It was also agreed that a guinea would be twenty-one shillings rather than thirty. By the late 1690s the currency had been stabilized, though some traders complained that there were insufficient coins in circulation.

Stable coinage was one of the requirements of a strong economy. The period after the Restoration also saw the development of some other prerequisites of commercial and economic strength. The stranglehold that trade guilds had exercised over manufacturing and commerce declined in the mid-seventeenth century. Cromwell and Charles II both permitted demobilized soldiers to enter trades without completing the seven-year apprenticeships required by most guilds. By the 1670s some guilds were entirely defunct and even the woollen and textile guilds were reduced to sending repeated petitions to Parliament to prevent the admission of weavers and other workers who had not served apprenticeships. The building trades were also badly affected by the rebuilding of London as the first Rebuilding Act dispensed with the requirements of the trade guilds, allowing unapprenticed builders to compete for work.

There were other instruments that helped commerce. Insurance policies, against fire, for example, grew after the Great Fire of London. This provided greater security for property. Double-entry book-keeping, used in Italy from the fifteenth century, was adopted so that companies knew both the profitability and value of their trade. Joint stock companies became widespread; these enabled people with savings to invest them in businesses without having to undertake the work of the company, by placing the money in the hands of the directors. In time, investment in such companies could be raised by public advertisement.

The government joined this financial revolution by the introduction of what was known as 'Dutch' finance. The Treasury needed to borrow money, but such loans were dependent on bankers' confidence in the country. In 1667 George Downing (1623–84) was made responsible for raising additional money by selling Treasury bonds with a guaranteed repayment date. This was the origin of today's government bonds. Such government debt was secured on the assumption that future taxation would provide the means to repay the loans, giving the lender a firmer degree of reassurance. It was, in effect, a mortgage of future taxes. The national debt had been born. In due course it was dramatically expanded to help pay for the British involvement in the French wars. And it survives healthily today.

The Poor
The system for dealing with the poor inherited by the Restoration was still controlled by the old Elizabethan Poor Law, which sought to keep them out of sight and gainfully occupied. Until 1665 it was lawful to transport paupers forcibly to the colonies as indentured labourers for up to seven years. Pauper children were apprenticed, and therefore became the dependants of their masters for food, clothing and training rather than the responsibility of the parish. Work was found for the unemployed, and the old and the disabled were relieved of the worst consequence of poverty. But the principle was that each parish should look after its own, and this was strengthened after the Restoration.

The Settlement Act of 1662 prevented vagrants and the itin-erant poor from wandering around the countryside, and particularly from drifting to the towns, by making their home parish responsible for the relief of their poverty. Each pauper was returned to their home parish for poverty to be relieved from the parish rates. Certificates were issued for paupers to pass through parishes on their way back to the parish in which they were legally 'settled'. In an attempt to encourage quicker 'settlement' of the poor, in 1662 the government reduced the period of residence to qualify for help from ratepayers from four years to forty days.

The 'settlement' of people suggests a desire to restrict people's mobility, and a fear of affluent areas being swamped by the poor and indigent. This fear was exacerbated by the large numbers of former soldiers who were likely to become a charge on their home parish. In 1660, 3,681 sailors were demobilized and the proceeds of the Poll Tax were used to settle their back-pay, at a cost of £128,000. In 1688 Gregory King estimated that there were 30,000 vagrants, thieves and beggars. But in times of harvest failure up to two-thirds of the population might be impoverished by scarcity and rising prices.

As always, the cost of supporting the poor was controversial. By 1700, about £700,000 a year was spent from the parish rates in England on help for the poor, although of course this fluctuated. There were two methods of relieving poverty. 'Outdoor relief' – which became known later as the Speenhamland system, after the village in which it was first practised – was a way of topping-up low wages and incomes when times were hard. The relief might be in the form of money, but could also be in food or clothing. The 'dole cupboard' in many churches was used to store bread for the poor and there were clothes stores in some parishes also. This is the origin of the word 'dole' for unemployment benefits.

The alternative was 'indoor relief' in almshouses or poorhouses, which were intended for the 'impotent poor' who could not support themselves even when there was work. These became known as 'houses of industry' for the 'idle poor', and gradually as 'workhouses'. The parish of St Giles in the Fields in London set up a workhouse as early as 1641.

Poor relief was one of the earliest forms of public administration, with the parish or borough officers charged with payment of relief or the operation of a workhouse. Public attitudes to poverty did not progress from the Puritan view that work brought spiritual benefits, and self-reliance was an element in a godly life. Poverty, then as sometimes now, could be associated with irresponsibility, sloth, vice and sin. In 1697 a law required paupers to wear a badge, usually a letter P sewn on to clothing. Later, the Privy Council required parishes to buy stocks in which to punish the idle poor.

Some, such as the philosopher John Locke and the MP Sir Humphrey Mackworth (1657–1727), advocated the profitable employment of the poor. The debate on the treatment of the poor swung in favour of indoor relief, and from 1723 workhouses were approved for all parishes that wished to establish them. The poor were also affected by the Game Laws, a series of laws passed from 1671 to 1723, which created new offences of trespass and poaching and eventually made poaching a hanging offence.

Restoration Culture
The Restoration has given its name to all sorts of cultural forms. Restoration comedy, theatre, poetry and satire are all distinct movements in British culture from this period. This was a time in which older and newer forms of culture were in tension. In the spheres of science and other fields of learning, the Restoration represented a break with the past. In 1660 Robert Boyle and Robert Hooke, two Oxford scientists, invented an air pump that enabled them to experiment on the nature of air and vacuums. Ideas of suction and the 'spring of air' (as Boyle called the ability of air to exert pressure) would be vital in the development of steam engines and other machinery that powered the industrial revolution.

In 1662 Charles II formed the Royal Society – Pepys called it the 'College of Virtuosos' – which quickly attracted the greatest minds of the period. Robert Boyle, Robert Hooke and fellow scientist Isaac Newton were among the fellows, together with Christopher Wren the architect, John Wilkins (1614–72) the mathematician, John Locke the philosopher and John Evelyn the diarist. John Dryden the poet was also elected but was later ejected for failing to pay his subscription. It also attracted aristocrats and socialites who were entertained by the discussions and experiments. Fairly quickly, the Royal Society established itself as a powerhouse of new ideas and its secretary corresponded with hundreds of European thinkers and scientists. The society also had the right to publish its own books without royal or episcopal permission.

The society met each week at Gresham College to discuss a wide range of scientific and speculative topics, which were recorded in its *Philosophical Transactions*. Some of the subjects represented 'old knowledge' such as witchcraft, alchemy and necromancy, but the Royal Society also became the cradle of new ideas in mathematics, astronomy and natural sciences.

These were not always theoretical subjects. The society explored maritime topics, navigation, the weather and forestry. Its members even conducted experiments with a diving-bell in 1664. Boyle's book *Sceptical Chymist* of 1661 earned him the nickname 'the father of Chemistry'. Isaac Newton's appointment as Lucasian Professor of Mathematics at Cambridge in 1669 enabled him to research a range of mathematical and physical ideas that were collected in his *Principia Mathematica*, published by the Society in 1687; in 1671 he had sent his design for a telescope to the society to be tested. Four years later Sir Christopher Wren asked the opinion of the society on the issue of the strength of arches and abutments, which was critical for the rebuilding of London. In this way, the Royal Society brought serious science and experimentation into the heart of Whitehall, where Charles II created a Physick Garden. He also sponsored the creation of a map of the heavens. John Flamsteed (1646–1719), Charles' astronomer royal and a fellow of the Royal Society, was the first to record a partial eclipse of the sun.

Charles II and the returning exiled cavaliers brought many ideas with them from the continent. Among them were distinctive architectural tastes. Restoration architects experimented with styles copied from Ancient Rome, Italy, France and Holland. They also adopted the Palladian style of Inigo Jones, the English builder who had died in 1652. These influences combined to form an 'English baroque' architectural style. Among the English baroque buildings were Greenwich Hospital, built as a hospital and almshouse for injured sailors in 1694, and the buildings designed by Nicholas Hawksmoor (1661–1736) and John Vanbrugh (1664–1726). In London, these houses grew up across the fields of Westminster, St James' and Piccadilly. Some of the aristocrats who built their grand houses here made money as property developers. Charles II was particularly keen to encourage grand architecture and sought initially to do so through the post of surveyor-general, but the Fire of London put paid to such plans.

Perhaps the greatest single building of post-Restoration Britain was St Paul's Cathedral, built after the Great Fire of London in 1666. At the top of Ludgate Hill, the huge new Palladian building captured the confidence of Restoration culture and took thirty-three years to build. This was partly because the 'little ice age' of the late seventeenth century meant that in the winters the ground was too frozen to work. Teams of horses were required to haul the huge forty-two-foot beams brought from Yorkshire and German forests to support the aisles. The cathedral's dome, started in 1700, towered over the building in emulation of St Peter's in Rome, though Wren had to reduce its size from his first plans. Indeed, Wren had wept when a committee had rejected his first designs. The cathedral was only finished in October 1708 when Sir Christopher Wren and his son fitted the cross to the top of the dome. In May 1709 the scaffolding was finally removed and the new edifice could be seen and admired by Londoners. A year later, driven to distraction by the process of working with governments and committees with their own tastes and desires, Wren gave up the office of architect and asked for his back-pay, suspended since 1675 to be paid. Ironically he died in 1723, having caught a cold on the way to visit his building. Under Queen Anne, St Paul's became a place of national thanksgiving for the successive victories in Europe and the 1707 Union with Scotland. For the men and women of Britain in the eighteenth and nineteenth centuries, St Paul's became a site of national rejoicing and mourning.

Despite Charles II's own French-influenced tastes, the leading poet of the day remained the distinctly English John Milton (1608–74), whose *Paradise Lost* was published in 1667. It quickly sold its first printing of 1,300 copies and ran through three further editions – though Milton received only £5 in advance and £15 in royalties. It coined an astonishing number of new words, including 'satanic' and 'pandemonium'. It was so popular that fellow poet Andrew Marvell (1621–78) proposed to adapt it for the stage, but could not get round the problem of Adam and Eve's nudity.

Poetry was increasingly popular as it became associated with satire and poking fun, with John Dryden and Andrew Marvell in the vanguard of this trend. Nevertheless, one of the best-selling poets of the day, Abraham Cowley (1618–67), was renowned for epic poetry and odes on serious topics such as the foundation of the Royal Society.

Although 'Restoration comedies' have become a byword for frivolity and vulgarity on the stage, Charles II's theatricals under his two licensed playmasters, William Davenant (1606–68) and Thomas Killigrew (1606–95), were dominated by tragicomedies, plays in which serious themes and moral dilemmas were worked out. Pepys noted in 1661 that he saw a woman acting on the stage for the first time; previously boys had been required to take women's roles. Plays were enormously popular: in 1661 Pepys attended sixty-six performances, many of which were to see a play more than once. He also attended one of the first Punch-and-Judy shows in Britain. Drama was one of the forms that united rich and poor. It was still the custom for people to be admitted free to the first act of a play, and consequently there was often a crush of poorer theatre-goers at the start of a play.

Music was also a form that united rich and poor. Released from the Puritan restrictions, music was heard in public again after 1660. There were public concerts and bands that played in inns, while the elite enjoyed chamber music and oratorios. Virginals, which were a sort of harpsichord small enough to carry in the streets, were also played in the grand drawing rooms of the aristocracy. Music from elite performances was often repeated in the streets for the poor to hear. Charles II introduced violins into the chapel royal, and, with the restoration of the Church of England, psalms were sung once again in parish churches, accompanied by bands of musicians. Popular composers like Henry Purcell (1658–95) received important commissions, such as to compose the music to accompany the funeral of Queen Mary in 1694, but to make ends meet they also had to compose popular secular works for theatres. Perhaps, as in all ages, those features of the Restoration that particularly made it seem new and differentiated from the past, were its culture and taste.

Dancing was also a pastime that transcended class. The wealthy might employ a dancing master so that they could learn the latest fashionable French dances, but popular jigs, reels, hops and sarabands were, like tunes, adopted at fairs and even in the streets.

Serious writing was the sphere of all, even the Lord Chancellor, Lord Clarendon, whose *History of the Great Rebellion,* was published in 1667. It earned so much money for Oxford University Press that it partly funded the Clarendon Building in Oxford. Samuel Butler's (1612–80) satirical poem, *Hudibras*, published in 1663, which recounted the adventures of Sir Hudibras and his squire Rappo, poked fun at the excesses of the Civil War. It was to be one of the most successful published works of the next century and a half. *Hudibras* was celebrated by Pepys, Voltaire (1694–1778), John Wesley

(1703–91) and William Hogarth (1697–1764) and sold in huge quantities and was widely pirated. But the dominant book of the period, running through eleven editions and more than 100,000 copies, was John Bunyan's *The Pilgrim's Progress*, an allegory of a good Christian life. Most people probably only had access to three or four books, all of them likely to be devotional: as well as the Bible, they might have had the *Whole Duty of Man* and the *Practice of Piety* – two religious handbooks produced and sold in huge quantities – and such works as *The Pilgrim's Progress* and Milton's *Paradise Lost*.

To return to the question posed at the start of this chapter: did 1660 mark a sharp change in Britain's history? With a new king, a reversal in religious policy and a new and vibrant culture, Britain had much that seemed new and fresh. This was especially so after the dour Commonwealth of Cromwell, which appeared to be so different. But there were longer-term changes that were already underway in Britain's economy and society, trends such as urbanization and increasing productivity in agriculture. These continued, and quickened, under the Restoration so that within a decade or so they added to the sense of change and difference from the years of the Commonwealth. Yet in some ways Britons looked backwards. In religion, the settlement of 1662 was highly conservative, seeking to turn back the clock to before the execution of Charles I. Charles II and later James II were monarchs who favoured the divine right of kings. So while 1660 is our starting point, we must not forget that for many people the restoration of Charles II on 25 May was just another day.

2

POLITICS AND THE STATE, 1660–1714

Fifty-four years after Charles II stepped ashore at Dover, another king from Europe arrived. He was Britain's second foreign ruler in twenty years. In September 1714, the new King, George I, set foot for the first time on English soil at Greenwich. One of the first people to greet him was the 64-year-old John Churchill, Duke of Marlborough (1650–1722). Marlborough was a great survivor and his career illustrates the dangerous times that many lived through during this period. Churchill had risen to Charles II's attention as a young army officer during the Dutch wars. He had been a gentleman of the bedchamber to James, Duke of York, and went into exile with him in 1679. When James became king in 1683 Churchill was made a lord and appointed second-in-command of the army. By 1688, however, he was conspiring against James and ultimately betrayed him. During the French wars of William and Mary's and Anne's reigns, Churchill became commander-in-chief, though he also experienced periods of deep disfavour, and was even imprisoned in the Tower in 1691. Under both

William and Queen Anne, Marlborough held political posts as
well as directing the war. To the public he appeared, in turn, to
be a hero and a villain. There were allegations that he made a
fortune from army contracts and embezzlement of army
expenditure. In 1711 he was dismissed by the Tory government
and retired from public life. In 1714, George I greeted him with
the words: 'My Lord Duke, I hope your troubles are now
over,' and, as his first act, restored him to the highly lucrative
post of master-general of the ordnance. Marlborough's career
is a barometer of the ebb and flow of political fortunes between
1660 and 1714 and exemplifies the remarkable changes that
affected Britain in this period. He gingerly stepped through the
minefield of politics, like the fictional vicar of Bray who also
changed his theology to reflect the changing religious politics
of this period.

The Reign of Charles II

The Restoration of Charles II is sometimes presented as
effortless and uncontested. Charles' joke, that he blamed
himself for not returning sooner as he met no one who said
anything other than that they had heartily wished for his
return to the throne, disguised the national ambivalence. In
fact, the return of the monarchy was not achieved without
some effort. As late as August 1659 there had been a royalist
uprising in Cheshire, led by Sir George Booth, but it did not
attract much support and was easily crushed. Republicanism
seemed to be alive and well. Five months later, when General
Monck crossed the border from Scotland to England, the
soldiers in his army still believed that they were following a
general committed to the parliamentary and republican cause.
When it became clear that Monck was likely to organize a
Stuart restoration, John Lambert, a hardened republican,
escaped from London and fielded troops at Edgehill to oppose
the Restoration of the monarchy. Monck quickly ended
Lambert's challenge. But, even after Charles II's arrival, there
were anti-monarchist risings in London in January 1661,

which took the city militia and a company of life guards to suppress. A further rising against the monarchy occurred in the north of England in 1663. Inevitably therefore, after the Restoration the royalists were concerned about the security of the new regime.

The new Parliament, which assembled in May 1661, was known as the Cavalier Parliament because it contained such a large royalist majority. It had few representatives of either the republicans or Presbyterians. It was a Parliament that was highly conservative and had little tolerance for political or religious minorities. Hence religious Dissenters – anyone not part of the established Church – were targeted in the Clarendon Code, a group of laws named after Charles' leading minister, Lord Clarendon, who framed them. The King's principal adviser, Clarendon was a stern monarchist and Anglican who had suffered the privations of exile during the Commonwealth. He and Charles were thought to be consciously seeking an expansion of the powers of the monarchy, following the example of Louis XIV of France, Charles' cousin. The Cavalier Parliament also passed the Licensing Act in 1662, which revived press censorship. Dominated by Anglicans, the Parliament resolutely supported the Church of England and refused to consider the King's Declaration of Breda, which had promised religious freedom to all. There was also legislation against 'tumultuous petitioning', restricting the right to petition the King to justices of the peace and petitions initiated by grand juries.

Fairly swiftly, Charles' attentions were drawn to dynastic and religious affairs. First, in May 1662, he married the Catholic Princess Catherine of Braganza (1638–1705), daughter of the King of Portugal. Catherine was said to have brought the fashion of tea drinking to Britain, and the first London coffee house, the Great Turk, opened in 1662. The marriage cemented England's alliance with Portugal and brought the garrisons of Tangier and Bombay to England as Catherine's dowry. John Churchill was an officer in the

English regiment sent to take possession of Tangier. The marriage was unpopular because Queen Catherine maintained a Catholic household, which fuelled concerns about Charles II's ambivalent religious views, seeming to favour Catholicism. Although Catherine had a number of pregnancies, she proved incapable of carrying a child to full term, leaving Charles heirless. As time went on, it became clear that Charles' brother, James, Duke of York, who had become a Catholic in 1669, would succeed him, causing growing anxiety to Protestants. The absence of a legitimate heir, perhaps, made people more tolerant of Charles' numerous infidelities, mistresses and bastards. There were also suggestive jokes giving Charles the nickname of 'Old Rowley', after his stallion.

The two principal concerns of foreign policy in the 1660s were trade and religion. Charles favoured France, an inclination that had developed during more than a decade in exile. He had spent much of the time France and his sister had married into the French royal family. The strongly Protestant instincts of the majority of Britons made Holland, rather than France, a natural ally. However, the Dutch were trading competitors and conflict grew between English merchants – particularly the Royal African Company – and Dutch traders. The Dutch were also the targets of English piracy and the mercantilist system. By 1665 the Royal Navy was obliged to defend private traders in their conflict with the Dutch. Although there was disquiet at the Crown's high levels of expenditure, Parliament agreed a budget of £2.5m to fight a maritime war against the Dutch – the First Dutch War. In August 1664 New Amsterdam was seized from the Dutch in America and renamed New York, in honour of the Duke of York. This was to strengthen Britain's strategic base in North America and marked the start of the decline of Dutch influence there.

In 1665 the Second Dutch War resulted in a series of inconclusive naval engagements. As a consequence of a diminished appetite for war, naval expenditure fell. This weakness enabled the Dutch to inflict a humiliation on the fleet in June 1667 by a raid on the Thames which destroyed some capital ships. The burning ships lit up the night sky, causing rumours in Gravesend of an invasion. In embarrassment, the King had to find a scapegoat, and found it in Clarendon, who was dismissed as a minister, impeached and exiled.

The Dutch wars, in which John Churchill also served, added to serious tension between the King and Parliament. Charles felt restricted by Parliament, and especially its unwillingness to vote sufficient funds for him. In turn, Parliament regarded Charles as profligate and viewed his pro-French views, and his desire for religious toleration, with concern. Charles replaced Clarendon with Lord Arlington (1618–85) and the Duke of Buckingham (1628–87), and, despite the King's misgivings, they ended the Dutch conflict and made the Triple Alliance with Holland and Sweden against France. The new government also persuaded the King to be more flexible and brokered better relations with Parliament. Charles' willingness to agree to the Conventicle Act, which outlawed worship by religious Nonconformists, encouraged Parliament to grant him a higher income in 1669–70.

While these compromises calmed tension between King and the Commons, it created a sense that the King would not obtain grants of taxes from Parliament without conceding something in return. This was an important factor in the government of the country. The compromises concealed Charles' fundamental duplicity: while his foreign policy ostensibly treated France as a threat, secretly he was negotiating a treaty with Louis XIV that pledged Charles to attack the Dutch alongside the French. Charles had already demonstrated an appetite for raising funds without Parliament – in 1662 he had sold Dunkirk to the French for £400,000.

The secret clauses of the 1670 Treaty of Dover, signed by Arlington and Thomas Clifford (1630–72), both Catholics, granted Charles an income from Louis XIV. This money gave Charles a degree of financial independence from Parliament. In exchange, Charles agreed to 'reconcile himself with the Church of Rome' as soon as the political affairs in England permitted, terms so shocking that Charles kept them secret, even from his other senior ministers, Buckingham, the Duke of Lauderdale and Anthony Ashley Cooper, Lord (later Earl of) Shaftesbury (1621–83). While the secrecy of the terms of the Treaty of Dover was maintained for some time, Parliament remained concerned that Charles showed undue interest in religious toleration.

In 1672, during a parliamentary recess, Charles acted alone and issued a Declaration of Indulgence. This asserted the King's claim to be able to suspend laws. It also allowed religious Dissenters, both Catholic and Protestant, to worship freely. Briefly, 1,400 licences for meeting houses were issued, which permitted freedom of worship. But the declaration was a challenge to both the constitution and the religious settlement of 1660. Charles' claim to be able to suspend laws was dubious, and was repeatedly denied by the Commons.

Parliament was determined to reverse the Declaration of Indulgence, which it saw as damaging the Church of England. When Parliament met again, early in 1673, the Commons forced Charles to withdraw his declaration. To enforce its insistence on an Anglican monopoly, the Commons passed the Test Act. This required all government officials and military officers to receive Holy Communion in the Church of England, or lose their posts. They also had to declare that they did not believe in the Catholic doctrine of transubstantiation in Holy Communion. Among those who were forced to resign as a result of the Test Act was the heir to the throne James, Duke of York. As a Catholic, he could no longer be lord high admiral. Worse still, the conflict coincided with a third Dutch war, which seemed to be a product of Anglo-French cooperation.

In addition to the humiliation over the abandonment of the Declaration of Indulgence, in 1674 Charles was obliged to settle the Third Dutch War. In consequence, Charles dismissed the 'Cabal Government' of Clifford, Arlington, Buckingham,

Ashley Cooper (Shaftesbury) and Lauderdale, and in their place chose the royalist Thomas Osborne, later Lord Danby (1631–1712). Danby strengthen royal finances and established the origins of the civil service. Danby also created a distinct 'court party' that would counter the criticisms of the emerging opposition to the King (or 'country party') that was led by Lord Shaftesbury. To create support for the King, Danby realized he needed to ally the King with the gentry, so he persuaded Charles that the opposition country party, in alliance with Protestant Dissenters, was challenging his authority and had to be sternly opposed. This persuaded the King that his desire for religious toleration merely gave the Dissenters power to undermine him. The King traded religious toleration for greater authority against his opponents.

At the same time, the country party MPs championed peace and an alliance with Protestant Holland. They warned of the dangers of a Catholic succession and of policies that flew too close to France. Charles never entirely gave his full support to Danby's strategy, but he came to share Danby's concern that the country party represented a serious threat to his inclination towards Louis XIV and France. However, Charles had a talent for tacking between the two sides. In 1677 he agreed that his niece, Mary, should marry the Dutch Stadtholder, Prince William of Orange.

By the middle of the 1670s, popular fear of Catholicism had reached most areas of society. The Church of England, in particular, was becoming strongly anti-Catholic. There was a rash of anti-Catholic tracts and sermons from leading Anglicans. In late 1678 the country was struck by a hysterical outburst of anti-Catholicism, known as the 'Popish Plot'. Titus Oates (1649–1705), a Dissenter, charlatan and plotter, claimed to have evidence of a conspiracy by the Jesuits to murder Charles and restore Roman Catholicism to England. Although the evidence and the plot were completely false, the country became gripped by anti-Catholic hysteria. This was largely because Oates' absurd claims fitted the psychological and religious tendencies of the times. The murder of Sir Edmund Berry Godfrey (1621–78), the London magistrate who had first heard Oates' claims, seemed to provide evidence of a dangerous conspiracy. London gave itself up to hysteria and violence. At the 5 November pope-burning processions, almost half the residents of the city, about 200,000 people, turned up to join in the celebration.

In the ensuing panic, thirty-five alleged conspirators in the plot were executed. Even the Archbishop of Canterbury, William Sancroft, urged some of the condemned to admit their parts in the plot. Anti-Catholic laws were revived, and Danby's political position was undermined when it was revealed that he had been in secret negotiation with France. Parliament voted for Danby's impeachment and investigated the Anglo-French negotiations.

In the wake of the Popish Plot, a second Test Act in 1678 barred any non-Anglican from sitting in Parliament. A clause granting an exception for the Duke of York, the heir to the throne, to sit in the House of Lords was carried by just two votes. This reflected considerable distrust of James personally. In response to what he saw as the worrying rise of the country party, Charles dissolved Parliament. He also saw that, in the wake of the Popish Plot, the presence of the Duke of York in London was a source of aggravation. So Charles asked James and his supporters, including John Churchill, to leave England. Initially James moved to Brussels, and in 1680 to Scotland, where he would not attract such extreme exclusionist opposition.

The Popish Plot focused attention on the succession because it had become clear that Charles and Catherine would have no legitimate heir. James, Duke of York, was not just a Catholic, he was inflexible and autocratic by temperament. He was seen by some as a future danger to English liberties and religion. The court party settled on the succession of James, whereas the country party demanded his exclusion from the throne. This issue dominated sittings of the next three parliaments elected in 1679, 1680 and 1681. In the first of these elections, John

Churchill stood as a court candidate for the seat of Newtown, Isle of Wight. Those court party supporters of Charles, like Churchill, who would not countenance any change in the succession of the Duke of York, were derided as 'Tories', from the Irish term *toraidhe* for a bandit or cattle thief. The country party's determination that James should be excluded from the throne earned them the nickname 'Whiggamore' – a term of abuse for a Scottish Presbyterian republican. The Whigs even introduced an Exclusion Bill, seeking to prevent James' succession to the throne.

In 1679, in this tense atmosphere, some wanted to protect themselves from a future Catholic ruler. Lord Shaftesbury introduced a bill to Parliament to prevent anyone from being imprisoned without trial. As a teller who counted votes in the House of Lords, Shaftesbury deliberately overstated the votes in favour of his bill by ten, thus ensuring that the bill would pass. He also sprinted through the House of Lords to ensure the bill got on to the list in time for the King to sign it, with just a few seconds to spare. On such cunning and guile Habeas Corpus – the legal right not to be imprisoned without a trial – rested. Later the Habeas Corpus Act would be exported with British colonialism to be a pillar of civil liberties across the world. Even with this to protect them, the Whigs remained opposed to James' succession.

The problem for the Protestant Dissenters, those excluded by the religious settlement of 1660–2, was that they supported the cause of religious toleration but opposed the King's new Anglican policy. As far as Charles II was concerned, this now placed them further beyond the pale of political respectability. In time, Protestant Dissenters came to provide an important plank of support for the Whigs. The Whigs' problem was that they were hampered by the absence of a realistic alternative to James to succeed to the throne. Charles' oldest illegitimate son, James Scott, Duke of Monmouth, was a Protestant and clearly ambitious for the crown, but it was unthinkable that an illegitimate son should succeed. The only other possibility was for the throne to jump a generation to Mary, daughter of James, Duke of York by his first wife. Mary had married the Protestant William of Orange – who was also Charles' nephew – and she had been brought up in the Church of England. But the common law ruled out any succession other than that of James. James was the rightful heir and Charles would not change the succession.

In 1673, James, a widower, had married a second wife, the Catholic Princess Mary of Modena (1658–1718). Over the next ten years she had a series of miscarriages. Some exclusionists were prepared to allow James to succeed to the throne because it seemed likely that James' Protestant daughter, Mary of Orange, would eventually succeed him. They assumed that the period of a Catholic kingship would be a temporary blip.

The Popish Plot had been a farrago of falsehoods, but it ushered in all sorts of real plots and rumoured conspiracies. In 1681, Lord Shaftesbury was indicted for treason, but was acquitted by a sympathetic jury and fled abroad. The Green Ribbon Club was established, with provincial off-shoots. It was a secret Whig club that aimed to prevent James' succession. In 1683, the Duke of Monmouth conducted a tour of the West Country, which clearly seemed to be a preparation for a military challenge to James' succession. Also in 1683, the Rye House Plot was uncovered, a conspiracy to assassinate both Charles and James. Leading Whigs such as Lord William Russell (1639–83) and Algernon Sidney (1622–83) were implicated in the plot and executed; other conspirators and their friends, including Monmouth, fled to Holland. In this tense atmosphere, Charles ignored the Triennial Act, which required elections to be held every three years. Neither did he call a meeting of Parliament, fearing it would have a Whig majority. Instead he relied on public trials and the purging of Whigs from all public offices to show his support for the Tory Anglicans. He also invited James to return to England from his exile.

Charles died unexpectedly in January 1685. He was exhausted by the pressure of ruling a turbulent country and balancing his own inclinations with those of Parliament, but died from mercury poisoning from inhaling its fumes in his private laboratory. On his deathbed he was received into the Roman Catholic Church, in fulfilment of his undertaking to Louis XIV. This was not widely known at the time.

If we compare the characters of Charles and James we can see the ways in which individual characters shaped the age they lived in. Charles possessed a mental agility and suppleness which enabled him to bend with the winds of fortune. He also had a personal charm which enabled him to slip out from under the worst recriminations. Despite his clear preference for Louis, France and Catholicism, he was brought to peace with the Protestant Dutch and formed alliances with them against the French. He also responded to the Commons' insistence on religious intolerance, despite the Declaration of Breda and his desire to permit Protestant and Catholic subjects freedom of conscience. Although towards the end of his reign he showed signs of increasing inflexibility, Charles remained personally popular, and was well regarded for the consideration he showed for his Queen.

In contrast, James' character was inflexible and brittle. He would not tolerate people who disagreed with him, and tended to be affronted by them. Such a reactionary and autocratic character did not bode well in the circumstances of his accession. It was feared that James wanted to return England to the Catholic Church and to restore the Catholic hierarchy. He believed that the Church of England would not oppose him in this. He also hoped to use religious toleration for all as a Trojan horse, to free Catholics from penal laws. James seemed to admire Louis XIV even more than Charles did, and appeared to believe that Catholic absolutism was the best model for Britain.

James II and the Glorious Revolution

Despite attempts to prevent his succession, James began his reign in fairly good circumstances. In a honeymoon period there was an upsurge of Tory feeling that was strongly favourable to him. He had the support of the bishops of the Church of England and, at his accession Council, he promised to protect the Church, as long as it did not oppose him. His first Parliament was strongly Tory, something that had eluded his brother. It voted him a generous Civil List payment, which had also been denied to Charles.

There were early cracks in the apparent harmony between the King and his leading subjects, however. Significant numbers of peers stayed away from James' coronation and many of them were shocked by his hearing Catholic Mass immediately after the ceremony. Accounts of the coronation claimed that the crown had rocked on James' head, because it was too big for him – people took this as a bad omen. James' installation of Catholic priests and confessors in Whitehall Palace, and the creation of a Catholic chapel there, were also sources of serious concern. Early in his reign, some Anglican clergy, who were hostile to Catholicism, preached against it. The Whig exclusionists' resolve, to prevent James from ruling, was soon tested by the Monmouth Rebellion.

In May 1685, Charles' illegitimate son, the Duke of Monmouth, invaded the West Country from Holland. The rising was planned to coincide with a second rebellion in Scotland, led by the Earl of Argyll, which quickly collapsed. There were also plans for uprisings in East Anglia and Cheshire, which never appeared. Monmouth was supported by a strongly Protestant army supplemented by local people with little military training, and he was declared king in Taunton on 18 June. But the royal army, commanded by Lord Faversham and John Churchill, wiped out the rebellion at the Battle of Sedgemoor in July 1685, the last pitched battle on English soil. Monmouth was captured and executed. The executioner botched the beheading, failing to kill him with three blows, and eventually resorted to a knife to separate the Duke's head from his body. The executioner had to be protected from the mob, who were appalled at his lack of skill.

Brutal justice was also meted out to the rebels in the West Country in the 'Bloody Assizes' of Judge Jeffreys. The bodies of rebels were cut into quarters and hanged from trees all over Somerset. The last woman to be burnt to death in England was Elizabeth Gaunt, who harboured some of the Monmouth rebels after Sedgemoor. As a result of the defeat of the Monmouth Rebellion, James thought that he enjoyed some divine protection. He believed he had been saved from the rebellion for a special purpose. This probably intensified his desire to restore Catholicism to England and his belief that he had been chosen to do so.

The Monmouth Rebellion showed that James had the support of most of the landed classes, who refused to help Monmouth. He also had the support of the Church, which actively defended the King. Bishop Mews (1619–1706) even lent the royal army his carriage horses to haul the King's artillery at Sedgemoor. The rebellion also gave James the opportunity to make emergency army commissions of Catholic officers, and to retain a standing army to defend him from other possible risings. In order to appoint Catholic army officers, James had to suspend the Test Act. In doing so, he also claimed to have the right to suspend any laws – something Charles had sought, but which Parliament had repeatedly refused to allow him. Now Parliament infuriated James by refusing to permit Catholic officers to retain their commissions in the army. Parliament also refused to recognize his claim to the right to suspend laws. Consequently James dissolved Parliament, and hoped elections would bring a Commons that would do his bidding.

James was also angered by the growing number of anti-Catholic sermons preached by Anglican clergy. He knew he had little chance of legalizing Catholicism if Anglicans stirred up hatred of Catholics in their sermons. James set up an Ecclesiastical Commission which suspended the Bishop of London, Henry Compton (1632–1713), for his failure to prevent such sermons. From this point on, James' relationship with the Church rapidly deteriorated, even to the point where he ordered Archbishop Sancroft to stay away from the court for his refusal to sit on the Ecclesiastical Commission. James misjudged people's disquiet at the rise of Catholicism. When the Duke of Somerset refused to greet the papal nuncio in London, reminding the King that it was illegal, James replied, 'I am above the law.' Somerset responded, 'but I am not'. He was sacked for doing so.

From 1687, James followed two principal policies. First, he tried to manipulate elections to Parliament. This was an attempt to get a majority of MPs in favour of repeal of the Test Act and of laws which would legalize religious freedom for Catholics. James did this by making what were called *quo warranto* changes to borough charters, restricting the right to vote to his supporters. The trouble was that this tactic was unsuccessful. Time after time, borough charters were amended, only for James to find that there was still insufficient support in the towns to elect MPs sympathetic to his plans. Some borough charters were changed three or four times. James also ejected lords lieutenant and magistrates who would not help in the effort to elect a Parliament that would do as he wanted. In some cases this removed so many magistrates that legal cases could not be heard.

James' second policy was to try to drive a wedge between the Anglicans and the Protestant Dissenters, who were drawing together to oppose James' Catholic agenda. He did this by issuing a Declaration of Indulgence in April 1687, as his brother had done unsuccessfully in 1672. James hoped that Protestant Dissenters would see that they could benefit from the declaration and might therefore support his policies and abandon the Anglicans. This attempt also failed, not least because the Protestant Dissenters realized what James was up to. Lord Halifax (1633–95) told the Dissenters that the King wanted to 'hug them now so that he could squeeze them later'.

James also began a campaign to force Catholics into senior positions in the universities. The resistance of the fellows of

Magdalen College, Oxford, to the appointment of a Catholic president led James to expel all of them from the college. James also sacked a number of ministers who were not in agreement with his policies. These included his brothers-in-law, Lord Clarendon (1638–1709) and Lord Rochester (1641–1711). He also invited Catholic bishops to England to try to convert the population. By the start of 1688 many of those who had previously supported James had grave reservations about his policies. John Churchill joined an association of Protestant army officers, which showed how much he felt alienated by the King. Like many others, Churchill had decided that James could no longer be King.

The events that precipitated the crisis of James' reign arose from his renewal of the Declaration of Indulgence in April 1688. This time, however, James ordered all Anglican bishops to ensure the declaration was read in all churches in their dioceses. Seven leading bishops petitioned James, asking him not to insist on this provision and questioning his right to suspend laws. The King reacted with fury and imprisoned them. Most clergy still refused to read his declaration, to James' irritation. In what James hoped would be a show trial, the seven bishops were prosecuted for sedition, but they were acquitted, and James was humiliated. On the evening after the acquittal, seven politicians, including Bishop Compton and Lord Danby, secretly wrote to James' son-in-law and nephew, William of Orange. They asked him to come to England and save the country from James' Catholicism. The association of Protestant army officers, led by John Churchill, also pledged their support for William.

It is clear that William, as the Dutch Stadtholder, had already decided that he needed to gain the English throne. Without it, Holland would be faced with the prospect of a dangerous military alliance between James and Louis XIV. The need to act in the summer of 1688 was partly a result of the trial of the seven bishops, which had created popular opposition to James. But there were also worries because James' wife, Queen Mary

Beatrice, had surprised everyone by giving birth to a son. This boy was now the Catholic heir to the throne and displaced James' Protestant daughters in the line of succession. What had once seemed likely to be only a temporary Catholic monarchy now looked as if it would be permanent. Those who were adamantly opposed to James claimed that the son was a 'changeling' or substitute baby. They claimed the child had been smuggled into the Queen's bedchamber in a bedpan when the real child was stillborn. Few believed the bedpan rumours, but they cast some suspicion on the legitimacy of the prince.

William invaded England in November 1688. His army was small, at most 20,000 troops – including a 200-strong contingent of black troops from Surinam. He quickly won support from the same nobles and gentry who had ignored Monmouth. For example, the Duke of Beaufort, who had led the West Country militias against Monmouth, refused to mobilize them against William of Orange. He chose, instead, to remain at home. James' policies had offended so many groups: the landed classes, the Church, politicians and even the Dissenters, who felt they had been manipulated by the King. James fielded an army on Salisbury Plain, but his resistance to William collapsed in the face of widespread desertion by many aristocrats and politicians. James was even abandoned by his own army commanders, led by John Churchill, and by his daughter, Princess Anne. Plagued by nosebleeds, James seemed to suffer from a mental collapse. His wife and son were evacuated to the safety of France.

As James' authority fell apart, the mob looked as if it would take control of London. In Scotland, gangs of Presbyterians 'rabbed' episcopal clergy, whom they regarded as too inclined to Catholicism, ransacking their houses and ejecting them from parishes. All sorts of rumours spread across the country. In December, Alderman Newton in Cambridge recorded that he had heard rumours of '5 or 6,000 of the Irish lately disbanded burnt Bedford and cutt all their throats there and they were coming to Cambridge to doe the like'. In December

1688 James fled to France. In February 1689 the Convention Parliament, called without the king's authority, claimed that James had abdicated, and reluctantly agreed that the only course was to offer the throne jointly to William and Mary of Orange. This unique dual monarchy married William's right of conquest with Mary's hereditary right as James' daughter. The ejection of James and the succession of William and Mary was known as the 'Glorious Revolution'.

During James' brief reign anti-Catholicism had become entrenched in people's minds. The Whig Green Ribbon Clubs had organized the burning of an effigy of the pope on 17 November each year, commemorating the accession of Elizabeth I. By November 1688, Catholics even petitioned James not to leave London with his army to face William of Orange's invasion until after 17 November. They feared that, without royal and military presence in London, anti-Catholic riots would be uncontrollable. Such anti-Catholicism became entrenched in the popular imagination of many Britons for over a century.

The Scottish Parliament followed the lead of the English, granting the throne of Scotland to William and Mary on 11 April 1689. But 12,000 'wild geese', Scottish and Irish supporters of James who would not swear loyalty to William, now King William III, left for the exiled Stuart court in France. The English Parliament passed a Bill of Rights which settled what should have been resolved in 1660. It accused James II of abusing his power. It denied the Crown the right to suspend laws, to maintain a standing army, to tax without parliamentary approval, or to interfere with legal processes. The bill also stipulated that no Catholic would be permitted to succeed to the throne, nor could a monarch marry a Catholic. The Bill of Rights was the embryo of human rights legislation, but was also highly discriminatory towards Catholics. Its provisions on succession to the throne remain intact today.

James did not give up his throne easily, however. From France, with help from Louis XIV, he landed in Ireland in the spring of 1690. The Parliament of Ireland had not recognized James' abdication and declared that James remained king, denouncing those who had rebelled against him. In Ireland, James introduced a law that granted religious freedom to all Catholics and Protestants. With French and Irish troops, James hoped, in time, to restore himself to the thrones of Scotland and England from Ireland, but he was defeated at the Battle of the Boyne in July 1690 by an army led by William. The Battle of the Boyne is often presented as a religious as well as a political battle. However, both armies contained Catholic and Protestant troops: some in William's army even carried papal banners.

Two days after the Battle of the Boyne, William's army entered Dublin. James abandoned his troops, fled to France again and never managed to regain his kingdoms. In Irish folk memory, James was nicknamed 'Seamus a' chaca', literally 'James the Shit'. He died eleven years later. His son, also James, called the Old Pretender, kept alive the hope of a restoration of the Stuarts and his supporters were known as Jacobites (from 'Jacobus', the Latin for James). Jacobitism could divide families. Samuel and Susanna Wesley, parents of John and Charles Wesley, were divided by the issue. When, in 1701, Samuel noticed that Susanna did not say 'amen' at the close of prayers for William and Mary, he challenged her. Susanna admitted that she did not regard William and Mary as the rightful monarchs. Samuel, in fury, refused to sleep with her any more, saying if they had two kings they would have to have two beds.

On the morning of their coronation, Mary received a letter from her father. He wrote that he understood that Mary might have been following William's instructions, but that if she allowed herself to be crowned she would earn the curse of her father and brother. The letter unsettled Mary enough for her to be two and a half hours late for the ceremony. Such fears of a curse on those who had sworn oaths to James cast long shadows over the next seventy years. At the coronation feast, when the King's Champion threw down the gauntlet for any to challenge the right of William and Mary to the throne, an elderly woman on crutches picked it up, then laid down a glove in response.

One of the reasons why the revolution of 1688–9 is called the Glorious Revolution is that it was, in England and Scotland – though not in Ireland – a relatively bloodless change of regime. But it contained other, more crucial, features that later came to be celebrated as 'glorious'. The revolution settled, for the most part, the lingering issue of the nature of government authority in Britain. Charles I, and his sons Charles II and James II, had maintained that they were God's anointed rulers and therefore their authority was derived from God. This implied that they were not bound by the will of the people, expressed in Parliament. But the events of 1688 showed that Parliament held that there had been an unwritten contract between James and his subjects. James had broken this contract and therefore overthrowing him was legitimate. This view suggested that the origin of government authority lay in the people. The people gave power to their rulers on condition that they govern responsibly. The Glorious Revolution did not achieve this in a single stroke; these issues were hotly debated for a score or more years. But within two decades there were few mainstream politicians, thinkers or churchmen who did not implicitly accept that the origin of government power lay in the contract between a ruler and the people. The Bill of Rights may have been vaguely worded constitutional principles, but the new monarchs' powers were also circumscribed by the Triennial Act, requiring elections to be held every three years.

An equally important feature of the Glorious Revolution was a change in the religious laws in Britain. Besides the exclusion of Catholics from the throne, the new regime sought to include or 'comprehend' as many Protestant Dissenters as possible into a broadened Anglican Church. This was natural perhaps, given that William III was a Dutch Calvinist

Protestant. Broadening the Church to include all Protestants would have returned Anglicanism to Elizabeth I's ideal of a national Church of which all people were members. The settlement also aimed to grant religious toleration to the few whose consciences would not permit them to be included in the Church. There was a feeling that this was the entitlement of the Dissenters for their part in resisting James. Nevertheless, the Anglicans felt that, having faced ruin from a Catholic monarch, the Church of England was also owed a measure of protection. As a result, in the Toleration Act of 1689, the Protestant Dissenters were permitted freedom of worship, as long as they were loyal to William and Mary and were Trinitarian (that is, they accepted the divinity of Christ). However, the comprehension of Dissenters into the Church was rejected by Anglicans who would not make the liturgical changes necessary to allow them to join the Church. So the Toleration Act of 1689 made permanent the separation of Dissenters from Anglicans begun in 1662. This was the source of considerable anxiety and tension in the years to come.

Within the Church of England there was a small, but vocal, minority, including some senior clergy, who would not accept William and Mary as sovereigns while James, the anointed King, was still alive. These included the Archbishop of Canterbury and some other bishops. These clergy, known as Non-jurors, refused to take the oath of allegiance required of all clergy and were ejected from their parishes and church offices in 1690. They continued to be active long into the eighteenth century. The Non-jurors challenged the right of Parliament to decide who should be the monarch, arguing that James and his son were the rightful kings. Jacobites also challenged the right of William and Mary, and later Queen Anne and George I to succeed to the throne. The Non-jurors provided the Jacobites with a theological argument to restore James II and his son.

In response to the Glorious Revolution and the Toleration Act, Anglicans were separating into High Church and Low

Church, although these were not hard and fast groupings. The High Church instinct was to defend a high view of the Church and the priesthood, and oppose the legitimacy of Dissent. Low Churchmen supported religious toleration and emphasized sincerity of belief over the importance of strict doctrinal purity.

The defeat of James in 1690 led to a series of vicious anti-Catholic laws in Ireland, ending a period of relative tolerance. Catholics were forbidden to own arms, or a horse worth more than £5 (in other words, anything other than a nag). Catholics could not be admitted to the army, navy, the universities, the bar, town corporations or become magistrates. Catholic bishops were banished and no Catholic churches were allowed to be built. Catholic landowners were only allowed thirty-one-year leases on land. All Catholic estates were subject to subdivision – rather than primogeniture, which bequeathed the estate intact to the eldest son. This was a systematic attempt to eliminate the Catholic landed classes. In 1727, Catholics were also denied the vote at elections. By 1775, Catholics had been so excluded from society that only 5 per cent of land was owned (as opposed to leased) by Catholics.

The Reign of William and Mary

In Scotland, when James fled, the Scottish Presbyterians declared he had forfeited the throne. Their principal grievance was that James had sought to force Episcopalianism on the Scots. The settlement they agreed with William in 1689 excluded bishops from the Church of Scotland, which became Presbyterian. In the summer of 1689, a coalition of Episcopalians, lowlanders, Catholics and clans staged a revolt on James' behalf. They had an initial victory at the Battle of Killiecrankie, at which 2,000 Highland troops led by Viscount Dundee (1649–89) attacked William's artillery before they could reload. But the coalition was eroded by bribery and military actions. Dundee's death at Killicrankie also robbed the Jacobites of an effective leader. William exploited divisions between the clans mercilessly, which led to the Campbells' brutal massacre of the MacDonalds at Glencoe in 1692. The Scottish Jacobites remained numerous, but any organized challenge to William's rule collapsed, in part due to a famine. From 1695, five years of harvest failures resulted in terrible famines in Scotland, resulting in a 15 per cent fall in the population. Visitors to Scotland in this period, such as Celia Fiennes (1662–1741) and Daniel Defoe, were shocked by the poverty, dirt and dereliction in the country.

Throughout the English colonial possessions, from India and the West Indies to New England, William had to establish the authority of his rule with the local officials who had been appointed by James. In this way, the revolution of 1688 was not just a London-focused event, or even a British event, it reverberated across the world as people found themselves ruled by a monarch with limited powers rather than the autocratic James.

It is easy to overstate the control Parliament now exerted over William and Mary. Although the Commons carefully oversaw taxation, it had no appetite for confrontation with William, and no desire at all for a Stuart restoration, which was the only alternative to him. Nevertheless, the fact that elections were held, on average, every two years between 1690 and 1710, focused attention on the struggle between the Whigs and Tories at the polls and in the Commons. This coincided with an increasingly literate electorate. After 1695, when the Licensing Act lapsed, government censorship before publication no longer existed and political tracts poured from the printing presses (see Chapter 3). One consequence of the heightened politics, the growing literacy and the freedom of the press was the beginning of newspapers. The first London newspaper, the *Daily Courant*, was first published in 1702, although there had been financial news-sheets circulating since 1692. Within two years, there were nine weekly newspapers in London with a circulation of over 40,000 between them, and a readership of perhaps a third of the city. Newspapers were passed from hand to hand, and were available to read in pubs and coffee houses.

By 1712 newspapers were so widespread that they attracted a halfpenny tax, and a century later newspaper advertisements were also taxed.

The reign of William III and Mary II introduced all sorts of innovations from Holland. Those keen to emulate the new sovereigns, and others attracted to novelties, adopted the new fashions. Dutch-inspired goods quickly made their way across Britain: pantiles for roofs, blue-and-white Delft china (which later developed into 'willow pattern'), tulips, chinoiserie designs from the Dutch East Indies, yellow silks, wallpaper and furniture on tall well-turned legs. All these, and more, were introduced to Britain, 'William and Mary' becoming a style of its own in silverware, architecture, china and furniture, and a precursor to 'Queen Anne' design.

Given the nature of the Glorious Revolution, it was surprising that William appointed leading Tories to his first government, including Lords Halifax, Danby and Nottingham. However, from 1696, William relied increasingly on the Whigs and a close-knit group of ministers, called the 'Junto', which included John Churchill. The support that James received from Louis XIV and the Dutch interests of William III meant that the diplomatic choice between Protestant Holland and Catholic France was resolved. England was allied with the Dutch against France, which was explicitly portrayed as a Catholic threat to Britain. From the summer of 1689 England joined Holland and Austria in the Nine Years War to block French ambitions to dominate the continent. The enormous costs of this military and naval venture led to the introduction of 'Dutch' finance. This system borrowed money based on future tax receipts to pay for current spending In other words, the taxation of as yet unborn people was pledged to pay back the debt. As Tory landowners and MPs opposed the costs of the war, William increasingly relied on Whig ministers to support him.

To manage the national debt, the Bank of England was established in 1694, founded by William Paterson to act as the government's bank. Paterson raised a loan of £1.2 million for the government. In return, the subscribers were incorporated as the Governor and Company of the Bank of England with banking privileges, including the right to issue banknotes.

In 1697, the Treaty of Ryswick ended the Nine Years War, and wrung from France recognition of William as King of England. The treaty gave no territory to Britain, in part because it was so clear that Britain had gained so much advantage in trade from the war. Consequently, and against his own desire, William was forced to demobilize the army.

The succession to the throne remained a worry. Mary had died childless in 1694, and in 1700 Princess Anne's only surviving child, William's nephew, William Duke of Gloucester (1689–1700), died; it was clear that Anne would be unlikely to bear a healthy child. As a result, in 1701, the Act of Settlement named the Electress Sophia of Hanover as the next heir after Princess Anne. Sophia had the advantage of being the daughter of the hugely popular Elizabeth, the 'Winter Queen' of Bohemia, who was herself a daughter of James I. Within a year both James II and William III were dead. William III died after falling from his horse when it stumbled on a molehill, which led Jacobites to drink toasts to the mole, who they called 'the black gentleman in the velvet coat'. Queen Anne, the last Stuart monarch, ascended the throne.

Good Queen Anne

Queen Anne was Mary's sister and James II's youngest daughter. However, she was much more acceptable to the Tories than William and Mary had been, because she was a Stuart and a staunch supporter of the Church of England, and some felt that William had only had the right of conquest on his side. With continuing suggestions that James II's son, the Old Pretender, was a false 'bedpan' baby, Queen Anne appeared to be the more legitimate ruler. Few, other than hardline Jacobites, contested her right to the throne. Anne was a wily ruler with, as Sir John Clerk described, the crafty ability to remember some facts in great detail and to forget other things which she ought 'in truth and honour' to remember. She had a tragic private life, having given birth to fourteen children, none of whom survived. At just 37 years of age she had to be carried into her own coronation service because she was so crippled by her size and illness. She found comfort in her friendship with the Duchess of Marlborough (1660–1744) and in huge quantities of food, even eating three large meals on the day her much-loved husband, George of Denmark (1653–1708), died. By the end of her life she was so fat she needed a hoist to help her go upstairs.

It would be wrong to assume that politics in Queen Anne's reign were similar to the two-party system of today. The Whig and Tory parties should not be compared to modern political parties. Like the High Church and Low Church parties, they were loose groupings, with people moving between the two. There were few rigid policy differences between them. The period known as the 'rage of party', between the Whigs and Tories was not wholly ideological. Politics under Queen Anne may have been dominated by party strife, but the electorate only comprised 300,000 adult males. Many others participated in the excitement and hurly-burly of elections, but the right to vote was only given to those with a 'stake' in the country, usually in the form of land ownership. Women were denied the vote, though sometimes they could exert an influence. In the election of 1741 the town clerk of Bridgwater, Somerset, recorded that the parson, the Revd James Knight, 'had an excellent method of influence in this election, called henpecking, by which is meant that the electors' wives bias'd their husbands ... on account of the private treats he gave them at his house.'

Just as it is today, it has been suggested that eighteenth-century politics was dominated by politicians' personalities, self-interest and exercise of the benefits of power. In fact, while personalities and the desire to exercise power played a role in politics, politicians in this period were motivated by a cluster of 'interests'. These interests included links between patrons and clients, which often comprised complex ties of obligations and commitments. There were religious interests, with Whigs and Tories holding distinctive views on the Church and the legitimacy of the toleration of Dissent. There were also regional and family networks that might associate a politician with a particular interest. For example, John Churchill, who was made Duke of Marlborough in 1702, was the father-in-law of Lord Sunderland (1674–1722) and a long-standing friend of Lords Godolphin (1645–1712), Somers (1651–1716), Halifax and Wharton (1648–1715), all of whom were ministers under Queen Anne. There were, of course, also policy issues that divided politicians. These included support or opposition to wars and foreign policy, economic policy and religious concerns, which caused the Whigs and Tories to hark back to their formation in 1679–80. Before 1714, there was also the issue of the succession of the Protestant House of Hanover, which divided Whigs and pro-Hanoverian Tories from Jacobite Tories.

Although Queen Anne seemed to be a contrast to William III, she continued his policy of strong support for the wars against France. In 1701 William had assembled an alliance to fight the French again, but it was left to Anne to declare war on France in the War of Spanish Succession. This was another attempt by England, the Holy Roman Empire, Portugal and Holland to prevent French expansionism. These allies wanted to prevent the succession of a French prince to the Spanish throne. Queen Anne's commitment to the war was largely due to her support for Marlborough, now the commander-in-chief and husband of her confidante, Sarah, Duchess of Marlborough. Marlborough was to prove one of Britain's greatest generals, leading a swift and energetic army across Europe and winning a succession of stunning victories.

Queen Anne resumed elaborate Stuart ceremonial, which William III had largely abandoned. She touched people for the 'King's Evil', because scrofula was superstitiously thought to be cured by the sovereign's touch; touching people thus endorsed the legitimacy of her rule. She also enjoyed the ritual and display associated with the royal levee, the State opening of Parliament and thanksgiving services – though her eyesight was so poor she could often not make out individual people's faces. She was committed to the Church and in 1704 granted 'Queen Anne's Bounty', which allowed the Church to retain fees formerly paid to the government. This money was used to supplement the income of poor clergymen. Above all, Queen Anne knew the importance of winning the hearts of the people, something William had neglected, and she became popular with the crowds, who nicknamed her 'Good Queen Anne'.

Emboldened by the belief that they might gain the support of the Queen, the Tories in Church and State aimed to turn back the clock to before the Toleration Act of 1689. They were alarmed by the large numbers of Dissenting meetings licensed under the Toleration Act. They also felt that the increase in people worshipping outside the Church of England was a threat to both Church and State. The Tories particularly resented that Dissenters had found a loophole in the Test Act, which was aimed at preventing Dissenters from holding public office. There had been a long tradition of Dissenters occasionally taking Holy Communion in the Church of England – this was now exploited to enable Dissenters to obtain a certificate showing that they had conformed, and this was all that they required under the Test Act to hold public office. Of course, such Dissenters tended to be Whigs. This practice of occasional conformity to the Church offended Tories and High Churchmen who felt that toleration had gone too far, and too many Dissenters were getting round the Test Act. Perhaps the Tories overlooked the fact the Queen Anne's husband, Prince George of Denmark, was an occasional conformist, having been raised a Lutheran.

After 1701, the High Churchmen used Convocation (the parliament of the Church) as a place in which to give voice to these concerns. Convocation was also the forum in which the

High Churchmen attacked the Dissenters. Eventually, William, and later Anne, permitted Convocation to meet, and from 1703 there were repeated attacks on occasional conformity from the clergy. Two attempts were made in Parliament to outlaw occasional conformity. Each time, the bills were defeated in the House of Lords, with the votes of Whig bishops preventing the bills from passing. Queen Anne, however, was unwilling to support the Tories as they were only half-hearted in their support of the French war, in spite of Marlborough's great victory at Blenheim in 1704.

As the Tories stirred up trouble in the Church and opposed the war, Queen Anne came to rely more heavily on the Whigs. In principle, she preferred mixed governments of Tory and Whig ministers, but from 1708 she was forced to accept a government dominated by Junto Whigs, such as Godolphin and Somers. They at least had the merit that they were friends of Marlborough and backed the war effort. Frustratingly, despite Marlborough's series of brilliant victories at Ramillies in 1706, Oudenarde in 1708 and Malplaquet in 1709, none of these delivered a blow that knocked France out of the war. The view in England grew that the war was protracted and expensive. The Tories particularly advanced this opinion.

Union with Scotland

The French war also drew attention to tensions between England and Scotland. Relations between the two countries had been uneasy after the Glorious Revolution of 1688. Like James I, William III had been content to allow the two kingdoms to remain separate. However, Jacobite loyalties in Scotland seemed stronger and England feared that Scotland, like Ireland, would be a 'back door' for invasions. This fear was heightened by the 'Auld Alliance' between Scotland and France. There was also competition between England and Scotland in overseas trade. In 1695 the Company of Scotland began a trading venture to the Darien Isthmus in Panama, where they founded the settlement of New Edinburgh. The venture was both risky and highly speculative with little chance of success. Fearing the company would become a trading competitor in India and Africa, William III withdrew Dutch and English investment and the company collapsed.

After Queen Anne's succession, the Scottish Estates, or Parliament, insisted on a separate foreign policy. Scotland passed a separate law of succession to the Scottish throne, apparently to be a threat to enable them to gain access to English and colonial trade. This irritated the English Parliament, which suspended trade with Scotland in 1705. Parliament also threatened to seize Scottish assets in England if Scotland repudiated the Hanoverian succession. Under this pressure, Scotland agreed to open negotiations for a union of the two countries, and commissioners from England and Scotland undertook protracted and difficult negotiations.

By a combination of threats and bribes the Scottish commissioners were brought to agree to a union. Part of the agreement was that England gave £400,000 compensation for the losses of the Darien venture. The Union established a single parliament for the 'United Kingdom', and it made considerable concessions to a separate Scottish identity. Scotland would retain its own separate legal, educational and religious structures, as well as gaining full access to trade with English colonies. Early versions of the Union were unacceptable to Queen Anne, who threatened to use her veto to prevent them. She was later to use the veto on a Militia Bill for Scotland – the last occasion on which the power was used by the sovereign.

The Act of Union was finally ratified by both countries in 1707, and celebrated by Queen Anne at a service of thanksgiving at St Paul's. The design for a flag, first devised by James I, superimposing the St George's cross on the St Andrew's cross became the Union flag. The new Parliament of the United Kingdom of Great Britain was also inaugurated. The post of secretary of state for Scotland, created under James I to connect the Estates in Edinburgh with the king in London, was retained as the official minister for Scotland. In Scotland, the

Union quickly became unpopular and Scottish politicians felt that they had been duped. Scotland remained a location for actual or planned Jacobite risings in 1708, 1715, 1719 and 1745, but the Union enabled the army to suppress these and none of these risings achieved sufficient purchase to threaten the new nation.

The Scottish MPs in the new Parliament, just forty-five of them, represented less than a tenth of the Commons. There were sixteen representative peers, elected by the Scottish lords, to sit in the united House of Lords. This number was smaller than the English and Welsh bishops who sat in the Lords. Their subsequent treatment by the British Parliament hardly inspired the Scots with confidence. In 1711 the House of Lords excluded Scottish peers who also held British peerages. A year later, a Toleration Act legalized the position of the Episcopalian clergy in Scotland, which infuriated the Presbyterian Church.

The Union with Scotland at least relieved Scotland of the blight of political in-fighting. Politics moved to Westminster, and Edinburgh was free of its intrigue and adversarial character. Some have suggested that this is what made the city the centre of the Scottish Enlightenment later in the eighteenth century. But stubborn Jacobitism meant that Scotland was also perceived as 'hapless Caledonia' by Tobias Smollett in his poem 'The Tears of Scotland' in 1746. Symbolically, the crown of Scotland was locked in an oak chest and bricked into a room in Edinburgh Castle, and was not seen for the next eighty-seven years.

The new United Kingdom did not alter the position of Ireland, which retained its own parliament and status as a separate kingdom, though it was very much subordinate to England and Scotland. The Westminster Parliament exerted far more control over Ireland's economy – by excluding Irish goods from Britain, which damaged Ireland financially – than the Irish Parliament could. Nevertheless, there were attempts to boost the Irish economy. These included the Linen Board, set up in 1711 to promote the use of linen, and the establishment of an Irish victualling industry supplying salt beef for British ships and colonies. Visitors to Ireland, like those to Scotland, found the countryside poor and depressed. In 1718 Bishop William Nicolson of Derry (1655–1727) found the hunger worse than he had seen in Scotland and northern Europe.

Wales, the third Celtic constituent of Britain, entered a period of cultural advance during the early years of the eighteenth century. Despite occasional English sneers at Welsh culture, St David's Day was still observed by the court in London, and Oxford remained a centre for Celtic study. There was a conscious effort to reclaim Welsh history and antiquities in the scholarly work of Edward Lhuyd (1660–1709) and Henry Rowlands (1655–1723). Lhuyd's main achievement, *Archaeologica Britannica*, was published in 1707 with the help of the historian Moses Williams (1686–1742). It recognized the linguistic connection between the Gaelic and the ancient British languages. Lhuyd also drew around him in Oxford an impressive array of Welsh scholars who studied the language, botany, archaeology, folklore and history of their native land.

Henry Rowlands' work explored the Druidic influence in North Wales. What Lhuyd and Rowlands achieved was the start of a widespread Welsh cultural revival during the eighteenth century. It coincided with some economic developments in the lead mines of Cardiganshire and the growth of maritime trade from the ports of Swansea and Neath. From the perspective of London, Wales remained backward, and a focus of Jacobite feeling. The shrine of St Winefride in Flintshire was a secret Catholic place of pilgrimage throughout the period. James II's son (the 'bedpan' baby) had been conceived after James' visit there in 1687, and it was therefore a place which implied the legitimacy of the Pretender. As a result, the appointments of lord lieutenant of Wales and of bishops in Wales were politically important. These dignitaries were expected to defend the settlement of 1688 and the Hanoverian succession.

Peace and Strife

Religious issues loomed large in the public sphere. Against the background of growing war-weariness, the Whigs misjudged the mood of the nation. In November 1709, Henry Sacheverell (1674–1724), a troublesome High Church clergyman, preached a controversial sermon before the Lord Mayor of London in St Paul's. In it, Sacheverell accused the Whigs and Low Churchmen, who agreed with the toleration of Dissent, of being 'false brethren' to the Church. He also questioned the legitimacy of the revolution of 1688. Sacheverell said that the role of the subject was to be unconditionally obedient to the ruler, and anyone who opposed the ruler was a traitor. He was thinking, of course, of James II, and this came close to questioning both Queen Anne's right to rule and the legitimacy of the Hanoverian succession. The Whig government was so outraged by Sacheverell's sermon that it chose to impeach him before the House of Lords. Sacheverell and his supporters turned the impeachment into an opportunity for popular and violent expressions of unrest. During the impeachment the mob sacked Dissenters' chapels and tracts poured from the presses arguing the case for and against Sacheverell.

The outcome of the impeachment was a legal victory – Sacheverell was found guilty. But it was also a political disaster as he was only sentenced to three years suspension from preaching. Sacheverell immediately began a countrywide tour stirring up High Church Tory feeling, with the cry of 'the Church in Danger!' Knowing that an election was due, this was a clever ploy. The impression that his supporters gave to the electors was that religious toleration threatened the Church of England. Clergy up and down the country supported Sacheverell's campaign and the Whigs faced almost impossible odds. In the autumn of 1710 the Whigs were swept from power in a landslide election and the Tories, under their leader Robert Harley (1661–1724), took power.

Queen Anne welcomed the Tories' insistence on defending the Church. A group of over 150 Tory MPs met regularly to plan how to eradicate Dissenters from public office and how to end the practice of occasional conformity, which they regarded as a fraud that allowed Dissenters to qualify for public office under the Test Act. In 1711 Dissenters' occasional conformity was outlawed, and in 1714 the Dissenters' schools, or academies, were suppressed in the Schism Act. The Act was hoped to be another means by which Dissent would be eradicated. In the Convocation of the Church, High Churchmen gained control and sought to take punitive action against those Low Churchmen who had been sympathetic to Dissenters.

After the 1710 election, the Tory policy of seeking to end the war with France occupied politicians' attention. The war had cost £150 million, at a time when the annual revenue from tax was just £2 million. Consequently, most of the money for the war had been raised by adding to the national debt. The war had enriched those who supplied the army, such as wool workers and cloth merchants, who had less competition from abroad and who had strong demand for the supply of uniforms and blankets. But politicians were naturally concerned at the ballooning of the national debt.

The servicing of the war had also created a great bureaucracy. Between 1689 and 1720 the number of permanent government employees grew from 4,000 to 12,000. At its height, the War of Spanish Succession also required an army of 171,000 and a navy of 48,000. These were the largest armed forces in English history to that point. Convicts, debtors and the unemployed were conscripted into the army. By the end of the war the Royal Navy had grown to over 110 ships of the line, with a tonnage twice the size of that of France. The Tories took advantage of their majority and the fact that the Queen had fallen out with the Duchess of Marlborough to dismiss the Duke as commander-in-chief.

It was the achievement of the leading Tory minister Robert Harley and his principal negotiator, Bishop John Robinson of Bristol (1650–1723), that Britain constructed a network of nine treaties to end the war with France. These agreements together formed the Peace of Utrecht, signed in 1713. Utrecht met England's principal war aims. Louis XIV repudiated the Stuart claims to the British throne and renounced France's right to the Spanish throne; the threat from France had thus been neutralized. Britain made substantial global territorial gains: St Kitts in the Caribbean; Hudson Bay, Newfoundland and Nova Scotia in North America; Gibraltar and Minorca in the Mediterranean, and access to trade with Spanish possessions in South America. An unintended but crucial outcome of the war was an enormous boost to Britain's global standing. Britain was becoming a world power, eclipsing her two rivals, France and Holland.

After 1712, Queen Anne became increasingly ill and weak. She was even too ill to attend the thanksgiving services for the Peace of Utrecht. She irascibly refused to permit discussion of the succession to the throne and denied her Hanoverian heirs any rights to come to Britain or to involve themselves in its affairs. Like Queen Elizabeth I, she saw this as having her own burial shroud laid out before her. Some believed that, if her half-brother James Stuart, the Old Pretender (1688–1766), abandoned his Catholicism and became an Anglican, Queen Anne would accept him as her heir. But in 1714 he confirmed he would not abandon his Catholic faith for the throne.

The second Tory landslide in 1713 brought at least fifty MPs to Westminster whose sympathies were with the restoration of the Stuarts, whether or not the Old Pretender converted. Among the High Churchmen active in Convocation was Francis Atterbury, Bishop of Rochester (1663–1732), who said he was willing to proclaim James Stuart king when Queen Anne died. Some leading figures, including the principal ministers Harley (now Lord Oxford) and Lord Bolingbroke (1678–1751), as well as Marlborough, maintained contact with the exiled Stuart court. They sought to keep their options open and were not convinced that the Hanoverian succession would take place when Queen Anne died. The anxiety regarding the future was palpable when, early in 1714, Anne fell ill, causing a stock market crash, as people considered whether there would be a fight for the succession.

The headstrong Bolingbroke attempted to lead a Tory faction that would pave the way for the succession of James Stuart, but neither Queen Anne nor the majority of the Tories were prepared to go along with him. Queen Anne ensured, as she lay dying in July 1714, that ministers who would support the Hanoverian succession held key government posts. Consequently, when she died on 1 August 1714, the Elector of Hanover was proclaimed King George I, Sophia, his mother, having died in May 1714. The 54-year-old George was an irascible man, set in his ways. He had been divorced from his wife for twenty years and imprisoned her in the Castle of Ahlden. George allowed a month before he set out on his journey to his new kingdom. He was waiting to see whether there would be a Jacobite rebellion; and he only arrived on 18 September 1714. The fundamental commitment of Whigs – and the majority of Tories – to the Glorious Revolution of 1688 and the Act of Succession had enabled a smooth transition. Queen Elizabeth I's adage that it was impossible to be a stiff papist and a loyal subject seemed to apply to the monarch in 1714.

3

AN ENLIGHTENMENT CULTURE

The Great Storm of 1703

On 26 November 1703 a storm of unique ferocity struck Britain. It remains the worst storm in British history and the benchmark against which all subsequent storms are measured. It was responsible for the deaths of more than 8,000 people. Twenty per cent of all sailors in the Royal Navy died as thirteen battleships sank and dozens of merchant ships and their crews were lost. Coastal towns were laid waste, some were described as looking as if they had been pillaged by foreign armies. Inland, towns, villages and the countryside were damaged by storm force winds and debris. Houses collapsed and trees were uprooted. Daniel Defoe counted 17,000 fallen trees in Kent alone. The diarist John Evelyn lost 2,000 oaks on his land in Surrey, and said he thought he heard a groan from the forest.

Then, as now, climate change on this scale worried people. In December Queen Anne issued a proclamation on the storm. She called for a national day of fasting and public prayer to assuage national guilt. Over the following decade, more than sixty sermons expressed similar religious responses to the storm. The great storm of November came at the end of a long series of meteorological depressions that crashed on to Britain in 1703. As early as May the vicar of Cheshunt, Hertfordshire, preached on 'the strange unseasonableness of the weather'. He could only conclude that Britain had attracted God's anger and displeasure, and predicted that worse would follow if people did not mend their ways and turn to God.

Scientists knew that storms were caused by atmospheric conditions and were propelled across the Atlantic by the Gulf Stream. Some meteorologists even tracked the storm of 1703 as it passed across Britain and wreaked similar havoc in Scandinavia and northern Europe. The journalist Daniel Defoe's book *The Storm* devoted its first chapter to what he called 'the national causes and original of winds'. He presented an explanation of wind as caused by the motion of the earth and talked of the 'elastic' property of air.

What these responses to the storm of 1703 represent were the past and the future. The old explanation for natural events as divine punishment (or reward) was falling away. It was being replaced by the new scientific knowledge of natural causes and consequences. This is an example of the Enlightenment in action.

A Slippery Idea

The Enlightenment is one of those historical ideas that can easily give the impression that history contains elements of inevitability, methodically working towards some pre-determined event or goal. Folk practices and ancient customs, it suggests, irresistibly gave way to science and the laws of nature. This feeling of inevitability is partly because of the way in which historians approach it. The Enlightenment in Britain, and in Europe, was not a single monolithic phenomenon. It was a collection of processes and movements, some of which coincided, some of which were connected; others were disconnected and occurred haphazardly. These events and movements were as contingent and prone to reversal and failure as any other parts of history. The word 'Enlightenment' adds to the sense of inevitability as it implies an emergence from darkness, and suggests a shedding of the light of reason on ignorance and superstition. In fact 'Enlightenment' was not used by people at the time and was only used much later to summarize all sorts of processes and trends in this period which were quite disparate. So we should restrain the tendency to see the Enlightenment as a victory of science over superstition.

The idea of the Enlightenment as a period of reason is challenged by much of the emotionalism of the period. The evangelical revival, the understanding of the human mind and the growing sense of individualism are examples of the way in which the Enlightenment was also preoccupied with emotions and feelings. How people felt, as opposed to how they thought, forms an important part of the Enlightenment. So while much of this chapter refers to 'reason', we should not discount the impact of emotions.

Two key themes that often appear in accounts of the Enlightenment are secularization and modernity. Some studies of the Enlightenment present it almost entirely as a process of secularizing society, and suggest that the grip that faith and belief held over society loosened as the Enlightenment gathered pace. In such accounts, new scientific ideas challenged and eroded faith and so religious beliefs exerted less hold on people. The laws of nature that the physicist Isaac Newton discovered, such as gravity, seemed to undermine religion. This implies that before Newton all people believed in a God-made world and after Newton they shook off that idea. The Enlightenment is also assumed to have ushered in 'modernity' and the start of modern society. In such interpretations, modern ideas about knowledge, causation and explanation emerged from the Enlightenment. Neither of these views is entirely realistic or accepted by most historians.

Some have seen the Enlightenment less as a set of ideas than as a tone of voice or a sensibility and a willingness to criticize.

In others words, it was a change in the *way* in which people thought, rather than *what* they thought. The toleration of other people's religious beliefs, for example, was not the same as faith or religion: it was an approach, or response, to religion. David Hume (1711–76) expressed this idea in his *Essays* in 1741: 'there has been a sudden and sensible change in the opinions of men within these last fifty years, by the progress of learning and of liberty'. If the Enlightenment had such a tone or sensibility, it explains why those who advocated progressive ideas could sometimes also support regressive and reactionary ones. In Europe, for example, there was a development in absolute monarchies known as 'enlightened despotism', in which autocratic rulers exercised power for the good of their subjects but they remained absolute rulers who expected complete obedience.

The existence of the Enlightenment has not been unchallenged. The Prussian philosopher Immanuel Kant (1724–1804) denied that this period was enlightened at all. More recently there has been controversy between those, such as the philosopher Michel Foucault (1926–84), who have seen the Enlightenment as focused on domination and control, and those who see the Enlightenment as broadminded and tolerant. Foucault, drawing on Kant, claimed that the seventeenth and eighteenth centuries were a period in which society was preoccupied by political control, imprisonment, confinement of the insane, punishment and the exercise of power over the individual. His account is one that is the opposite of 'enlightenment'.

Historians have also often debated whether we should even talk of 'an Enlightenment' or 'the Enlightenment'; or whether we should drop the capital E, which suggests a single event or moment, in favour of 'enlightenments'. There are debates as to whether there were Scottish or English Enlightenments that were separate from those of Europe and North America. It is clear that the Enlightenments were not always uniformly progressive; many contained contradictory, unenlightened forces and experienced setbacks in their acceptance. The Enlightenment was a series of connected but separate trends and processes.

The Enlightenment and Europe

One of the features of Britain, unlike the continent, was that few people consciously referred to, or thought of, themselves as *'illuminati'* or *'philosophes'* – the people who in Europe appeared to lead and inspire the Enlightenment. Paradoxically, however, many of the European leaders of the Enlightenment, such as the French thinkers Charles Montesquieu (1689–1755), François-Marie Arouet (1694–1778, better known by his pen-name Voltaire), Denis Diderot (1713–84), Giacomo Casanova (1725–98) and Jean-Jacques Rousseau (1712–78), looked to Britain as a source of inspiration for the Enlightenment.

There are important differences between the British and continental Enlightenments. The French and other European Enlightenments tended to focus on abstract ideas of liberty and equality. In contrast, the British Enlightenment focused on the concrete effects of social virtues, such as economic, scientific, and literary advances. The British Enlightenment was also undogmatic and not wedded to an ideology, whereas the French Enlightenment seemed to have a definite agenda. In Britain, the Enlightenment was a lived experience as well as a movement of big ideas. People at many levels in society could experience the Enlightenment through all manner of objects and materials. Another important difference was that, in Britain, the Churches espoused the Enlightenment. In France the Church saw reason as a threat and reacted against it.

Between 1726 and 1728 the French philosopher Voltaire visited Britain, and viewed it through rose-tinted spectacles. He saw Britain as a model of freedom and tolerance; he idealized Milton, Newton, Locke and Shakespeare and relished the London theatre. As a man whose work was often censored in France, he loved the freedom of the press and wanted the laws that guaranteed British freedoms to be adopted everywhere. He supported the idea of Britain as a chosen nation and the embodiment of the civic virtues of Ancient Rome: trade, freedom and an enlightened elite. Despite witnessing the crime and grime of London, Voltaire believed that Britain was a much less class-ridden society than France, and he admired a system that held noblemen and paupers equally accountable for the same offence. He believed that the separation of the government from the legislature encouraged popular participation in law-making. Reason and liberty seemed, to Voltaire, to be everywhere. It was embodied in trade and commerce and in the British enjoyment of grumbling and complaining. In 1733 Voltaire published *Letters Concerning the English Nation*. Its praise of a nation so different from France led to the imprisonment of its French printer and it was publicly burnt in Paris. But its English translation was naturally popular in Britain, and popularized the story of Isaac Newton and the falling apple. Voltaire claimed to have introduced English gardening and even a taste for roast beef to France. Naturally, his home in retirement in Ferney, near the Swiss border, became a regular stop on the Grand Tour. The radical John Wilkes (1727–97), the writer Edward Gibbon (1737–94) and the politician Charles James Fox (1749–1806) all visited him.

The Grand Tour in the eighteenth century was a cross between a finishing school, a cultural tour and an aristocratic rite of passage. Often accompanied by a tutor, chaplain or older friend, a young gentleman – and by the Victorian period a chaperoned young lady – would tour the principal cultural sites of Europe, particularly the classical Roman and Greek sites. The tour enabled an affluent youth to improve his French and other languages and to learn fencing, riding and dancing. Such young men often bought artefacts or commissioned paintings, which were brought home for display. Artists such as Canaletto earned many commissions from grand tourists. More serious-minded young men might benefit from the liberal education in museums, galleries and even from invitations to meet individuals such as Voltaire. They might even spend some time in a university. Those with more physical interests would climb the Alps and indulge in some of the notorious flesh-pots of France and Italy. Archaeological ruins were often popular, and those of Pompeii especially so. Few grand tourists omitted a visit to Venice from their itineraries. Most tours lasted a few months, but for some – especially those with a desire or need to get out of Britain – the experience could last for years.

The Grand Tour provided opportunities for the affluent to experience a wide variety of arts and ideas. More importantly, they brought these things back to Britain. Connoisseurship and the development of 'high' taste were partly products of this continental influence – and the numbers experiencing it were growing. In 1765 France estimated that 40,000 Britons had passed through Calais in two years. Connoisseurship was depicted in Hugh Douglas Hamilton's painting *Sir Rowland and Lady Winn, Nostell Priory* (1767). In it, Sir Rowland consciously displays his own experiences on the Grand Tour by showing his purchases of sculpture, paintings and books to his wife. The Grand Tour also heightened awareness of nature. In 1741 William Windham's exploration of the glacier in Chamonix was widely published and created a sensation. It began a craze for mountain climbing and tourism in Savoy and Geneva. Mountains were gradually treated as part of the Romantic landscape.

Enlightenment Ideas of Government
The Glorious Revolution of 1688 spurred on some of the ideas of government that had been emerging in the preceding years. Sir Robert Filmer's *Patriarcha, or the Natural Power of Kings*, which was written in the 1630s but published in 1680 (twenty-seven years after Filmer's death), opened with the phrase: 'the first kings were the fathers of families ...' Filmer argued that divine authority descended to kings from God, in the same way that fathers were ordained to govern their families by

God. It was the fullest statement of the divine and 'natural' autocratic authority of the king and appeared during the attempt to exclude the Duke of York from the throne as an attempt to buttress the divine right of kings and hereditary monarchy. But James II's reign witnessed the crumbling and collapse of such ideas of kingship and the divine origins of authority.

The natural replacement for Filmer's *Patriacha* as a rationale for the nature of government, and written in response to it, was John Locke's *Two Treatises on Government*. This was published in 1690, but was written between 1679 and 1680. Locke was a Whig who had been forced to live in Holland for much of the 1680s because he was suspected of involvement in the plots against Charles II. He returned to London with William and Mary. Locke's *Treatises* rejected patriarchalism, divine right and the need for passive obedience from subjects. While not a democrat, Locke argued that in early societies men banded together for security and, as a practical measure, handed government to those best equipped to discharge it. They retained the right, however, if the contract between ruler and ruled was broken, to take back the government of society. This is what happened in 1688. Locke's ideas were founded on the assumption of a contract between the ruler and the ruled, and on property rights, which entitled the individual to defend himself and his property from a bad ruler.

Locke's ideas sparked a debate on how to become free from a tyrannical ruler. He suggested that people had the right to determine the system of government under which they lived, rather than simply to accept whatever tyrannical system their rulers imposed on them. Freedom from such tyranny took centre-stage in philosophical and political theory throughout the eighteenth century. From Britain it became the founding discourse of the American republic, where it remains strong today.

The importance of freedom was that it guaranteed citizens' participation in politics. By implication it also gave men and women licence to attack and criticize their rulers. Criticism of rulers was an important ingredient in the Enlightenment. In Britain it was expressed in such publications as the *Spectator*, *Cato's Letters* and the *London Journal*. In the 1720s, as a reflection of the power of this new medium, the government bought the *London Journal* to become the government's media response to such attacks. The *Spectator* was also influential on the European stage, and was widely translated. Rousseau paid tribute to the influence the journal had on his early thinking.

Attacks on the government became an important element in the development of the system of politics. The Tory Jacobite Lord Bolingbroke, who returned to Britain from the Stuart court in France in 1744, believed that freedom could only be protected by the existence of an opposition party. Such a party could use constitutional methods to restrain the government and hold it accountable. He argued that the aim of the opposition party was to try to obtain power from the government. He also argued that in order to do so the opposition needed to be united and had to be permanent to ensure that it was regarded as a part of daily politics. It had to offer an alternative, on every occasion, to the government. This opposition had to prepare itself to control government. These ideas may seem common today, but in the mid-eighteenth century they represented a new way of thinking of politics.

The philosopher and politician Edmund Burke (1729–97) is often associated with a 'counter-enlightenment' – a reaction against the ideas of the Enlightenment. In fact, he epitomized the Enlightenment's often-contradictory political elements. Burke showed signs of opposing Enlightenment ideas: he rejected the radical demands for liberty of the French Revolution and supported moderate conservative opinion on many issues, including the benefits of the spread of Christianizing 'Englishness'. Yet he embraced many elements of the Enlightenment. He supported free trade as a replacement for the mercantilist system; he championed the reform of Parliament; he denounced the East India Company's rule in India, claiming that Britain had done nothing but exploit Indians; he opposed the conflict with colonial America, preferring conciliation of the colonists, and advocated religious toleration, including that of Catholics. He is also credited with inventing the phrase 'moral indignation'.

The Scientific Enlightenment

One of the key features of the Enlightenment was a revolution in ideas in science. At the centre of science in England at the end of the seventeenth century was Isaac Newton. In 1669 he became Lucasian Professor of Mathematics at Cambridge; he had already established the basis of calculus, pulling together a wide range of mathematical ideas into a coherent system. He had also discovered that light comprised the spectrum of colours. His contemporaries recognized Newton as a genius. Students in Cambridge were said to be careful to avoid scuffing his markings in the gravel in case they contained the workings of some brilliant theory. Newton's reputation for rational science, especially mathematics and physics, is so great that it often masks the fact that he also had wide-ranging mystical and religious interests. He experimented with alchemy – the idea that base metal could be turned into gold through the use of the 'philosopher's stone' – and he read scripture with a keen eye, privately deciding that the doctrine of the Trinity was false. More mundanely, he is also credited with inventing the cat-flap in doors. On his death in 1727 Alexander Pope (1688–1744) captured his ambivalence between science and religion:

> Nature and Nature's laws lay hid in night,
> God said 'Let Newton be!' and all was light.

It is quite clear that Newton was not seeking to undermine religion – in fact Newton was a committed Christian who saw his work as buttressing religion and faith.

Newton's central achievement was his *Principia Mathematica* of 1687 (which had originally been rejected for publication by the Royal Society in favour of a book on fish). The *Principia* identified the forces that operated in the universe, combining the ideas of Galileo and Kepler with his own laws of gravity. Gravity, Newton argued, operated on all particles and exerted a force in direct ratio to its mass. It was a scientific rule of striking clarity, and on it Newton's reputation was built. His famous claim to Robert Hooke in 1676 that 'If I have seen a little further it is by standing on the shoulders of giants' was unduly modest. Newton may have built on the ideas of others but he was a truly gifted thinker and scientist. He was knighted, made Master of the Mint and elected president of the Royal Society. A host of subsequent authors discussed, explained and explored the *Principia* and its consequences. Newton's subsequent book on *Opticks* in 1704 was far more experimental, and promoted the crucial idea that science was based on careful experimentation and observation.

Opportunities to pursue Newton's ideas were also developed. The Boyle Lectures were founded by the scientist Robert Boyle, who was a friend of Newton and who denied the extreme rationalism of the Portuguese philosopher Spinoza. The lectures were designed as a forum to explore Newtonian science, and to use it to prove and defend the existence of God. Boyle lecturers advanced rational ideas that supported Christianity; they were a roll-call of leading theologians, including, in the first two decades of the lectures, Richard Bentley, Samuel Clarke, William Whiston, Josiah Woodward, Benjamin Ibbot, John Leng, William Derham and Thomas Burnet. Bentley, the first lecturer, used Newton's *Principia* to show that God's providential aims for mankind were benevolent and reasonable.

Newton's ideas radiated reason and rationalism outward into all sorts of fields. These were ideas in tune with the rational Christianity of latitudinarian Anglicans – those who supported reasonableness in religion and religious toleration – and Protestant Nonconformists. They abandoned mysticism and superstition in favour of religion that was empirical and sincere. Newton's ideas cast a death blow to older Aristotelian ideas of metaphysics and bodily humours. Later in the century Newton's ideas attracted theologians such as William Paley (1743–1805), whose *Natural Theology*, published in 1802, used Newton's ideas to argue for the existence of God as the 'watchmaker' of the universe.

One of Newton's favoured ideas was calendar reform. Since 1583 Britain had been separated from most of Europe, which had adopted the Gregorian calendar at the end of the seventeenth century. This meant that Britain was eleven days behind the rest of Europe. By the early eighteenth century this disconcerted people such as Newton. It caused havoc with some, like the Duke of Marlborough, who had to use both dates in writing to Britain from campaigns on the continent. Merchants who had commercial relations with Europe also had to cope with two calendars. However, Newton's proposals to adopt the Gregorian calendar did not command support. But by the 1740s the *Gentleman's Magazine* threw its weight behind reform of the calendar. Only the Church, which associated the Gregorian calendar with popery and Catholic intolerance, defended what it saw as the Protestant Julian calendar.

In 1752 Lord Chesterfield (1694–1773) piloted a calendar reform bill through Parliament and did so as a consciously scientific and enlightened measure. In 1753, eleven days were lost from the calendar overnight and the opportunity was taken to bring the numbering of each new year from Lady Day in March to 1 January. (Before this the number of the year changed on 25 March). There was widespread consternation about the 'loss' of eleven days, though the suggestion that there were riots has been disproved. When it was realized that some events, such as fairs, mayoral elections and even royal anniversaries were in the eleven days that had been lost, a hurried amendment Act had to be passed to accommodate them. The amendment Act also dealt with the issue of the 'loss' of the eleven days in lease renewals and other property and financial issues. But superstition and lore died out slowly. For decades, fairs and events were held on the same days, ignoring the loss of the eleven days. In some areas there was even the celebration of 'old Christmas'. The last of these events which ignored the reform of 1753 was in Oldham in 1879.

Science and scientific speculation became popular and many people engaged in them. The *Gentleman's Magazine* regularly carried scientific articles. Science was the subject of discussion and public lectures in such venues as the Spaulding Gentleman's Society in Lincolnshire, and there was a profusion of scientific and mechanical societies. By the middle of the eighteenth century Bath, Birmingham, Bristol, Chichester, Gloucester, Newbury, Norwich, Oxford, Reading, Scarborough and York each had public lectures, sometimes from itinerant lecturers on all manner of scientific subjects. It was lectures of this kind that inspired the penniless William Herschel (1738–1822) to pursue his interest in astronomy. Later, as a renowned astronomer, he proposed naming a newly discovered planet 'Georgium Sidus' (George's Star) after George III; it was never a popular idea, and by 1850 the planet became known as Uranus.

At the other end of the social spectrum Charles II's Royal Society held experiments on clocks, barometers, thermometers, air pumps and a wide range of instruments that had popular applications. It also held public discussions on such curious topics as the creation of a new universal artificial language which all people could learn. From 1754 the Society for the Encouragement of Arts, Commerce and Manufactures (now known as the RSA) offered premiums and bounties for scientific inventions and experiments with commercial applications. The number of inventions grew dramatically. Between 1760 and 1785, 776 patents for new inventions were registered, compared with 697 for the period 1617–1760.

Science and knowledge were not just pursued for their own sake; the exploitation of commercial applications was as important. The interest in the diffusion of science resulted in the foundation of a number of organizations, such as the Royal

Humane Society, established in 1774, to resuscitate the drowned and, in 1773, the Medical Society of London. Science could also be beautiful. Orreries and globes, among other things, were astronomical instruments that were also beautifully made in brass and decorated with elaborate embellishments. Thomas Turner, a Sussex shopkeeper, recorded in his diary in August 1758 that he entertained his wife and sister-in-law with a clockwork 'microcosm' – an orrery – which was 'a very pretty curious sight'.

Nature in the Enlightenment

Much scientific progress displaced the traditional theology that identified mankind as fallen, sinful and corrupt. The scientific Enlightenment was much more in tune with the prevailing optimistic theology of mankind. This regarded society as a means to bring about the happiness of humanity, and mankind as God's agency to achieve it. David Hume's *Treatise of Human Nature* of 1739–40 advocated the scientific exploration of humanity. Perhaps because of his own mental illness as a young man, Hume was fascinated by the working of the mind. He concluded that we can only understand the world and ourselves from observation and perception, not from divine revelation. He also advanced a highly contingent and insecure view of humanity, which recognized that people were less consistent and more changeable than previously thought.

These views of mankind were confirmed by a plethora of anatomical experiments that advanced from the discovery in 1628 of the circulation of the blood by William Hervey (1578–1657) to William Hewson's work on the lymphatic system in the 1760s. Medical studies emphasized the complexity and beauty of the human body, as well as the natural laws that controlled it. In such an environment, it became customary for philosophers such as Locke, Hume and Ferguson to emphasize the unspoiled nature of humanity, derived from science. If mankind and nature were not fallen and corrupt, as the Bible taught, they could unequivocally be objects of beauty, celebrated in poetry, painting and all the arts. It also meant that entertainment and art could be disconnected from sin and temptation. Puritan disapproval of beauty and pleasure died.

Scientific ideas of nature were also explored during the Enlightenment. Nature connected with, and could affirm, faith and religion. It could also confirm Newton's view of the universe, and frame new ideas of a benevolent environment. Nature also stimulated human reactions, which formed a significant element in the Enlightenment, such as Romanticism. Nature could be seen as familiar, comforting and kindly, as the Revd Gilbert White (1720–93) did in his *Natural History of Selborne* (1789), which presented a view of nature as centred on the people of the parish. Not all nature was quite as benign; nature could be regarded as disordered. Thomas Burnet's *Sacred Theory of the Earth* of 1689 asked how much more beautiful the earth and skies would be if the land, sea and stars had been organized in a regular symmetrical design. As we have seen, the Enlightenment witnessed a change in explanations for dangerous natural phenomena, such as earthquakes, fire, flood and storms.

Just as the storm of 1703 had provoked religious responses, there was a similarly religious reaction to the 90,000 deaths in the Lisbon earthquake of 1755. This produced major responses in Britain. One of these was the anonymous book *An Old Remedy New Reviv'd: or, an Infallible Method to Prevent this City from Sharing in the Calamities of Lisbon*, which advocated national obedience to God and the need for prayer to avoid a similar divine punishment for sin in Britain. However, by 1795, an altogether different response was elicited by a minor earthquake in Britain. Edward Grey's *Account of the Earthquake Felt in Various Parts of England, November 18, 1795; with Some Observations Thereon* was a thoroughly scientific analysis of the earthquake, focusing on observation and measurement of the quake, and made no suggestion that it was God's doing.

While the clergy described the earth as entrusted to man's stewardship, this did not discount the view that nature was subject to exploitation and 'improvement'. Enclosure and forest clearance had for many years been a means to improve land. *The Gentleman Farmer, Being an Attempt to Improve Agriculture by Subjecting it to the Test of Rational Principles*, published in 1776 by Lord Kames (1696–1782), was so popular that it ran to a fourth edition by 1798. Even George III was associated with the land and nicknamed 'Farmer George' for his rural interests.

During the eighteenth century there was also a more aesthetic improvement of land in the form of landscaping. The works of Lancelot 'Capability' Brown (1716–83) and later the Scotsman Thomas Blaikie (1753–1838) were evidence of the eighteenth-century fascination with creating landscapes. In more than a hundred estates, Brown perfected nature by adding and removing hills, diverting streams and rivers, creating avenues and lakes. Nature was increasingly thought of as picturesque. William Gilpin (1724–1804) argued that Britain could be experienced and enjoyed by spending leisure time in the countryside. Responses to picturesque landscape were not uniform, however. Edmund Burke likened the soft gentle curves of some landscapes to objects of sexual desire, whereas Thomas Gray (1716–71) claimed that the Scottish mountains produced ecstasy as only God could combine beauty with horror.

A natural consequence of the work of Capability Brown was James Hutton's (1726–97) geological studies. In 1695 John Woodward (1665–1728), Gresham Professor of Physick, accepted that sedimentary rock contained fossils, and assumed that they were caused by Noah's flood. But Hutton found the Biblical view of the earth as being 4,000 years old and formed by Noah's flood was at variance with the evidence. Hutton's *Theory of the Earth or an Investigation of the Laws Observable in the Composition, Dissolution, and Restoration of Land upon the Globe* of 1788 advanced the new idea of 'deep time'. Hutton argued that his observations of rock formation, volcanic activity and erosion showed that the earth had to be much older than 4,000 years. It was Hutton who inspired later scientists, including Charles Lyell and Charles Darwin, in their development of ideas of evolution and natural selection. What Hutton proposed were ideas that challenged the Biblical views of the earth as pre-ordained and planned. By 1802, when his *Illustrations of the Huttonian Theory of the Earth* was published, his views were becoming widely accepted in scientific circles.

The Enlightenment also promoted the development of education. It is no coincidence that John Locke, one of the prime movers of much Enlightenment thinking, also wrote on education, since education was central to the Enlightenment. In *Some Thoughts Concerning Education* (1693), Locke argued that people were neither wicked nor good, but could be motivated either way by their education. He argued that education should abandon fact-learning and should instead aim to inculcate understanding and self-control. Above all, what he desired was the development of the rational, thinking individual. By 1775 over twenty-five editions of the book had been sold. The value of education was not uncontested: in 1751 Lord Chancellor Hardwicke (1690–1764) argued that, while the Reformation had seen the creation of schools for poor scholars, it would be better for the poor to be trained to work on farms and not taught to read.

Education lay at the heart of the self-improvement that many Enlightenment writers supported. Knowledge was sought out, and often made the subject of wide dissemination rather than kept as the preserve of the few. Self-help manuals were widely printed, public lectures spread knowledge and experiments on animals became public entertainment. Joseph Wright's (1734–97) painting *Experiment on a Bird in an Air Pump* (1768) showed a scientist recreating Boyle's air-pump experiments, in which a bird was deprived of oxygen and then revived. The painting showed a group of onlookers with varying reactions but, for most, scientific curiosity exceeded concern for the bird. The scientist looked out of the picture, inviting the viewer's participation in both the experiment and the compassion.

The British Museum, established by Act of Parliament in 1753, was consciously developed to exhibit artefacts and knowledge, both artistic and scientific, for the enjoyment and education of the public. Ethnographic collections, such as Hans Sloane's (1660–1753) collection of shoes from the Coromandel coast in India, were also exhibited for the interest of the public.

The Religious Enlightenment

The stereotype of the seventeenth-century Puritan is of a disapproving, dour individual, wearing dark clothes and wagging a finger at the misbehaviour of others. Theatre, alcohol, sport, games, sex, in fact almost any pleasure or enjoyment, were condemned by Puritans. Leisure and pleasure could only lead to temptation and sin. The claim that Puritans abolished Christmas during the Commonwealth, however, is perhaps an exaggeration, but an official proclamation certainly ordered that no special celebrations were to be held, and that all fairs should be held as usual on each 25 December. The Puritan concern about enjoyment and pleasure arose from the belief that the salvation and afterlife of the whole 'godly community' of Christians was endangered by the sins of any one individual. Consequently Puritanical disapproval and the determination to seek out others' sins was important for the decent ordering of society, and vital for achieving the promise of heaven for all.

In the years after 1660, however, stimulated by the growth of rational thought and by toleration, this idea, of the dependence of the salvation of the whole community on the behaviour of individuals, fell away. Each man and woman was seen as responsible for his or her own salvation, and their behaviour could not rob another of redemption. This was an important change, promoting religious toleration and the individualism that were central to the Enlightenment.

The Enlightenment did not usher in, as is so often assumed, indifference to religion. Britain in this period was a secularizing but certainly not a secular society. Religion remained important and highly controversial. Most of the print culture of the period was focused on the hotly contested features of religion and belief. The Enlightenment connected religion to reason, which is not the same as secularization. The Cambridge philosopher, Benjamin Whichcote (1609–83), argued that religion was rational. His ideas inspired John Locke, who proposed that the scriptures were to be understood and interpreted only in plain and direct language. Locke argued that religion had to accommodate man's limitations – one of which was an unwillingness to accept things, especially religious teachings, on trust. Locke could not accept that faith and reason were in conflict with one another, and he rejected religion based heavily on revelation. In 1695 he published *The Reasonableness of Christianity*, in which he separated knowledge from faith, claiming that ideas came from external stimuli and were understood in the same way as faith. Both were voluntary acts and therefore faith could not be enforced or made compulsory. Nor could punishments for spiritual or religious beliefs have any validity. This naturally supported arguments for religious freedom.

What Whichcote and Locke brought to rational ideas of religion was an optimistic view of mankind in which the salvation of souls and the happiness of society were brought together. Their ideas were pursued by the latitudinarian Anglican churchmen, among them Archbishop John Tillotson (1630–94). Tillotson was a friend of Locke, and his sermons were widely read. He argued that the demands of religion and its obligations were the same as man's natural instincts. Therefore the laws of God were reasonable and, in modern language, intuitive.

Locke also held that ideas of virtue, both private and public, were essentially moral ideas that were derived from, and informed by, religion. So although Locke is sometimes portrayed as lukewarm towards religion, this was not the case. In fact, he inspired Bishop Joseph Butler (1692–1752) to advance the idea that reason alone was not sufficient to promote virtue. Reason had to be allied with compassion, fellow-feeling and a natural benevolence that was derived from religion. Locke's ideas entered the mainstream of religious thought, notably through another latitudinarian, Bishop Benjamin Hoadly (1676–1761), who championed his ideas. They also a strong influence on Nonconformist writers, who found their separation from the Church endorsed and legitimized by Locke's emphasis on voluntary religion. In the next century, the philosopher Jeremy Bentham (1748–1832) said he could have known nothing without Locke.

Beyond the confines of orthodox Christianity lay Deism, a belief in God that stripped away all Christian doctrine and focused on minimalist beliefs such as that God created the earth. A leading Deist, John Toland (1670–1722), who was a convert from Catholicism, published *Christianity not Mysterious* in 1696. This argued that nothing in the Gospels was contrary to reason, and the doctrine of the Trinity was unreasonable. Toland also claimed that anything in the Bible that was irrational, such as miracles, had to be rejected. These ideas were so controversial that the book was burnt by the public hangman in Dublin and indicted by the Grand Jury of Middlesex. By 1710 Deism seemed to be on the rise and a serious challenge to orthodox Christianity. Within two decades it was in decay, but Deism had raised questions in people's minds about the importance of reason in religion.

The work of many clergymen was at the centre of the Enlightenment diffusion of knowledge. Indeed, the Royal Society was dominated by clerical fellows, and clergy were at the forefront of Enlightenment thought. In natural history were William Derham (1657–1735) and Gilbert White; in scholarship Richard Bentley (1662–1742), Conyers Middleton (1683–1750) and William Warburton (1698–1779); in philosophy George Berkeley (1685–1753) and John Horne

Tooke (1736–1812); in literature Thomas Percy (1729–1811) and Laurence Sterne (1713–68); in poetry Edward Young (1683–1765) and George Crabbe (1754–1832); in economics Josiah Tucker (1713–99) and Thomas Malthus (1766–1834); and in travel and tourism William Gilpin. Clergy were especially prominent in making meteorological observations in the 1770s, and formed a network of weather observers. These examples show that the clergy were not always opponents of the Enlightenment; they were, for the most part, its agents and mediators.

In the later eighteenth century the radical inheritors of the revolution of 1688 such as Richard Price (1723–91) and Joseph Priestley (1733–1804) embraced civil liberty in defence of the cause of religious freedom. The Toleration Act of 1689 had excluded those who were not Trinitarian, and Priestley advocated the extension of toleration to include Unitarians, who rejected the divinity of Christ. Priestley's friend and supporter, Richard Price, compared the arguments in favour of toleration of Unitarians with those for free trade and for conciliation of the American colonists. There were also moves to allow the Church of England to be broader and more inclusive. A campaign was organized to abandon the need for clergy to subscribe to the Thirty-Nine Articles – which were the formal statements of the Church's doctrine. After 1772 the 'subscription debate' also expressed itself as a campaign for freedom of individual conscience.

The regulation of religion by the State, however, remained. Throughout the early years of the eighteenth century the common hangman burnt sermons and religious tracts that offended the Church. Thomas Emlyn (1663–1741), one of the first Unitarians, was imprisoned in Dublin for expressing his doubts about the divinity of Christ. Churches also imposed severe penalties. In 1737 the Glasgow Presbytery prosecuted a minister for arguing that happiness was a legitimate objective and that good and evil were independent of God. Church courts also continued to regulate people's behaviour. Adultery, bastardy, fornication, defamation and other moral offences were prosecuted and punished by church courts. Offenders were disciplined, often appearing in their parish church in a white sheet, before the whole congregation, to admit their sins. Reoffenders and recalcitrants could be excommunicated – which meant being cut off from the Church. There was also the Blasphemy Act of 1698, which laid down that to deny the doctrine of the Trinity, or to suggest that there is more than one god, or to deny the truth of the Bible or Christianity was a criminal offence. However, the terms of the Act, which is still in force though much misunderstood, only applied to 'any person, educated in or having made profession of the Christian religion'. In fact, very few people were prosecuted under the Act, partly because it allowed only a very short period for lodging a formal complaint and for bringing a complaint to court.

Those Enlightenment writers who attacked religion often found that their ideas were not well-received. One of these was Edward Gibbon, whose *Decline and Fall of the Roman Empire* was a huge project, appearing in six large volumes between 1776 and 1788. Gibbon's book is claimed to be part of the Enlightenment because he associated the collapse of the Roman Empire with the erosion of reason and civic virtue. But he misjudged his own age. Gibbon portrayed the final years of the empire as decadent and claimed that a cause of this was the influence of religion, including Christianity. While early Christianity was pure and worthy, Gibbon claimed that in subsequent years it became degenerate and prone to super-stition. He also claimed that stories of Christian martyrs during the Roman Empire were myths. His criticism of Christianity attracted a storm of controversy. Gibbon later wrote in his autobiography:

> Had I believed that the majority of English readers were so fondly attached even to the name and shadow of Christianity ... I might perhaps have softened the two invidious chapters.

There were significant features of religious life in eighteenth-century England that appeared to run counter to the Enlightenment. One of these was the evangelical revival. It has been argued that the emphasis of Methodism on good works and its provision of an emotional outlet to poverty and distress was a conservative force that resulted in the deradicalization of men and women. Methodism thereby contributed to the failure of Britain to produce the sort of revolution that was seen in France. Methodism has been seen as profoundly anti-intellectual and dominated by the prejudices and preoccupations of the uneducated, but there were undoubtedly elements of enlightened thought in Methodism. It promoted religious toleration, it emphasized liberty of conscience and showed compassion for the lot of the poor; it also advocated the abolition of slavery and promoted the cause of education.

Methodism also endorsed 'emotional religion', in which people *felt* converted to Christianity. Moreover John Wesley, one of the founders of Methodism, remained a Tory, and – like the Puritans – was suspicious of the temptations that leisure would grant the poor, seeing work as their source of redemption. In political matters he acknowledged his own conservatism: 'I am a High Churchman, the son of a High Churchman, bred up from my childhood in the highest notions of passive obedience and non resistance.' By the time of John Wesley's death in 1791 there were only 57,000 Methodists, though the movement had perhaps 120,000 followers. It was to grow significantly in the nineteenth century.

There was also an erosion of folk religion during the eighteenth century. Bishop Edward Fowler of Gloucester, who died in 1714, was firm in his belief in fairies, and John Wesley said that a world without witches was one without the Bible. But these were fading ideas. As we have seen, superstitious explanations for everything from illness to earthquakes – beliefs that had been a potent force before the eighteenth century – gave way to rational explanations. Bishop Francis

Hutchinson's book *An Historical Essay Concerning Witchcraft* of 1718 argued against the existence of spirits and challenged the credulity that ascribed all unexplained events to witchcraft. Nature and misdirected humanity became the things to fear much more than 'things that went bump in the night'. Providential intervention in everyday events was gradually replaced by a sense that cause and effect were more earthly, and commerce exploited this with the growth of life and fire insurance. Nevertheless, popular beliefs in faith healing, magic and mysticism survived to be an important feature of society today. Superstitious attitudes to madness, which linked it with sin and the lapsarian nature of mankind, gave way to a sense that madness was an organic affliction of the mind.

The Enlightenment of Luxury and Pleasure

One of the features that marked the Enlightenment in Britain was the growth of pleasure and consumption in both experience and the acquisition of goods. Consuming goods often went hand in hand with the development of new ideas. Which was cause and which effect is a moot point. For example, consumption of food and drink was associated with the new enlightened ideas of 'politeness' and 'sociability' and was experienced in places such as coffee houses and in clubs. Such social values could also be experienced at performances of oratorios, at exhibitions, in pleasure gardens and on promenades. All of these were new experiences in the eighteenth century.

The prejudice against wealth, derived from Puritan ideas of the spiritual advantages of poverty, was swiftly eroded. The Enlightenment elevated wealth and prosperity just as it did pleasure. Even those from a Puritan or Dissenting background, such as Daniel Defoe, came to praise the pursuit of wealth. In 1714 the philosopher Bernard Mandeville (1670–1733) published *The Fable of the Bees: or, Private Vices, Publick Benefits*. It was a satire, comparing society to a hive of bees. Mandeville argued that the bees' desire for personal gain bene-fited the hive and that without the private 'vice' of consumption there would be no public benefit for the hive. Society was stimulated by the pursuit of luxury and pleasure. As in the 1980s, greed was good. While most Enlightenment thinkers sought to wed self-interest and social virtue, Mandeville did not. Mandeville's views were attacked as cynical and likely to degrade society; but they also promoted the division of labour and the circulation of money which were the precursors of an industrial economy. Commercial activity also brought together different sorts of people in a common endeavour. Voltaire, for example, described the Royal Exchange in London, where all manner of Christians traded with Jews and Muslims. Old prejudices and divisions between Presbyterians, Baptists, Quakers and Anglicans faded away in the pursuit of wealth.

Luxury was an ambivalent idea in the eighteenth century. On the one hand it implied wealth and taste and perhaps a life of ease and comfort. It meant the consumption and enjoyment of rare and expensive items of furniture, clothing, art or food. But luxury was also associated with excess, vice and self-indulgence. Eighteenth-century writers often indicated that luxury was a French and effeminate ideal. It was the object of attacks in the *Spectator* and in public prints – the broadsheets and engravings that flooded London streets in the early eighteenth century. It was also principally an urban experience, whereas rural and provincial life was regarded as simple and wholesome. The novelist Henry Fielding believed that luxury bred envy and materialism among the poor.

For many people, prosperity became legitimate when it contributed to the benefit of all. The historian William Maitland wrote in 1739: 'as opulency and riches are the result of commerce, so are learning, hospitality and charity the effects thereof'. Trade and wealth were also justified when they were linked to benevolence and philanthropy. Voluntary philanthropy of private donations seemed more worthy than the State philanthropy of the Poor Law. Thomas Coram's (1668–1751) establishment of the Foundling Hospital in 1739 attracted private patrons and the support of many aristocrats. However, the public ballots to decide which children were to be saved from destitution – which do not seem compassionate today – attracted many women patrons. Philanthropy could expand and change as the needs grew. Hanway's Humane Society, established in 1756 to provide warm clothes for boys in the navy, grew to run a number of schools. Similarly the Society for Promoting Christian Knowledge, founded in 1698, established 2,000 schools, which educated 22,000 pupils. Charity schools and Sunday schools reached 200,000 enrolments by the end of the century and by 1833 there were 16,000 Sunday schools educating 1.5 million children.

Pleasure was no longer frowned on. When latitudinarians and Nonconformists claimed that God was a benevolent force, keen to ensure the happiness of his creations, theology could support the idea of pleasure. Pleasure could include the consumption of goods and services, but it could also be found in leisure. Older ritualized leisure was focused on the church, and religious and agricultural lore. This was replaced by new leisure forms of organized games, such as cricket, horse racing and prize fighting, and by social activities such as promenades, assemblies and theatres. The pleasure gardens at Vauxhall and Ranelagh attracted rich and poor alike, and enabled all classes to share the pursuit of pleasure. This interaction was an important feature of society and reduced social tensions. A cross between circus, promenade, place of romantic assignation and street theatre, the pleasure gardens were open all day, and at night the thousands of lights in the gardens were a major attraction. Vauxhall also contained a *trompe l'oeil* of the ruins of Palmyra that caused a sensation. Shopping also became a leisure activity for the moneyed rather than a chore for their servants.

An economist who challenged some of the consuming assumptions of the Enlightenment was the Revd Thomas Malthus. His 1798 *Essay on the Principles of Population* argued that population was regulated by a law of nature: population could increase geometrically but food only grew mathematically. This natural law kept the population down to the level of the means of subsistence available. Malthus suggested that this was almost a biological law, and indicated that there was a natural element to poverty and famine, which could not be overturned by government action. Malthus' ideas were used by the economist David Ricardo (1772–1823) to suggest that wages also had a natural level, which simply depended on the supply and demand of labour. The ideas of Malthus and Ricardo seemed to stigmatize the poor and legitimize poverty and deprivation as market forces that could not be ameliorated.

Such ideas also challenged the mercantilist system of the seventeenth century. Other writers, such as Adam Smith (1723–90), whose *Wealth of Nations* was published in 1776, advocated free trade between nations as the natural replacement of mercantilism. Josiah Tucker, the Dean of Gloucester, likened market forces and the flow of money to the pull of the planets and the force of gravity. Like water, money found its own level. Smith grounded new economic ideas in the mathematics of supply and demand and in the belief that the freedom to be wealthy was the greatest blessing a country could bestow. Smith naturally also hated dependence and the inability to be self-reliant. Smith calculated that the division of labour would enable ten men, who individually could only make 20 pins each, to make 48,000 pins. There was also a moral overtone to Smith's thought. Although he felt that high wages were good because they would motivate others to work hard, he claimed that they had the danger of encouraging sloth in some. He also recognized that much wealth was built on the worst aspects of people's characters: envy, greed and a delight in riches – as he famously wrote: 'the chief enjoyment of riches consists in the parade of riches'.

The Literary Enlightenment
From 1660 to 1695 there had been censorship in England under the Licensing Act, which enabled books to be censored before

they were published. Only the monarch or bishops could authorize the publication of books, and they could only be printed in London, York, Oxford or Cambridge. The Stationers' Company also controlled the supply of paper to printers. In 1694 John Locke used his friends in Parliament to campaign for freedom of the press. In a *Memorandum* Locke spelled out the restrictions that the Stationers' Company exerted on printing and he also argued that the Licensing Act gave sweeping powers that had been abused, including the right to search houses. The inability of the various factions to agree on whether to renew the law, or to amend it, meant that it lapsed in 1695 and censorship ended.

One of the effects of this was to enable publishing to be undertaken beyond the confines of London, Oxford, Cambridge and York. Any provincial town could have its own printing press and publish books and other items. The consequence was a boom in publishing. By 1740 there were 400 printers in 200 provincial towns, and by the end of the century 1,000 printers in 300 towns. Whereas in the 1620s about 6,000 titles were published, by 1710 this had risen to 21,000 and by the 1790s to 56,000. Altogether, between 1660 and 1800, 200 million copies of books were sold. Britons became voracious readers: by the 1780s, more books were printed each year in Britain than were printed in the whole century in Spain. There was also a growth in booksellers – Newcastle-upon-Tyne had twelve in 1800. Booksellers were a combination of printer, literary agent, serialist, advertiser and stationer. In many towns, before the bookshop and the library separated, booksellers served both markets. Newspapers also played an important role in the book trade. Booksellers had complex relationships with London stationers, often buying paper from them, advertising their books in the newspapers and acting as their agents in the provinces in supplying of books for sale.

The reading of books promoted the development of printing as an important part of the economy. Even those who could not read were thrilled by books. In 1741 a blacksmith in Slough read Samuel Richardson's (1689–1761) novel *Pamela* aloud to his fellow townsfolk, and the marriage of Pamela was publicly celebrated when it was read to them. Such was the enchantment with books that Jonathan Swift (1667–1745), in *Gulliver's Travels*, described a fictional professor in the academy of Lagado working on the invention of a device that in a far-off day would make it possible to write books mechanically and cheaply. He also predicted that doing so would not need the slightest talent or education.

Individual books were sold in increasingly large quantities. Throughout the eighteenth century sermons were the single largest literary form; on average three sermons were published each week. Henry Sacheverell's controversial 1709 sermon sold 40,000 copies. Interest in the Bangorian controversy of 1717, which was stimulated by a sermon, was so great that the stock exchange in London closed for two days to enable people to read the tracts that poured from the press. It is from this date that, for the first time, initial print runs for individual items were in excess of 1,000 copies. During the century the number and variety of published work grew dramatically and were read more widely than ever before. In 1790 John Lackington, a bookseller, claimed that four times as many books were sold than twenty years previously and that even poor farmers and labourers bought books and read them to their families. As today, book clubs were also popular as a means of sharing and discussing books.

What this growth of published works indicated was that reading had shifted as a pastime. Previously, reading had been an 'intensive' activity – people repeatedly read a few familiar books. These included the Bible and devotional works. During the Enlightenment, reading became 'extensive', with people reading more and more widely, and their reading including religious tracts, poetry, novels, periodicals and newspapers. To supply this voracious interest in the printed word, paper production in the eighteenth century rose six-fold. The most popular works were accounts of travels, histories, letters and novels. John

Hawkesworth, who wrote the official accounts of the travels of Captain Cook (1728–79) and others, earned £6,000 from his books (more than £0.5 million in today's money). By the 1780s, however, the novel was growing in popularity. Phillip Skelton, an Irish theologian, said that the novel had become the chief form of education for those 'between the court and the spade'. There was also a thriving underground print culture. The pornographic book *Onania; or, The Heinous Sin of Self-Pollution, and All its Frightful Consequences in Both Sexes, Considered*, begun as a moral instruction but later embellished with lurid accounts of sexual activity, went through nineteen editions between 1707 and 1759.

The rise in printing was closely linked to a growth in literacy. By the middle of the eighteenth century, about 60 per cent of men and 40 per cent of women could read. The great boost in these figure occurred between 1670 and 1730, a period in which about 40 per cent of men learned to read. A significant element in the growth of literacy was the need for apprentices to be taught to read by masters. There was also an encouragement to literacy among Nonconformists, who read the Bible in chapels. By 1856 illiteracy rates fell to 26 per cent of men and 36 per cent of women. The spread of literacy in the eighteenth century was not uncontested. For example, Bishop Samuel Horsley (1733–1806), in the last decade of the eighteenth century, regarded education for the masses as likely to spread dangerous revolutionary ideas from France. Consequently he argued against teaching the poor to read. Some individuals who were unable to take advantage of education were self-taught. Stephen Duck (1705–56) and John Clare (1793–1864), the poets, and William Cobbett (1763–1835), the writer, educated themselves. All three were farm labourers whose thirst for reading and desire to write overcame the absence of education. Illiteracy was not necessarily a bar to advancement: as late as 1831 Cobbett claimed that many people were successful in business without knowing how to read.

For those without the natural genius of Duck, Clare or Cobbett, there were growing opportunities to learn to read and to obtain books. In 1684 Thomas Tenison (1636–1715), later Archbishop of Canterbury, established a parish library in St Martins in the Fields, London. Parochial libraries, which were originally intended to be clerical libraries, became a major source of books for the rural poor. During the eighteenth century, subscription and lending libraries were also formed, some of which became major libraries. The Bristol Library Society, founded in 1773, had 130 members who paid a guinea each and recorded 13,000 loans in a decade. Subscription libraries opened in Liverpool in 1757, Leeds in 1763, Bradford in 1774 and Hull in 1775. In the 1770s Bell's circulating library in the Strand in London contained 150,000 books. This growth did not always happen without some resistance; in 1765 the author Joseph Craddock wrote that 'turnpike roads and circulating libraries are the great inlets of vice and debauchery'.

Newspapers were also part of the growth of a literary culture. The first provincial newspaper, the *Norwich Post*, was founded in 1701 and within sixty years there were thirty-five provincial newspapers. Some provincial newspapers reached an extraordinarily wide readership: the *Salisbury Journal* sold 4,000 copies a week and made Benjamin Collins, its proprietor, a very wealthy man. By 1760, about 200,000 newspapers were sold in Britain each week. Newspapers fuelled the culture of consumption through advertising services, inventions and products. In 1775, Josiah Tucker said that Britain was suffering from a mania for news. By 1800, there were 129 regular newspapers and periodicals in Britain and over the next century this was to rise to 4,800. It has been estimated that each newspaper might be read by up to fifteen people.

Another important part of the literary culture of Enlightenment Britain was the wide range of periodicals that were published from the first decade of the eighteenth century. Daniel Defoe's *Review*, which started in 1704 and was followed soon after by Richard Steele's (1672–1729) *Tatler* and

Joseph Addison's *Spectator*, were hugely popular and influential. These periodicals consciously promoted manners, refinement and civility. Defoe's *Review* discussed politics in a way that laid aside the overwrought and violent struggles of the past. Satire and wit replaced calls to civil strife. The readers of these periodicals experienced a shared world of politeness. They had their imitators. In 1709 Mary Manley (1670–1724) published the *Female Tatler* to provide news and ideas of interest to women. We should not be too quick to assume that all books promoted politeness; there was a thriving market in 'impolite' books for the working classes.

By the middle of the eighteenth century, the *Gentleman's Magazine*, which was established in 1731, was one of a number of publications that provided an astonishingly broad range of topics for its readers. Initially selling 9,000, and by 1744 15,000 copies, the *Gentleman's Magazine* summarized the contents of other journals, and published obituaries as well as foreign and domestic news, and original reports and articles. Like newspapers, these periodicals had a wider circulation beyond the subscribers; many copies were passed to friends and neighbours. One new type of journal was the literary magazine. In 1749 the *Monthly Review* and in 1756 the *Critical Review* were established. These were journals that specialized in book reviews. For the first time, readers could read about books before they read the books themselves. As today, reputation and recommendation became important in the choice of books to read.

Alongside such periodicals there were other sorts of publication. At one end of the market were chapbooks. These were cheap, flimsy, paper-covered books that were widely read by the poor. For the barely literate, chapbooks were illustrated with often crude, wood-cut pictures. They provided a combination of bible stories, folklore, romance, ballads, advice for illnesses and pastimes. Such books were the foothills of the literate culture of the eighteenth century and show how the Enlightenment penetrated deep into popular culture. In the middle of the market were books that were small enough to fit into a pocket. There were also sensational books. In 1791, William Lane set up the Minerva Press specifically to supply the market for melodramatic and sentimental novels for the masses. At the top end of the market were the great monumental works of the period. Samuel Johnson's (1709–84) *Dictionary of the English Language*, published in 1755, was literally a huge work. Each volume stood 18 inches (45 cm) tall and 20 inches (51 cm) wide, and contained definitions of 42,773 words. It also sold for the enormous sum of £4/10s – more than £500 today. Another such work was *Encyclopaedia Britannica*, first published in Edinburgh in 1768, which became so popular that its third edition in 1787 sold 10,000 copies. The *Biographia Britannica*, which appeared as a series of six volumes between 1747 and 1766, was also a luxury book bought by libraries and connoisseur collectors.

Novels were, as their name suggests, a new form of literature that burgeoned during the Enlightenment. They were formed around narratives, usually focusing on an individual, such as Robinson Crusoe, Moll Flanders, Fanny Hill and Tristram Shandy. These were fictional people making sense of the world for the entertainment of the reader. Usually the hero or heroine was buffeted by forces outside their control, and had to make moral choices and deal with the consequences of their own and others' actions. Readers shared their experiences and could imagine themselves in the same situations – this is familiar to us, but was an entirely new experience in the eighteenth century. Before this, the main outlets were biblical stories and folk legends, which quickly became formulaic. Individualism and humanity were endorsed by novels, and happiness was assumed to be a goal in their narratives. Novels, like most literary forms, promoted an 'interior' life in their readers, a life of imagination and complex possibilities, and one in which everyday shackles could be thrown off.

It has been assumed that the market for novels was domi-nated by women. It is true that the diaries of women such as

Anna Larpent (1758–1832) noted the novels they read, but Larpent also read Shakespeare, French works, philosophy, political economy and history. Moreover some novels consciously appealed to men, especially those that emphasized adventure and exploits in foreign lands. Thomas Turner, the Sussex shopkeeper, read a number of novels as well as histories and works of theology. In 1772 *New and Elegant Amusements for the Ladies of Great Britain* urged women to avoid frivolous novels in favour of poetry and journals. Evangelical writers also warned of the dangers of novels, which were too worldly and cynical.

Novels were part of a wider literary culture that included the printing of pictures. Hogarth's popular print series *The Rake's Progress* (1732–3), *The Harlot's Progress* (1731–2) and *Marriage ... la Mode* (1745) were what would today be called 'graphic novels', telling a story in pictures. These were narratives that appealed to wide audiences: they often had a 'moral' and some pointed out the similarities between the high and low born.

The Scottish Enlightenment
The degree to which the Scottish Enlightenment can be completely separated from that of the rest of Britain is doubtful because most Scottish thinkers in this period owed a debt to ideas and publications from England as well as the continent. English writers, such as Shaftesbury and Hutchinson, corresponded with Scotsmen throughout the period. A number of leading Scottish publishers, such as Andrew Millar and Strahan and Cadell, owned London printing houses, allowing Scottish books to be jointly published in England rather than simply in Scotland. This also enabled them to pay large royalties because they could access a bigger market. In this way not only did publishers help to promote the Scottish Enlightenment, but the Scottish Enlightenment also helped to shape publishing as a multinational, multi-city business.

The Scottish Enlightenment had a strong educational base since there were four Scottish universities compared to England's two; it was the product of a clearly identifiable intelligentsia and happened later than in the rest of Britain, perhaps because there remained two regressive forces in Scotland – Covenanters and Jacobites – which remained strong until the mid-eighteenth century. As late as 1755 the architect Robert Adam called Scotland 'a narrow place where scarce will ever happen the opportunity of putting one noble thought in execution'.

Once underway, however, the Scottish Enlightenment had a major impact. The moderate rational Christianity of the sermons of Hugh Blair (1718–1800) and William Robertson (1721–93) played an important role in the Enlightenment because they sold so well. Blair's collected sermons of 1777 focused on morality, rather than theology. They emphasized patriotism, action in the public sphere, and the virtues promoted by a polite secular culture. Blair, who was socially conservative, encouraged people to improve their natural talents through hard work, but he also encouraged them to be content with their appointed status in society. He urged people to play an active role in society, to enjoy the pleasures of life, to do good works and to maintain their faith. Blair was also at the centre of a group of Scottish Enlightenment figures including David Hume, Thomas Carlyle (1795–1881), Adam Smith and Adam Ferguson (1723–1816).

The Scottish Enlightenment was also marked, as in England, by the growth of debating and social clubs. The Easy Club, founded in 1712, was the first of many, including the Mirror Club, the Select Society and the Poker Club. The latter was established in 1757 to stir up ideas like a poker stirring the fire. Among these ideas was the desire for Scotland to have its own institutions, such as a militia rather than being garrisoned from England. David Hume claimed that such clubs helped to relieve his depression; he enjoyed the discussions of new ideas in a social setting which sometimes ran to more than four or five hours each evening. He also believed that there was nothing to be learned from professors that could not be gleaned from books. Such discussions and clubs spawned a range of publications. Among these was the *Edinburgh Review*, founded in 1754 by Adam Smith and Hugh Blair. It lasted for just two months initially but established firm foundations for a later revival in 1773. In its first edition, the lawyer Alexander Wedderburn (1733–1805) suggested that, if countries had ages, then Scotland was a youth guided by her mature kindred nation.

The leading figures of the Enlightenment in Scotland were David Hume, Allan Ramsay (1713–84), Adam Ferguson and Adam Smith. David Hume was a brilliant child who had attended Edinburgh University as a boy of just 14. He turned to philosophy following a failed romance that led him into a lifelong struggle with depression. Hume created a rational natural philosophy that rejected the idea that humanity was a reflection of the divine, especially in thinking and mental processes. Hume's atheism led him to reject divine and mystical explanations of cause and effect, though in later years it was said he turned back to belief in an afterlife. His ideas were to influence generations of philosophers. Allan Ramsay, who painted Hume's portrait in 1766, was Scotland's best-known portraitist, producing a series of Scottish portraits that attracted attention for their eye for detail. Ramsay's exquisite draughtsmanship caught the shine on drapery and the details of the faces he painted. He became 'painter in ordinary' to George III in 1761 and dominated painting for the three decades before the end of the century. His later work was affected by a badly dislocated shoulder, which made painting painful and slow for him. Ramsay was committed to the abolition of slavery and it was said that his portrait of Queen Charlotte, George III's wife, deliberately exaggerated her mulatto features, which he believed had been inherited from a sixteenth-century African ancestor.

Adam Ferguson is known as the father of sociology. After a period as an army chaplain he abandoned the Church and became tutor to Lord Bute's family. In 1767 Ferguson published his *Essay on the History of Civil Society*, which sought to describe the history of nations from an analysis of societies. This book brought him a European reputation since it was widely translated into other languages and was said to be especially popular in Russia. Ferguson advocated a view that has become widely adopted: that of the progress of mankind. He believed that mankind was on an upward path from ignorance and deprivation to one of knowledge and prosperity. In some respects he was conservative. He supported the British cause during the American War of Independence, and his views led successive thinkers to focus on materialism.

Adam Smith was a highly influential figure whose ideas have continued to inspire modern politics. Smith had been educated at Glasgow and Oxford universities, where he encountered the ideas of David Hume. From 1748 he delivered a series of lectures in Edinburgh, and, although he was a poor public speaker, his ideas of a 'natural liberty' attracted attention. He has been claimed to be the father of modern capitalism; he championed the consumer over the monopoly of producers. There are sometimes said to be two Adam Smiths. He is usually remembered for his seminal work, *An Inquiry into the Nature and Causes of the Wealth of Nations*, which advocated free trade and the benefits of self-interest for economic advancement. Famously, Smith claimed that it was not to the benevolence of the baker and the butcher that people owed their dinner but to self-interest. Smith's ideas have been blamed for the decline of the 'moral economy', which sought to meet the social obligations of feeding the poor before making a profit for individuals, and prevented wealthy farmers from charging high prices in times of want.

But Smith did not advocate unfettered free market economics. Seventeen years before he published *The Wealth of Nations* he had published *The Theory of Moral Sentiments*. He returned to revise it in his final years. It was hugely popular, running through four editions in as many years. In it, Smith argued that, however selfish people were, they possessed compassion and sympathy for the misery and suffering of others. The perfection of mankind, Smith argued, was to restrain selfishness and promote benevolence. It was a doctrine of civic humanism which promoted general prosperity, and it is often forgotten that Smith sought a balance between self-interest and the interests of others.

Smith's ideas also promoted the idea of nations and nationhood, as he argued for a replacement of the mercantilist system with free trade and national self-interest. His ideas were also strongly meritocratic. Although Smith wrote of the 'lower orders', he held that men and women could advance themselves through their own efforts and deserved to be able to rise through society. Social advancement was not the preserve of a closed aristocratic class, but open to any people of talent. Like Hume, Smith's absorption with ideas meant that he never married, and on one occasion he was so engrossed by his thoughts that he walked into a tanning pit.

While Scotland may have had its own Enlightenment like England, that did not mean it was an enlightened nation. 'Bonded labour' – in effect slavery – remained legal in Scotland until the 1790s. Bonded labourers worked in mines and in a variety of trades. They were the lowest form of labour, tied to their masters for terms of years, often a lifetime; any children born to them were also bonded labourers. Sometimes, especially in times of famine, such bonded labourers had the advantage that they might be fed since they were a valuable commodity for their masters. But in other times and in all other respects they lived lives of legalized slavery. And bonded labourers were lower than the meanest peasant in not having the liberty to choose how to live their lives.

The 'Sociability' of the Enlightenment

The Enlightenment was both a cause and a consequence of the growth of sociability or 'politeness' – the quality of enjoying the company of others and avoiding open conflict. As we have seen, the desire for an interaction which was more gentle, polite, inspiring and stimulating was expressed in coffee houses and a whole range of clubs and societies in the seventeenth century. For the elite, clubs were places in which men could meet and talk about political and social views. But coffee houses were places where the elite and working classes could meet. De Saussure, a Swiss visitor to Britain in the 1720s, wrote that 'workmen habitually begin the day by going to coffee-rooms in order to read the news. I have often seen shoeblacks ... club together to purchase a farthing paper.' About the same time, Abbé Prévost recalled seeing some lords, a baronet, a shoemaker, a tailor and some shopkeepers in a coffee house discussing the news.

Before 1688, clubs, such as the Green Ribbon Club, had been dangerous clandestine places of plotting. But from the 1690s such clubs took on a social purpose. The Kit-Cat Club, a Whig club of politicians, aristocrats and writers, was founded in the 1690s. It had begun as a group of friends who sought to support the Glorious Revolution, but within a few years its toasts were to the beautiful women of the day. It was immortalized in portraits of its members and sponsorship of publishers. By 1750 it was said that every night in London 20,000 men met in clubs of all sorts. Sociability went hand in hand with politeness. This was encouraged by the growth of the titles 'mister' and 'missus'. By the second half of the eighteenth century almost everyone enjoyed these titles, whereas in the seventeenth century few were accorded such honours. Almost anyone wearing a wig and clean clothes might be addressed as 'sir' or 'your honour'.

Clubs could also become a place of debauchery and dissipation – such as the Hell-Fire Club, which met in the ruins of Medmenham Abbey, for drinking and sex – but they were more usually the places where serious ideas were discussed, as at the Lunar Society. The Lunar Society was so called because it met for dinner on nights when there was a full moon to make travelling home easier and safer. It was formed in 1765 in

Birmingham and brought together industrialists such as Matthew Boulton (1728–1809), James Watt (1736–1819), Richard Arkwright (1733–92) and Josiah Wedgwood (1730–95), and philosophers and intellectuals such as Benjamin Franklin (1706–90), Richard Lovell Edgeworth (1744–1817) and Joseph Priestley. They formed a 'Midlands Enlightenment' that focused on promoting the industrial revolution and bettering the lot of all men and women.

Perhaps the most remarkable club was the Spalding Gentlemen's Society, founded in 1710 as an antiquarian and literary weekly meeting of local gentry. It also aimed to run local libraries and share news from London, but it grew from these small beginnings into a body which, by 1770 had some 400 members. It included many new professional men, including apothecaries, engineers and scientists, as well as lawyers, physicians and clergy. In time it attracted leading national figures and by the middle of the century included members in Greece and a West African Muslim scholar. The society meetings included discussions of numismatics and readings of Royal Society scientific papers. Natural history was a popular topic at meetings, as were accounts of exploration, music and art. The success of the society was due in part to its comprehensive character: it avoided religious intolerance and disputes and had an absolute ban on the discussion of politics. The society continues to this day.

The sociability of the Enlightenment for men was also expressed in the growth of Freemasonry after the Grand Lodge of England was formed in 1717. Within eight years there were 52 lodges and by 1768 there were 300. Lodges brought together men of different social backgrounds and faiths. They also provided hospitality to visitors from other lodges. Freemasonry was built on foundations of liberalism, economic stability, constitutional monarchy, social mobility and religious toleration. Its rituals and garb added an element of solemnity and dignity that elevated masons' social encounters. The charitable objects of freemasonry included widows, poor men, children and education and it promoted a sense that one of the reasons for sociability was pity and social inclusivity. The Oddfellows, a friendly society that survives today, was founded in 1745 as a popular alternative to the Freemasons, though it omitted Freemasonry's claim to secret knowledge.

Sociability also focused peoples' minds on religion. Above all, sociability made people think about other people's lives. Obituaries, for example, grew into an art form, with lengthy obituaries published in journals and magazines for the first time. A number of tracts, most notably the popular *Friendships in Death*, written in 1728 by Elizabeth Rowe, argued that friendships transcended death.

Some social organizations were consciously focused on modernity and progress. The RSA's prizes or premiums that we have already mentioned were offered for a number of public challenges, which were listed in the *Daily Advertiser* and the *Gentleman's Magazine*. Captain Bligh, commander of HMS *Bounty*, was seeking to win the society's premium for shipping breadfruit trees to the West Indies when the mutiny occurred in 1789. After the abortive *Bounty* voyage, he repeated the attempt and, having successfully transported the plants, was awarded the prize. Other premiums were offered for such ventures as devising new forms of machinery and agricultural improvements. The society's prizes were also awarded for inventions such as semaphore, power looms and lifeboats, and discoveries including cobalt and the North-West Passage from Canada to the Pacific. Its Irish forerunner was the Dublin Society for Improving Husbandry, Manufactures and other Useful Arts, founded in 1731. In addition to inventions and 'improvements', the Dublin society included social occasions such as sporting and equestrian events.

Friendly societies, the forerunners of trades unions and health insurance, were perhaps the most widespread expressions of the purposeful sociability of the age. There were also organizations most widely known to ordinary people. Cow societies, which insured a rural worker's cow for a year, and burial societies, which paid funeral expenses, were popular in rural parishes. Most societies were small because they restricted membership to people in a local area, or a particular industry. They often took the medieval guild as their model of organization and varied in the financial provision they made for unemployment, illness and bereavement. Friendly societies were so popular that the Friendly Societies Act of 1793 licensed them through a system of registration and regulation, which prevented them from becoming trades unions. By 1801 there were 7,200 societies, with a total membership of 650,000.

Women in the Enlightenment

An important feature of the Enlightenment was not just the participation of women, but the growing sense that the exclusion and marginalization of women in parts of society was unjust and untenable. There was increasing visibility of women in a number of spheres in Restoration Britain: Aphra Behn in drama and poetry (and as a royal spy in Antwerp during the Dutch Wars, code-named 'Astrea'); Eliza Haywood (1693–1756) in writing, acting and publishing; Angelica Kauffman (1741–1807) and Sarah Hoadly in painting and portraiture; Elizabeth Elstob (1683–1756) and Catharine Macaulay (1731–91) in scholarship, and Lady Mary Wortley Montagu (1689–1762) and Elizabeth Montagu (1718–1800) as patrons and in a plethora of spheres. These achievements were important in a male-dominated economy and society. Nevertheless, for men such as John Evelyn these women, especially those who chose not to marry, were abnormal.

Women had to overcome the manifold difficulties described in Judith Drake's *Essay in Defence of the Female Sex* published in 1696. Drake's *Essay* was laid out as a letter to a friend, in which she challenged the discrimination of contemporary writers, including Locke, for their dismissal of women. Drake showed that men could be as ill-informed as women, but without the excuse of poor education. She also drew on the new discoveries in science. For example, in describing her conversations with physicians, she used studies of anatomy to show that there was no physical difference between the brains of men and women. She also argued from nature that female animals were just as intelligent as male. Drake argued that class and income were more likely to make a difference in intelligence than sex. In a challenge to the male hegemony, she suggested that women's physical weakness, relative to men, might suggest that they were designed for intellectual activity and men merely for the physical.

Drake's ideas naturally drew the ire of men such as the author Jonathan Swift and the playwright Colley Cibber (1671–1757). But they also influenced women such as Mary Astell (1666–1731), who argued for women's right to education, and Lady Mary Chudleigh (1656–1710), who challenged the idea that women were the weaker intellectual sex. Increasingly satire pointed out the anomalous position of women: John Gay's *Beggar's Opera* included the witty line: 'the comfortable estate of widowhood is the only hope that keeps up a wife's spirit'. Some women simply refused to be dominated. In 1739 one author, known only as 'Sophia', commented in *Woman not Inferior to Man* that there was not a single sphere of skill in which women could not prove to be the equal of men.

Women were as keen as men on the opportunities for improvement and sociability. In 1717 three Edinburgh women formed the Fair Intellectual Club 'for improvement of one another in the study and practice of such things as might contribute most effectually to our accomplishment'. They also opposed the 'injustice to deprive us of those means of knowledge'. Initially it was a secret society but eventually the Fair Intellectual Club published reading lists and members viewed themselves as sharing and producing knowledge. Weekly meetings under a speaker continued for some years, and in time members of the club were hailed as muses; it gained some respect from men, and by 1742 Aaron Hill observed that the club was for improvement not for entertainment.

The Fair Intellectual Club was confined to women of a certain class who were strongly Protestant, but this kind of restriction did not apply to all such clubs. Some women's clubs were designed to have wide and popular membership. In London, for example, wives' clubs were very popular in the eighteenth century. There were clubs for the wives of weavers, butchers, shoemakers, barbers and other trades. There were also occupational clubs for women, such as the Milliners' Club in the Royal Exchange, the Basket Women's Club in St Giles, the Mantua Makers' Club in St Martin's Lane and the Quilters' Club in Long Acre. There was even a Whores' and Bawds' Club in Drury Lane. These were largely social and entertainment clubs and their existence was promoted in the 1756 publication *The New Art and Mysteries of Gossiping, Being an Account of All the Women's Clubs in and About the City and Suburbs of London.*

Ideas about the oppression of women were most fully developed and advanced by Mary Wollstonecraft (1759–97), who wrote two important works that promoted ideas about women. In 1787 her *Thoughts on the Education of a Daughter* was written as a manual for women raising their daughters. It addressed what, at the time, were controversial issues, such as breastfeeding. She rejected the impoverished education given to most affluent women, in painting, dancing, card playing and clothes fashions. Drawing on her own experience, she argued that poor, respectable women with no income were forced to become governesses. With a better education they might have whole worlds open to them. Nevertheless, even within an enlightened framework, Wollstonecraft was a woman of her age, arguing for strict observance of the Sabbath and the benefit of stoically bearing the suffering sent by God.

Wollstonecraft's most widely read book, *A Vindication of the Rights of Woman*, was written in 1792. It was a response to Prince Talleyrand's report to the French National Assembly that women ought only to be educated in domestic matters. While Wollstonecraft did not regard men and women as equal, she saw that both sexes could make complementary contributions to society. Women's roles in raising children and as companions and helps to their husbands – rather than simply drudges who were to be kept in ignorance – made them, she claimed, a national resource. This gave them an entitlement to the same fundamental rights as men, and especially to that of a good education.

Despite its challenging views, Wollstonecraft's *Vindication* was well received and went into a second edition within the year. It was influential with many women, such as the poet Mary Robinson (1757–1800), but attracted considerable opposition from conservative women, including the evangelical writer and bluestocking Hannah More (1745–1833). When she died in 1797, Wollstonecraft's husband, William Godwin (1756–1836), wrote her biography, which mentioned her love affairs, illegitimate children and suicide bids. Consequently some women, like the novelist Maria Edgeworth (1767–1849), actively distanced themselves from her ideas. Nevertheless Wollstonecraft became enormously influential and her impact can still be seen in the work of later writers such as Virginia Woolf (1882–1941).

Women were also becoming aware of their own history and past roles in society. The physician William Alexander's *History of Women*, published in 1779 and reprinted in 1782 (and even translated into German and French), was written for women and sought to show them how their sex had fared in earlier times. But it was also a conduct book, seeking to show women how they should behave. Alexander argued that women had a civilizing impact on men; without them, men would be brutal and coarse. Yet in that mixture of regressive and progressive, Alexander concluded that 'women are in some degree every where the slaves of superior power' and that progress was dependent on improvement in the condition of women in society.

This discussion should not distract us from the essential misogyny of life in this period. As late as the 1770s some West Country towns still had ducking stools, in which 'disorderly or scolding' women were drenched in the river. Men's authority was also endorsed by the State: in 1782, Judge Francis Buller (1746–1800) ruled that a husband might legally thrash his wife, as long as the stick he used was no wider than his thumb. James Gillray (1757–1815) published a caricature in 1783 of Buller as 'Judge Thumb', carrying two bundles of sticks, described as 'for family correction: warranted lawful!' Wife-selling was also used as a crude form of divorce, sometimes with wives' agreement. In was said that the Second Duke of Chandos had scandalized polite society by buying his wife at such a wife sale in 1744. Such practices continued into the nineteenth century, even featuring in Thomas Hardy's *The Mayor of Casterbridge* in 1886.

For many women, life was blighted by such attitudes. Elizabeth Ashbridge, for example, born in 1713 the daughter of a Cheshire surgeon, said that sometimes she wept because she had not been born a boy. In the 1850s Mary Ann Evans (1819–80) had to adopt the pen-name 'George Eliot' and used her husband as her agent before she was taken seriously as a novelist. It was many years before society was prepared to accept John Stuart Mill's view that 'the legal subordination of one sex to another is wrong in itself.'

The Enlightenment was not a linear, single upward movement of ideas. There were switch-backs and opposition to some processes. Prejudice, irrationality and superstition continued to exert a strong pull on minds and imaginations. Many people could be both enlightened and regressive at the same time. Edward Long (1734–1813), a West India merchant, wrote articles for London newspapers and tracts explaining the sugar trade. He was a committed Whig who made sure his family had a good education and was an accomplished musician who played the violin. He took a keen interest in science and gathered materials to write a history of Jamaica. But Long was also an advocate of slavery and regarded African slaves as a subhuman species.

The Enlightenment also threw up, at its edges, radicals whose ideas were more influential in later years than they were at the time. Thomas Paine (1737–1809) was unrepresentative of many thinkers. He was attracted to dramatic events, having visited America during the Revolution of 1776 and France on the over-throw of the king. He was also a 'late' Enlightenment figure, who published his most influential work, *The Rights of Man* in 1792. Paine consciously detached himself from the past and adopted views that few others did. He advocated a republic, rather than monarchy. In tandem with an economy free of government control, Paine proposed a welfare system for the poorest fifth of society, providing free education and support for the poor. This would be funded by a three-penny tax on incomes up to £500 a year and a confiscation of profits above this sum. It was over a century before his ideas began to win political support in Britain. Yet even Paine, a Unitarian, saw the power of religion, and wrote 'my own mind is my own church'.

Finally, the Enlightenment also literally brought more light to people. The Georgian sash window and plate glass brought light into homes for the first time. Lamps lit streets, so that the dangers of the night, real or imagined, were reduced. From 1684 in London lamps were required outside every tenth house. In 1716 the Corporation of London ordered all shops facing the streets to hang a lamp outside their premises from six to eleven o'clock in the evening. New forms of oil lamps, such as the Argand lamp, invented in 1780, lit interiors also. In 1792 the engineer William Murdoch lit his house with gas and in 1802 Boulton's factory in Birmingham was also lit with gas lamps. Darkness was gradually being overcome. Street-lighting with gas lamps was first introduced in London in Pall Mall in January 1807. Five years later, Parliament granted a charter to the London and Westminster Gas Light and Coke Company, which was the world's first gas company. The effect was a significant reduction in crime in Westminster. Such well-lit streets were the first to become fashionable and respectable areas because lighting forced out street crime.

4

THE EMERGENCE OF A
WORLD POWER

A Trading Empire

In September and October 1676 Edward Randolph, a
merchant trading with Massachusetts, recorded his trade
between England and the American colonies. The range of
produce he traded was remarkable: he sent beef, peas, flour,
biscuits, salted pork, cod, mackerel, horses, deal boards and
house frames to the West Indies and America. His ships then
brought back timber for masts and yardarms, fir and oak
planks, furs, tobacco, sugar, indigo, ginger, fustic (a dye), cacao
and rum. His trade with the colonies was such that 'His
Majesty need not be beholden to other nations for naval
stores.' The volume of British trade with the growing overseas
colonies was astonishing; the Canadian beaver trade alone sent
150,000 furs to London in 1693.

In 1660 Britain's formal overseas possessions were relatively
modest and they hardly constituted those of a world power.
The colonies consisted of scattered islands in the West Indies
and Atlantic: Anguilla, Antigua, Barbados, Bahamas, Belize,

Bermuda, Jamaica, Montserrat, St Christopher and Nevis, St Vincent. There were also Connecticut, Maryland, Massachusetts, Rhode Island, Virginia and Newfoundland in North America, and Surinam in the East Indies. Of course, the East India Company operated four forts in India.

The acquisition of land in the early years of this period was haphazard and, like later gains, achieved without an eye to establishing a worldwide empire. Bombay and Tangiers came with Catherine of Braganza's dowry in 1662, and it was said that Portugal was glad to be rid of the troublesome North African port. New Amsterdam – or New York – was won as a result of conflict with the Dutch in the Second Anglo-Dutch War. Nevertheless in 1660 the global architecture of Britain's later possessions was already laid down. Trade with America and the West Indies helped to develop interests in West Africa, where the slave trade grew up to supply labour. Britain's interests in India led to important trade routes around the Cape of Good Hope in southern Africa. The need to guard the route required naval bases in the Mediterranean and the Indian Ocean. The same would later develop with the overland and canal routes through Suez.

Over the century, the Atlantic shrank, as a regular postal service was developed, and became faster and more frequent. An important improvement to shipping was the improved rudder control that came from helm wheels, and, over the eighteenth century, the numbers of ships crossing the Atlantic doubled. Depending on the trade winds, England to Newfoundland could be a five-week voyage, to the Caribbean might be seven or eight weeks, and to Jamaica twelve weeks.

The Glorious Revolution also affected the direction of Britain's overseas territories. The accession of William of Orange brought to the throne a king with European interests. Unlike the Stuarts, William regarded France as his main competitor and rival. This established a pattern of rivalry with France for over a century. It was unclear, though, how Britain's relationships with her colonies would be managed. The mercantilist system ensured that the colonies served Britain economically, and was adjusted from time to time, by such measures as the Naval Store Act of 1705, which provided bounties to colonies for supplying Britain's war needs, such as timber for ship masts, pitch and tar. Greater control of the colonies was not easily achieved. William sought to take over the direction of commerce with the colonies as part of his royal prerogative over foreign policy. In 1696 Parliament established the Board of Trade to do this and increasingly Britain regulated colonial trade by passing laws. Between 1689 and 1714, twenty-seven laws regulated colonial trade, whereas in the period between the Restoration and the Glorious Revolution only five such acts had been passed.

The twenty-six years between the revolution and the Hanoverian succession were not favourable for the development of Britain's colonies. Between the 1690s and 1713 Britain was too preoccupied by the military engagement with France to consider the strategic development of its colonial possessions. Religious ties between Britain and its Puritan colonies in New England were neglected. This was partly because the Church of England focused on the domestic issues of toleration and the theological aftershocks of the revolution in the conflict between High and Low Churchmen. Queen Anne's support for the High Church did not conciliate the Puritans of North America either. Later governments withheld the appointment of a bishop for North America as a way to put pressure on the colonies, in the hope that they would be more compliant with Britain. Nevertheless there were some who saw already Britain's emerging global interests as a means to spread religion. Edmund Bohun (1645–99) wrote in his autobiography in 1696 that it was clearly God's design to spread Christianity through the world using British trade and commerce.

It was, then, largely left to trade and commerce to act as the stitching that sewed Britain to the colonies. Britain's economy was undoubtedly stimulated by its colonial trade. In 1700 its overseas imports were valued at £5.8 million; by 1730 this had risen to £7.3 million. Growth in trade with the North American and West Indian colonies between these two dates were 76 per cent and 104 per cent respectively. The dependence of Britain on its colonies as a source of trade heightened Britain's need to exclude French, Spanish and Dutch traders from them. Economic growth was felt most keenly in the maritime trades and in the western ports, as well as in London, but gradually inland manufacturers needed to be connected to these ports to trade with the colonies. Birmingham iron-masters, for example, agitated for the river Severn to be made fully navigable to give them access to Bristol's overseas trade. Equally, the growth of colonial imports turned luxury goods, such as rice, tea, sugar and tobacco, into products that could be bought by more than just the rich.

Ireland

Britain's closest overseas possession was Ireland. After the defeat of James II by William III, the English ascendancy in Ireland was strengthened for fear of further invasions of Britain through Ireland. In Ireland, therefore, Protestantism was associated with loyalty to Britain, and Catholicism with disloyalty, more strongly than in the rest of Britain. A series of laws passed by the Irish Parliament sought to prevent the growth of Catholicism, notably the Test Act of 1704. This law, as in England, restricted public office to those who had taken communion in the Church of Ireland, thus excluding Presbyterians as well as Catholics from power. Catholics also had to conform in order to be able to inherit land.

So began the period known in Ireland as the 'long *briseadh*', or shipwreck. Although there was no formal union of Britain and Ireland until 1801, the Declaratory Act of 1720 laid down the right of the British Parliament to pass laws for Ireland. It also transferred the power of the final court of appeal in Irish cases to the House of Lords in London. Together, the Protestant ascendancy and the country's treatment as a colony by London led to considerable Irish resentment.

In addition to this political situation, Anglo-Irish landlords, who owned 95 per cent of all land – and were often non-resident – extracted large sums from the estates in Ireland. So did the Anglican clergy in the form of tithes. In the first two decades of the eighteenth century, rent payments of £800,000 were taken by landlords. The best Irish agricultural produce was exported to supply Britain and its navy with beef, pork, butter, cheese and timber, sometimes leaving native Irishmen in a state of starvation. Serious shortages occurred in 1726 and 1741, the latter leading to the deaths of 400,000 people. In such circumstances, those who could often fled to America to start a new life. Benjamin Franklin estimated that a third of the population of Pennsylvania was made up of Irish refugees. Many of them were disinclined to support the British in the American War of Independence. After American independence, cheaper US meat exports undermined the Irish meat market and gradually drove Irish landlords to switch to potatoes and oats.

Those rural workers who chose to stay in Ireland, especially tenant farmers, often joined secret organizations such as the Whiteboys (named from the white smocks they dressed in), the Hearts of Oak (or Oakboys) and the Steelboys. These groups resisted rent increases, tithe payments and enclosure of common land; the loss of common land reduced the income that could be made from grazing their own animals. When economic conditions worsened, the secret organizations attacked enclosure fences, maimed cattle and sheep, attacked landlords and even resisted the militia.

After 1766, when the papacy recognized the legitimacy of the Hanoverian dynasty, some penal laws against Catholics were relaxed. Catholic Committees were established to represent moderate Catholic gentry, promoting the repeal of the penal laws. Complete freedom from the anti-Catholic laws had to wait until 1828.

The Protestant ascendancy in Ireland had also steadily come to resent English rule. In 1719 Jonathan Swift called on his fellow Irishmen to burn everything from England except the people and their coal. In 1722–4 there were further protests at the monopoly on minting copper coinage granted to William Wood (1671–1730), an ironmonger and merchant. A violent campaign against the prospect of the use of the Irish coinage as a profit-making business for an Englishman led to the withdrawal of the grant to Wood. But there remained a lingering sense that Ireland was prey to British interests. In 1751 a group of Irish politicians sought to prevent government resolutions that appropriated Irish tax for English purposes.

Opposition to English rule grew significantly from the 1770s under the Irish MP Henry Gratton, who led resistance to the Navigation Acts, which treated the Irish economy as a colonial dependence of Britain. During the American War of Independence, the Irish Volunteer Movement, which established militias to guard against invasion from France, provided Gratton with a military force to agitate in favour of his demands. In 1782, therefore, free trade was granted between Britain and Ireland and the Declaratory Act was repealed, restoring control over Ireland exclusively to the Irish Parliament. By 1793, in an attempt to liberalize Ireland to safeguard it against French revolutionary ideas, Britain amended the Test Act, permitting Catholics to vote and hold some public offices. Two years later a government grant was made to establish a Catholic seminary in Maynooth.

The aftershocks of the French Revolution, like those of America's independence, were profound in Ireland. Inspired by the French, Theobald Wolfe Tone (1763–98), a Whig politician, formed an alliance of Catholics and Presbyterians seeking political reform, known as the societies of United Irishmen. They advocated universal suffrage and espoused some of the radical ideas from France, including republicanism. It was at this time that the Orange Order was founded in Ulster to defend Protestantism against the freedoms granted to Catholics. When it quickly became clear that the United Irishmen would not attract support from the political establishment, Wolfe Tone sought military support from France. In

1796 and 1798 French (and in 1797 Dutch) invasions were attempted, but all failed. Finally a rebellion planned by the United Irishmen broke out in May 1798, but only gained a hold in Ulster. The rebellion was swiftly put down, and Wolfe Tone was court-marshalled, having been caught in a French uniform. He committed suicide before he could be executed.

The rebellion of 1798 attracted Prime Minister William Pitt's (1759–1806, known as Pitt the Younger) attention to Ireland. His solution was to unite Britain and Ireland into a single kingdom with one parliament. The Act of Union of 1801 abolished the Irish Parliament and formed the United Kingdom of Great Britain and Ireland. Like the Union with Scotland in 1707, it was forced through the Irish Parliament with the help of bribes and the threat of further rebellions. Catholics were encouraged to support the Union, which their bishops did, with the promise of greater civil freedoms.

The political and economic problems of Ireland in the eighteenth century often obscure the fact that it also had a thriving cultural life. There was an Anglo-Irish strand in this, dominated in the first half of the century by Jonathan Swift, and including other Anglo-Irish figures such as the radical politician John Toland and the Whig political thinker Edmund Burke. Swift's poetry and satires, such as *Gulliver's Travels*, were enormously popular in England as well as Ireland. There was also an indigenous Gaelic strand to Irish culture that was largely Catholic, often Jacobite, and produced the '*aisling*', or dream, poetry that depicted Ireland as a woman in need of rescue by its young men. This poetic movement was led by Aogn Ó Rathaille (1670–1728) and Brian Merriman (1749–1805), who often strayed into political themes, as in Ó Rathaille's 'The Drenching Night Drags On', which looked back to a time when Irishmen ruled themselves in a land that was wealthy and undivided by bitterness.

The West Indies and North America

As with Ireland, trade and commerce dominated Britain's relationship with its transatlantic possessions. Even in the early years of the Hanoverian regime, the government was quick to spot that, although North America was becoming much more populous, the trade with the West Indies and Caribbean was far more valuable. In 1700 North America's settler population was 234,000 and it accounted for 26 per cent of Britain's imports and 49 per cent of exports. But the West Indies and Caribbean islands, with fewer than 33,000 settlers, accounted for 74 per cent of imports and 51 per cent of exports.

The wealth to be earned in the West Indies was similarly striking. Alderman William Beckford was said to earn an astonishing £50,000 a year from his Jamaican estates; his son, also William, built Fonthill Abbey in Wiltshire with the proceeds. It was a common practice to use plantations as a source of income to buy estates in Britain rather than settle permanently in the West Indies. The Barbados plantation owner, Christopher Codrington, who died in 1710, left £10,000 to All Souls College, Oxford, and his vast estate, worth £100,000, built on sugar and slaves, to found Codrington College in Barbados. The British appetite for sugar, which the Codrington and other plantations supplied, seemed unquenchable. After 1700 the value of Britain's sugar imports always exceeded the combined total of all other imports. In the fifty years after 1730 sugar consumption in Britain quadrupled. The roots of Western over-consumption run deep in history.

This trade in sugar and other commodities was first built on the labour of indentured labourers and then African slaves, though the first Barbados slaves were taken from Guiana in the mid-seventeenth century. From 1720 the triangular trade from London, Bristol and Liverpool to West Africa and then to the Caribbean and North America became the dynamo that powered much of the British economy. This was in part because West Indies merchants were not, for the most part, settlers who sought to establish a local elite. Rather, they hoped to come 'home' after their time in the colonies – the West Indies were regarded as a white man's grave, as many died working in the plantations.

The dependence of the West Indies and Caribbean economy on slaves was visible in the ratio of white workers to slaves. In 1675 they were equal in number; by 1722 there were eleven slaves for every white worker. As exports from the islands grew, and increased production reduced prices, the slaves were forced to work harder and were exploited unmercifully to provide profits for the traders and plantation owners. Besides this, about 20 per cent of all slaves died during transportation across the Atlantic as they were packed into the holds of ships where disease was rife; this was more than three times the mortality rate for ordinary passengers.

In North America, the problem for Britain in imposing some sort of control was the way in which the colonies had grown up piecemeal. In consequence, each colony had a very different character. Some, like Carolina, were royal foundations, others, like Virginia, were formed by chartered companies. One, Maryland, was the property of Lord Baltimore, and New York had been gained as the spoils of the war with the Dutch. Their religious character was also starkly contrasting: Virginia was Anglican and had even been considered as the probable seat for a colonial bishop in 1672, whereas in New England stern Puritans regarded a bishop as something they had crossed the Atlantic to escape. Nevertheless there were some who regarded America in an idealistic light. George Berkeley (1685–1753) in his *Verses on the Prospect of Planting Arts and Learning in America* (1752) wrote:

> In happy climes the seat of innocence
> Where nature guides and virtue rules
> Where men shall not impose for truth and sense
> The pedantry of courts and schools.

There was also an emerging colonial spirit of independence. In 1688, when James II slipped out of England, the colonists of

Massachusetts, New York and Maryland rose to throw off his newly created 'Dominion of New England'. This had been an attempt by James II to make local assemblies subject to the control of royal governors. Instead, the colonies reverted to local assemblies that controlled taxation and therefore constrained the role of governors. Three attempts were made in the first decade of the eighteenth century to bring the disparate colonies into a single structure, with oversight by the Board of Trade. All three failed due to the very effective colonial lobbying at Westminster. All that bound the colonies to Britain was their residual sense of being children of a mother country, a common heritage and economic self-interest. The existence of the French in Canada and their capture of Quebec in 1690 strengthened these ties. The efforts of the French to spread south remained an important threat up to, and beyond, the Treaty of Utrecht, which ceded Newfoundland and Nova Scotia to Britain.

Colonies and European Wars

For the first half of the eighteenth century, colonies might have dominated trade and commerce, but Europe was the focus of British foreign policy. The fact that Britain's colonies were subject to events in Europe was underscored during the War of Spanish Succession. In 1689 the Irish settlers in St Christopher Island in the Caribbean rose in support of James II, and the French took the opportunity to seize the island. They used it as a base to plunder nearby Nevis in 1706. But in 1713, at the Peace of Utrecht, France surrendered half of St Christopher and confirmed British ownership of Nevis.

If William III viewed his British possessions through Dutch eyes, George I did so through Hanoverian eyes. Both saw colonies as principally an aspect of commerce and a secondary issue to Britain's European role. In 1718 Britain joined the Quadruple Alliance with Holland, France and Austria against a resurgent Spain, which had decided to reassert its dominance of the Mediterranean. For a short interlude, Spain replaced France as Britain's principal rival. Prime Minister Robert Walpole (1676–1745), however, keen to secure the longevity of his Whig regime, and to avoid the disruption to trade and the high taxes which war would entail, evaded military conflicts.

During the 1730s public opinion and political pressure from MPs and ministers led to greater resentment of the practice of the Spanish boarding British ships to verify that they were not trading with Spanish colonies. This was an attempt by the Spanish to claw back trade concessions made at Utrecht in 1713. In 1738 Captain Robert Jenkins displayed his pickled ear, which the Spanish had sliced off during one boarding, in the House of Commons. The effect was to whip up anti-Spanish feeling, and Walpole was forced to declare war. The War of Jenkins' Ear, as it became known, lasted until 1748, though from 1742 it merged into the War of Austrian Succession. It was in this war that, in 1740, after a victory at the Battle of Porto Bello in Panama, the first public performance of 'God Save the King' was played as the national anthem. It was also during this conflict that Commodore George Anson (1697–1762), over three years, circumnavigated the globe in pursuit of Spanish ships. The war was ultimately a military stalemate in which neither side gaining the upper hand.

The degree to which colonial ventures were subsidiary to European interests was also demonstrated by the War of Austrian Succession. Its origins lay in the Prussian challenge to Maria Theresa's claim to the throne of Austria, and spread as the French supported Prussia, while Britain, Holland and Russia backed Austria. The British involvement was, in part, a reaction to French sponsorship of a Jacobite plan to invade Britain. The war ranged across central Europe, and the notable victory at Dettingen 1744 was the last battle in which a British king, George II, personally led his troops. The war also spread to North America, where the British and French clashed at the fortress of Louisbourg in 1745.

By the end of the war, Britain had thrown off its relative disadvantage and had re-emerged as the leading naval power. The 1748 Treaty of Aix-la-Chapelle that ended the conflict turned the clock back to 1740. It included the return of Louisbourg to France, and did not resolve any of the competitive commercial issues between Britain, France and Spain over their colonies. The only major concession from France was the expulsion of the Jacobites from Paris and recognition of the legitimacy of the Hanoverian succession. The peace was celebrated by the first performance of Handel's *Music for the Royal Fireworks* on the Thames, in April 1749.

The principal threat facing Britain overseas was once again French rivalry. France had regained its position in North America and viewed British and colonial expansion along the St Lawrence, Ohio and Mississippi rivers with alarm. In the following years, there were repeated skirmishes between the British and French in North America, the Caribbean and in India, which culminated in the humiliating loss of Minorca in 1756.

Minorca had been obtained by Britain as a base in the Mediterranean in 1708, and was confirmed as a British possession at the Peace of Utrecht in 1713. In 1756 the British lost the island to a French force, after Admiral John Byng failed to repel a French naval landing. In an effort to protect his fleet, Byng also failed to pursue the French. It was a national humiliation and, despite the attempted intervention of the House of Commons, Byng was court-marshalled and shot on the quarterdeck of his own ship, prompting Voltaire to say that the English shot their admirals from time to time *'pour encourager les autres'* (and thereby coining the phrase). The loss of the island was taken very hard in the country: Thomas Turner recorded in his diary:

Oh my country! Oh my country! Oh Albion! Albion! I doubt thou art tottering on the brink of ruin and desolation this day! The nation is all in a foment upon account of losing dear Minorca.

In Parliament, the government of the Duke of Newcastle (1693–1768) was replaced by William Pitt, an opposition Whig MP who had led the attacks on the government. But it would require Newcastle and Pitt to join in a coalition before it was possible to prosecute the competition with France effectively. In a diplomatic triumph, Britain detached Prussia from France and joined it in an alliance against Austria and France. The combination of Prussian land and British sea power was to be significant in the ensuing Seven Years War. The war was sparked by French building of forts in Pennsylvania and the Prussian invasion of Saxony. The Seven Years War ranged across the world and can legitimately be thought of as an early world war. It was fought out in North America, India and Africa as well as in Europe. There were a number of reverses early in the war, but by 1758 the tide turned decisively in Britain's favour.

The peak of British military success occurred in 1759, the 'year of three victories', and much of this was down to impressive generalship. British troops defeated the French in Canada, Guadeloupe and West Africa. In India, East India Company troops led by Robert Clive (1725–74) defeated the French at the Battle of Plassey, where Company guns had a longer range than the French, who had allowed their muskets to get damp in the tropical weather, preventing any effective response.

In Canada, General Wolfe (1727–59) won the Battle of the Plains of Abraham, in part due to the good luck of discovering the French battle plans. In a surprise attack lasting just twenty minutes the fate of Canada was decided; Quebec surrendered to the British. The drama of Wolfe's victory was heightened by his own death (and that of the opposing General Montcalm), and by accounts of the impressive volleys of the British muskets. The war entered the literature of the nineteenth century in Fennimore Cooper's *The Last of the Mohicans* (1826). In Sussex, the shopkeeper Turner recorded in his diary on hearing the news from Quebec:

> Oh what a pleasure it is to every true Briton, to see with what success it pleases God Almighty to bless his majesty's arms, they having success at this time in Europe, Asia, Africa and America!

During the Seven Years War the British outspent the French, and British military and naval command outpaced its rivals. In the last years of the war Britain captured Montreal, Martinique, Havana and Manila. But the war was costly in terms of human life, accounting for around a million deaths, and it was also enormously expensive in financial terms. The British national debt, which stood at £74.6 million at the start of the war, grew to £132.6 million by its end. This represented a dramatic strain on British finance, and one that troubled the government.

Surprisingly, the Treaty of Paris that concluded the war in 1763 did not see a commensurate stripping of French territory. Nor was there great loss of territory by Spain, which had joined on the French side. This further underscores how little the British government's eyes were set on global acquisition. A century later, in contrast, the sense of the door closing on global land-grabbing led nations to snatch at any colonies they could. But in 1763 the British government's aim was the defence of existing possessions. Consequently, Guadeloupe, Martinique and Goree in West Africa were restored to France and Cuba, and the Philippines to Spain. Nevertheless, Britain gained most of New France in Canada, all lands to the east of the Mississippi, as well as Florida and Minorca. Britain's position in India was also strengthened, and its use of the subcontinent as a base for the conquest of the Philippines confirmed that India could not be regarded as the sole preserve of the East India Company. Without Britain's victory in the

Seven Years War, French presence in North America and India would have resulted in a very different future for the American colonies and the British Raj in India.

Though victorious in North America in the Seven Years War, Britain still had to face resistance from Native Americans. The Ottawa tribe, led by Pontiac, brought together a group of northern nations to resist the British colonists' expansion. Colonists drew back across the Appalachians, and Pontiac laid siege to a number of garrisons and forts. However, the absence of French-supplied gunpowder for the Native Americans after the Treaty of Paris limited their advance. Eventually, after about a year, George III made a proclamation limiting the westward expansion of the colonists and, with the resumption of payments of presents to Native Americans, a peace was agreed. It did not, of course, please the King's American subjects.

The Loss of America

The expansion of colonies in North America had resulted in the charter for the last of the thirteen colonies, the Province of Georgia, named after George II, in 1732. In conception, Georgia was designed as a refuge for Protestants escaping persecution in Europe and debtors freed from England. The new colony also acted as a buffer between the Carolinas and the Spanish in Florida and the French in Louisiana. However, the European wars had been costly and had seen the British national debt balloon. For some time there were fears of national bankruptcy which naturally made British politicians anxious. The politicians' response was to expect the colonies to contribute to the cost of their own defence. After all, it was argued, British defence expenditure had ensured the colonists' freedom from foreign rule and protection from the predation of foreign trade.

The options for relieving the costs that the British taxpayers had to bear for colonies were few. Constraining the westward expansion of the North American colonies reduced the expense, but would leave the way open to France or Spain. Alternatively, a stricter application of the mercantilist principle would recoup some of the money that 'leaked' from the system as it was believed that there was much illicit trade between the colonies and other European powers; this would inevitably affect both colonists and merchants.

In 1764 George Grenville (1712–70), the British prime minister, renewed the sugar and molasses tariff in America. He halved the rate charged, but made it clear that strict enforcement would be required. He also passed a Currency Act that outlawed the issuing of paper money in America. Both were measures designed to recoup funds and return the colonial economy to dependence on Britain. A year later he passed a stamp tax, which imposed a duty on newspapers, books, pamphlets and all official documents. The colonists resisted the taxes, claiming in their 'Declaration of Rights and Grievances' that while they were subjects of the king, the Westminster Parliament could not impose taxes on them since they were not represented in it. The colonists began to boycott British goods.

When, a year later, Grenville was succeeded by Lord Rockingham (1730–82), the government response changed. In London, Benjamin Franklin made the case that the American colonies had paid heavily, in manpower, money and blood to defend their territory in a series of wars against the French and Native American nations. Further taxes to pay for those wars were unjust, and might bring about a rebellion. Rockingham conceded and lifted the taxes, but passed a Declaratory Act that restated the right of the British Parliament to impose colonial taxes. In this relatively conciliatory atmosphere, the colonists lifted the boycott they had imposed on British exports, and transatlantic trade picked up again. George III was one of the few who remained implacably offended by the colonists, in part because of their support for John Wilkes, whom they regarded as a fellow agitator for liberty. The goodwill was squandered, however, by the Townshend Act of

1767, which placed taxes on some essential goods, including paper, glass and tea. Angered at these new taxes, the colonists resumed their boycott of British goods.

In 1770, Lord North (1732–92), the new prime minister, brought greater political stability to Britain, but he was more inclined to a policy of coercion towards the American colonists. In June 1772 HMS *Gaspée*, a British revenue-collection ship that had been vigorously enforcing mercantilist and tax regulations was burnt by American colonists. Soon afterwards, the governor of Massachusetts, Thomas Hutchinson, reported that he and the royal judges would be paid directly from London. This would avoid any control by the colonial legislature and asserted the independence of the governor and judges from it. To the American colonists this looked as if Britain was planning to control them through their governors and judges.

In December 1773 Samuel Adams led a group of men, disguised as Native Americans, to board three ships of British East India Company tea merchants. They dumped an estimated £10,000 worth of tea into the harbour in protest at the British attempt to sell cheap Indian tea in America; despite the fact that there had been a reduction in duty from 1 shilling to 3 pence, the Tea Act of 1773 imposed a tax on tea that the colonists opposed. This event, known as the Boston Tea Party, remains a significant part of American patriotic lore.

At Westminster, opinion swung behind Lord North and against the colonists. The government argued that the supremacy of Parliament had been infringed. In North America, meanwhile, the colonists' right to representation in matters of taxation was asserted; both sides claimed that they were the true heirs of the Glorious Revolution of 1688. The British government pressed on with measures that they did not appreciate would further inflame the colonists. In 1774 the Quebec Act, which recognized French civil law and toleration for Catholics in Quebec, was a further source of concern in America. American Protestants, especially in Massachusetts, feared that their liberties would be threatened by Catholics to the north. Some British laws were undeniably inflammatory, and a group of them were named the 'intolerable acts'. One of these, the Quartering Act of 1774, allowed governors to quarter troops in any unoccupied buildings. One loyalist was shocked that 'the King is openly cursed, and his authority set at defiance', and Lord North's effigy was paraded round Alexandria, Virginia, shot at and burnt.

In response to the 'intolerable acts', the American opposition began to harden. Initially colonial assemblies, such as the Stamp Act Congress, were the focus of opposition. But soon the Sons of Liberty, a secret society that had been formed in 1765, threatened violence to ensure that the British taxes were unenforceable. From 1772 Samuel Adams created new 'committees of correspondence' to establish a network of like-minded colonists in all thirteen colonies, and in due course these committees provided the framework for the rebel government. A year later, even loyalist Virginia, the largest colony, set up its committee of correspondence, on which Thomas Jefferson served.

The spark that fell on to this dry tinder was the skirmish between Massachusetts militiamen and British troops at Lexington and Concord in 1775, when the British sought to confiscate colonists' arms. During the conflict that followed, London badly underestimated the colonists' organization and determination. London also overlooked the almost impossible logistics of conducting a war against insurgents over 3,000 miles away. The British dismissal of the Olive Branch Petition from the colonists in 1775 was a grave error, and led to a refusal to consider negotiations on either side until 1783.

It is estimated that about a quarter of the American colonists remained loyal to Britain during the war. These 'loyalists' or 'king's men' were those who were unwilling to break with Britain for a number of reasons. Some were Anglicans who felt obliged to support the king as head of the Church, others were merchants with business connections back in Britain.

Immigrants who had not been fully absorbed into American society were also inclined to support Britain, as were many of the Native American nations. The war was, in effect, a civil war. Benjamin Franklin's son, William, remained loyal to George III and never spoke to his father again. In the Church of England, Archbishop William Markham of York (1719–1807), who owned land in America, preached a sermon sternly criticizing opponents of the war in 1777, but Bishop Keppel of Exeter (1728–77) preached a sermon in front of the King, urging him to make peace with the colonists.

In July 1776 the Congress adopted the Declaration of Independence and, thereafter, articles of confederation were circulated to all the colonies. The central blow of the war for Britain was General Burgoyne's surrender to the rebels at Saratoga in New York in October 1777, after he had been outnumbered three to one and suffered casualties twice that of the revolutionaries. This event triggered the entry of France, and later Spain and Holland, into the war on the American side. Although the British made advances in the south, after 1778 Britain suffered two setbacks. First was the failure of sufficient loyalists to come to their aid, and then the destruction of the British fleet, which was coming to relieve the army, by the French. General Cornwallis was forced to surrender in 1781 at Yorktown, Virginia.

In Britain, Lord North was concerned that, while the majority of public opinion backed the war, a vocal and well-organized minority – largely made up of merchants and religious dissenters – opposed the war in sermons and addresses to the King and Parliament. Two army camps were formed at Coxheath in Kent and Warley in Essex to defend London from any attack. As the war dragged on, all the bogeymen of foreign wars came to the fore. Merchants decried the disruption to trade, the national debt rose further, there were fears of French invasion and Irish unrest. Worse still, a Franco-American privateer force bombarded Edinburgh and briefly even captured Whitehaven. Lord North was furiously attacked in

Parliament by the 'old Whig' Edmund Burke, the 'new Whig' Charles James Fox and Lords Rockingham and Shelburne. After Yorktown, in an attempt to end the war, North proposed the Conciliation Plan, in which he promised to eliminate all the Acts that the colonists opposed, in order to end the war. But this was too little, too late: the colonies were determined to gain their independence from Britain.

In 1783, the Treaty of Paris recognized the independence of the United States of America, and gave it all land east of the Mississippi River and south of the Great Lakes, excluding Florida. Britain made a separate treaty with Spain that ceded Florida to Spain. It was the end of Britain's political connection with those former colonies and the end of aspirations for an expansion of its colonies in the west. The loss of the territory temporarily dashed British confidence, and indicated the future directions of the British Empire.

After the American War of Independence, British trade with America resumed and continued to grow. In 1751–5 British exports to American were worth £1.3 million, but by 1786–90 this had grown to £2 million, as America lacked access to credit and industrial production, remaining largely dependent on Britain. Nevertheless, after 1770 India became much more prominent in British ideas of empire and trade.

India

In the east, the speed with which the East India Company exploited trade with Asia surprised investors and government alike. By 1690 about 13 per cent of Britain's imports came from Asia. British merchants were also quickly opening access to China as a market. By 1720 about 10 per cent of the East India Company's trade was with China. It is easy to forget how flimsy the foundations of the East India Company in India were. In 1713 the Company owned only a score of 'factories'. In Calcutta – as in most other cities – there were only a few hundred Britons in each factory. In such circumstances, the Company was obliged to work with the local populations; any other strategy would not work. An attempt to be more dominant in Bengal in 1688 had led to opposition from the local population and a sharp reversal in policy.

In 1698 an attempt by other English merchants to break the East India Company's monopoly on Asian trade by chartering a new company failed. The old East India Company simply bought the majority shareholding in the new company and restored its hugely valuable monopoly. Thereafter, any threats to its dominance of Asian trade were fought in the courts, which imposed heavy fines on incursions into the East India Company's chartered area.

Although India is often thought of as the quintessential British imperial possession, at the end of the seventeenth century it was still an open field. The Dutch Verenigde Oost-Indische Compagnie (from 1601) and the French Compagnie des Indes Orientales (from 1664) traded alongside the East India Company for cotton, indigo and silk. What permitted the European merchants to gain such a foothold in India were long-range trading ships with navigational and maritime skills; commerce at such a distance would have been impossible without these. The Europeans also possessed firearms, which could be used to enforce their interests. India was receptive to colonial and commercial advances because there were local merchants and producers who could supply European traders. Moreover, local rulers in India were prepared to grant concessions to the traders in exchange for customs duties or support in dynastic feuds.

The East India Company found that India possessed some of the key economic structures that facilitated trade. The subcontinent had a mobile labour force, some of which was organized in merchant guilds, and much of which could be directed to work by rulers and bureaucratic systems. India also had a well-developed financial system, including credit notes and banks. Indian merchants lent funds to rulers, and Europeans were also willing to do so. Additionally, although the Mughal Empire was in rapid decline, the British were able to adopt the systems and bureaucracy that the Mughals had establish to reinforce and sustain their control over the territories into which they expanded.

In south India, the British base in Madras was less significant than the French fort at Pondicherry. The French strength in south India was based, in part, on their intervention in Indian domestic affairs. This enabled France to capture Madras in 1746 during the War of Austrian Succession, although it was handed back to the British in 1749. In Hyderabad, in central India, similarly, France allied itself with the local ruler, the Nizam, and this led to reduced influence for the British, who were allied to the ruler of Peshwa, the Nizam's enemy. This pattern was reversed in Carnatic, in south India, where the British support for Muhammad Ali, the successful claimant to be the Nawab of Carnatic, produced a ruler sympathetic to the East India Company in 1751.

The Seven Years War in India witnessed the rise of Robert Clive, who had come to Madras in 1744 as a 'writer' – a combination of clerk and accountant – for the East India Company. He had distinguished himself during the 1746 attack by the French on Madras, but depression forced him to leave India in 1748. He returned in 1755, as deputy governor of Fort St David, south of Madras. From here, he evicted the French from Hyderabad, eventually being commissioned as a colonel. During the war, the ruler of Bengal, in eastern India, had chosen to oppose the British. With impressive diplomatic and military action, he was defeated by Clive at Plassey in 1757. It was a stunning victory, in which Clive's army, numbering just 1,100 Europeans and 2,100 sepoy troops with nine field-pieces, faced 18,000 cavalry, 50,000 infantry and fifty-three heavy guns operated by French fusiliers. Clive was victorious, largely due to the scattering of the Bengali troops. He then captured the Bengali treasury and distributed enormous sums in spoils. Clive himself gained £160,000, while £500,000 was distributed among the East India Company troops, and £24,000 was given to each member of the Company's committee – worth several million pounds in today's values. By the end of his career, Clive was the first self-made millionaire.

It was during this war that the Nawab of Bengal incarcerated 146 English prisoners in the 'Black Hole of Calcutta', from which only twenty-three emerged alive. The only eye-witness account of the ordeal of the prisoners was published in the *Annual Register* in 1758, which created a wave of anger in Britain, although later investigations questioned the truth of the report. Clive also defeated an opportunistic Dutch action. During the war with France, Britain was responsible for another great colonial victory, by capturing their historic base at Pondicherry in 1761.

One of the outcomes of the Seven Years War in India was British dominance over Bengal. This led to the establishment of the system whereby the East India Company troops were paid from Bengali tax revenues rather than from British taxes or Company profits. This was a blueprint for the financing of the administration of India; it was also this model that the Americans would refuse to tolerate a decade later. While British relations with America declined during the 1760s, the East India Company conducted four wars against Mysore and, after some setbacks, reached an alliance with the ruler of Delhi. But Mysore and Hyderabad, having allied themselves with France, remained a source of conflict with Britain until the end of the century, when Arthur Wellesley (1769–1852), later the Duke of Wellington, defeated the ruler of Mysore, Tipu Sultan, and brought them under British control.

The British rule in India was established through a combination of effective leadership, a policy of divide and rule between feuding dynasties in India, superior firepower, the use of mercenaries, the exploitation of Indian revenues against the country itself and the incentivization of local entrepreneurs. After 1773, when a governor general was established by the British government, the government of India gradually became better organized and less improvised.

Warren Hastings (1732–1818), the first governor general, was alert to the opportunities to expand British territory. He also was determined to plan and organize British control of the subcontinent carefully. The East India Company continued the practice of using Mughal tax collectors to raise revenue, but bribes, protection payments and corruption affected the Company's finances. Under Hastings, tax collection was extended in south India and a Board of Revenue was established in Calcutta. The East India Company officials were merciless in their extraction of funds from India. Consequently, despite a famine in Bengal in 1769–70, the tax yield was unaffected. At the same time, the payments to princes and to the Mughal emperors were reduced and eventually stopped. In time, pensions for some princes were resumed to maintain order, and to ensure their dependence on the British.

The British gradually introduced the instruments of imperial government. In 1765 in Murshidabad, the East India Company resident established a high court to deal with disputes. By an Act of 1773 English law was established in India as the system for British subjects and their trade and commerce. Thereafter, criminal courts also gradually adopted English law. However, the British also encouraged some indigenous institutions. In 1781 Hastings supported the development of Muslim *madrassas* in India, with the first in Calcutta – to strengthen education for Indians.

Ironically, given Hastings' commitment to the use of native officials to avoid exploitation, when he retired as governor general, Hastings was accused of corruption. The accusation was fuelled in part by Sir Philip Francis, whom Hasting had wounded in a duel in India. Hastings was impeached in 1788, and the trial dragged on until his acquittal in 1795. Nevertheless Hastings had enriched himself, like many others, and later writers accused him of lax principles and a hard heart towards his Indian duties.

Africa

Africa was the last continent to be systematically explored by the British. This was partly because, with the exception of West Africa, there were few economic and commercial incentives to exploration. European interests were principally coastal, and an unwritten understanding defined the interior as exclusively for Africans. This was possibly because, as the Royal African Company's employees discovered, there was a high mortality rate for those who ventured too far from the coast. This was in part because the interior was unmapped and unknown. In fact, the Europeans tended to rely on African intermediaries if they ventured more than a few miles inland. The Royal African Company depended on sixteenth-century travellers' accounts of the interior, such as those of Leo Africanus (Hasan ibn Muhammed al-Wazzan al-Fasi), which mixed myth and fact and created a frightening imaginary account of the African interior.

By the mid-eighteenth century such fearful descriptions gave way to the assumption that the whole world should be open to European exploration. There seemed to be a natural right to explore and travel. In 1771 Joseph Banks (1743–1820), the naturalist and president of the Royal Society, sent Henry Smeathman, an entomologist, to the Banana Islands off the coast of Sierra Leone to collect plant and insect samples. Smeathman quickly became one of the few experts on African matters. In 1788 Banks formed the Association for Promoting the Discovery of the Interior Part of Africa, known as the African Association. The establishment of the association was a consciously progressive venture; the association proclaimed that it was 'desireous of rescuing the age from a charge of ignorance, which in other respects belongs so little to its character'. In its first year, the association sponsored three expeditions by John Ledyard, Simon Lucas and Daniel Houghton into different parts of the western Sahara. Lucas discovered little, and Ledyard and Houghton died on their expeditions.

The first significant African exploration was by Mungo Park (1771–1806) in 1795. Park, a member of the Linnaean Society,

had already become an expert on fish in India. Park was sponsored by the African Association and the government to
explore West Africa, between the rivers Gambia and Niger. His
account of *Travels in the Interior Districts of Africa* was hugely
popular. Park described large cities in West Africa, prosperous
farms and beautiful landscapes. He embellished the book with
rumours of the fabled city of Timbuktu and of his own imprisonment by a local chieftain. Park's book, which was lavishly
illustrated with engravings based on his own sketches of
African villages and landscapes, inspired poems and prints.

Park's second expedition in 1805 to the Gambia followed the
river Niger into the interior, which he erroneously thought
was part of the Congo. Park was drowned when his boat hit a
rock on the Bussa rapids, however. Two subsequent
government-sponsored expeditions in 1816 and 1817 to the
Gambia and Congo failed to achieve anything of significance.

Mapmakers also turned their attention to Africa. James
Rennell, sponsored by the African Association, pieced
together much of the speculative geography of the interior of
Africa, but his first map of 1796 included the belief that the
river Niger flowed into a inland sea. James Bruce's account of
Ethiopia, published in 1790, was also littered with myths,
including that Ethiopia was the location of the mythical
Christian kingdom of Prester John.

Global Exploration

Exploration was at the heart of the British overseas endeavour.
It was common for privateers such as William Dampier
(1651–1715), who had previously been a pirate in North and
South America, to be employed by the government. In 1699,
Dampier was given command of the ship *Roebuck* to explore
the coast of New Guinea. In doing so, he also charted the coast
of Western Australia. He was the first man to circumnavigate
the globe twice. In Dampier's second expedition, the seaman,
Alexander Selkirk (1676–1721) was shipwrecked on the island
of Juan Fernandez from 1704 to 1709. His account of the

wreck and life on Juan Fernandez was the origin of Daniel Defoe's *Robinson Crusoe*, published in 1719. Within a year the book had sold out four editions. *Robinson Crusoe* was also responsible for much of the interest in travel and 'discovery' of new worlds.

Exploration also provided some of the important information on which mariners came to rely. The astronomer Edmund Halley (1656–1742) had also been an explorer, having worked in the South Atlantic, using St Helena in 1686 as the base for charting the trade winds. The government remained keen to pursue exploration, especially where it would support trade. The search for a North-West Passage from the northern coast of America into the Pacific had long been the goal of travellers, and had engaged the British since the time of Martin Frobisher in 1576. In 1719 James Knight failed to find a passage and, in 1741, the Admiralty sent out two ships, *Discovery* and *Furnace*, under Christopher Middleton to find it. While Middleton travelled further north than earlier voyagers, he also failed. By 1745, the Admiralty offered a reward for anyone who found the passage, increasing the prize to £20,000 in 1775, but even Captain James Cook failed.

Cook is more usually associated with the South Seas than with North America. He had been employed by the Royal Society in 1766, after a distinguished naval career, to make astrological observations. Cook reached Tahiti in 1769 and, under secret orders from the Admiralty, also sought to verify the existence of a southern continent. He charted and circumnavigated New Zealand, and landed on the east coast of Australia. At Botany Bay in 1770 Cook claimed the territory for George III. On his return, he published diaries, which were very popular accounts of his voyages and discoveries. In later expeditions, he discovered Christmas Island, landed on Antarctica and he was able to lay to rest the myth of the existence of the North-West Passage; and he found the northern Pacific to be ice-bound. Cook was also significant because of the protégés he inspired, who also found fame in exploration:

among them William Bligh (1754–1817) in the Pacific and Australia, George Vancouver (1757–98) in the Pacific north-west and Charles Dixon (1728–86) in North America.

James Cook's death at the hands of Hawaiians in 1779 illus-trates the ways in which colonial history has been variously depicted. The most famous version of Robert Cleveley's *Death of Cook* (which hangs in the Honolulu Academy of Arts) shows Cook as a peacemaker killed by aggressive Hawaiians; but the original, found in 2004, shows Cook attacking the Hawaiians. Cook, and other explorers, confirmed British dominance of the Pacific in the eighteenth century, and the discovery and claiming of such key islands as Lord Howe Island (1785), the Gilbert and Marshall Islands (1788) and Chatham Island (1799) provided Britain with a string of possessions across the Pacific.

The Experience of Empire

Empire and overseas expansion was experienced in all sorts of ways by Britons in the eighteenth century. In the early years of the century, colonies were sometimes associated with financial speculation. John Law's fraudulent Mississippi scheme of 1710 and the South Sea Bubble of the 1720s exploited some of the wilder speculations of what riches could be amassed from colonies. These ventures were perhaps as outlandish as the literary speculation of what non-Europeans were like. *The Foreign Travels of Sir John Mandeville*, a chapbook of the early eighteenth century, included tales of pygmies, giants, dragons and 'people that have heads like hounds', as well as extravagant stories of their exploits. As the century progressed, the sense of confidence in imperial matters grew. Edward Gibbon's *Decline and Fall of the Roman Empire* argued that Europe would never be overrun by barbarian hordes, as the Roman Empire was. Gibbon implied that there was, in imperial ventures, the opportunity for a reversal of the process, with civilization being exported to barbarian lands by European powers.

The public appetite and interest in overseas knowledge was remarkable. In 1737 a sale of animals brought back from a long African voyage attracted enormous interest in London. Among them were a camel, a panther, a hyena, a crocodile, an armadillo (described as 'a hog in armour') and an ape. Handbills were issued and the animals were exhibited to the public before the sale at a 'great booth' in Chelsea. The descriptions of the animals were designed to create a sensation: the hyena was described as having a voice like a human, which seduced natives to leave their huts before they were eaten by it. Crowds flocked to see the exotic animals. The sale was an odd mixture of melodramatic myths of what were depicted as barbarian lands and an expression of the desire to learn more about these animals.

The most enduring features of Britain's imperial ventures are linguistic, cultural and constitutional imports and exports. The English language was an intangible aspect of imperial conquest. In North America it survived in a form closer to its seventeenth- and eighteenth-century roots than it did in Britain. From India, in particular, the English language was enriched by all manner of words and phrases. Britain also exported a political culture to the colonies, and more consciously in the parliamentary structures that endure in many former British colonies across the world.

The experience of empire was also a religious one: William III promised £20 to each clergyman who went to the 'western plantations', and in 1715 George I funded chaplains and clergy in Virginia, Philadelphia, Boston, Algiers and Montserrat. This was partly from a desire to exclude Catholic powers from British colonies, but it was also from a wish to spread Protestantism. The Society for the Propagation of the Gospel in Foreign Parts (SPG) was founded in 1701 by the Revd Thomas Bray (1658–1730) at the request of the Bishop of London. It was chartered to send schoolteachers and clergy to the West Indies and American colonies to promote Christianity among the colonists. By 1710 the SPG decided that its principal mission was to convert 'heathens' and in 1776 had 300 missionary priests in America.

The growth of Britain's overseas possessions had an economic and cultural impact at home. Britain's relations with its colonies were shot through with implications of superiority. In 1757 the monument to Admiral Watson in Westminster Abbey depicted Calcutta, represented by an Indian woman, presenting a petition to Watson, on her knees. European explorers brought back more than just foodstuffs and the raw materials of manufacturing – though the impact of these should not be underestimated. Houses of the wealthy were decorated with paintings, engravings, furniture and carpets from India, China and elsewhere. The architect William Chambers (1723–96), who had visited China, built a pagoda in the Oriental manner at Kew. In 1757 Chambers published the *Design of Chinese Buildings*, and in 1772 a book on Oriental gardening. He incorporated the designs derived from his colonial experiences into Somerset House and the gilded state coronation coach. Clothing for rich and poor respectively used Chinese silk and Indian cotton.

News from Britain's colonies appeared in newspapers and periodicals in increasing amounts as the century went on. The arrivals of ships in ports were often recorded, as were events and economic developments. This subtly developed a culture of imperial sensibility in Britain. Places beyond Europe became part of a wider imperial understanding that broadened British minds and horizons. Knowledge of British exploration also bolstered a sense of national destiny and mission. Adam Smith's *Wealth of Nations* argued that the skill and dexterity of pre-modern armies were vital in earlier victories, but firearms and technology made these skills obsolete. In Persia, Serbia, Afghanistan and India, however, it was clear that firearms were not always the deciding factor in colonial warfare in the eighteenth century.

Foreign encounters also developed ideas of race in Britain. People from India, China, North America and Africa were gradually seen in London, and more widely across the country. This tended to reinforce ideas of alien paganism and European superiority. But it also emphasized the similarity of peoples: the scientist and writer Dr John Arbuthnot (1667–1735), the philosopher Baron de Montesquieu and the novelist Oliver Goldsmith (1730–74) all argued that skin colour was a result of the climates of foreign lands and that all babies were born white. Such prejudices became ingrained.

In the same way that Britain sought to convert foreigners, they also Europeanized many peoples that they came into contact with. The epitome of this was Omai (?1751–80), a Polynesian who returned with Captain Cook to London between 1774 and 1776. Omai was received as a 'natural man', but he became thoroughly Europeanized. He was taught to read and write, to ride and shoot, he was clothed and converted to Christianity. In 1776 Sir Joshua Reynolds painted him as a patrician in classical costume. In a metaphor for the age, when Omai returned to his homeland he did so wearing armour.

Britons sometimes idealized the 'noble savages' of colonial exploration, and were prepared to learn from them. In 1784, the Asiatic Society of Bengal was established by William Jones (1746–94) to promote Oriental research and collect a library and museum of Indian culture. In India, China and elsewhere, British explorers found highly developed cultures and civilizations. Oriental cultures were treated as the Ottomans were: foreign and pagan, but to be respected. Warren Hastings' treatment of India exemplified this approach, paying – sometimes grudging – respect to Indian culture and heritage.

Attitudes to empire germinated quickly in Britain. Joseph Banks, director of the Royal Botanic Gardens at Kew, made it the centre of botanical colonialism, aiming to improve agriculture and horticulture in Britain from information and samples gathered from the empire. This was seen as a thoroughly Enlightenment harnessing of empire to the material progress and improvement of Britain. Banks believed it could enlighten the dark continents of Africa and Asia at the same time as it enriched the metropolitan.

The Instruments of Global Power

The growth of Britain as a world power was both a cause and consequence of the growth of government. The authority of the State became far more centralized and less focused on provincial power. This centralization was principally because the State needed far more money to sustain the costs of foreign ventures. Unlike its enemies, Britain used credit on a huge scale to fund its war efforts. The number of government employees had already risen to 12,000 by 1720, and this growth continued to 16,000 by 1760. The number of revenue officers alone increased from 2,500 in 1690 to over 8,000 in the eighteenth century. This reflected the fact that excise supplied 55 per cent of government income by 1733. The growing numbers of excise officers, rewarded and promoted on the basis of their ability, also contributed to the growth of a meritocratic society.

The income raised by this expanding bureaucracy was spent on the army and navy. Each capital ship cost tens of thousands of pounds to build, the equivalent of tens of millions today, and needed regular repairs. Few, if any, saw many battles, and more sailors died in storms and accidents than in warfare. In fact, in 1805 more sailors died in the storms a few days after Trafalgar than in the battle itself. By the 1740s Portsmouth dockyards employed 2,000 workers and the shipboard force of the navy reached 40,000. Even in times of peace the army rarely fell below 10,000.

The royal dockyards were a good example of the complex pre-industrial economy. Before 1720 there were 6,500 dockyard workers maintaining 430 ships at sea. The dockyards included dry docks and by 1720 the navy introduced prefabricated dock buildings for overseas naval bases. But at the end of the Napoleonic wars there were 17,500 dockyard workers supporting 900 ships. This growth of activity often had an impact on the local economy. Rope-making, for example, which was important for ships, was often 'outsourced' to local companies. In workhouses and prisons inmates picked oakum fibres from used ropes to make it into caulking, which water-proofed ships.

Once Britain had acquired colonial possessions, techno-logical advances developed to support their maintenance. In 1795 the Admiralty formed a hydrographic department to draw up charts for the use of its ships. By 1819 these charts were made available to merchant vessels for a fee; by 1855 there were 1,981 charts, covering the whole earth. In 1802 the head of the hydrographic department, Rear Admiral Sir Francis Beaufort (1774–1857), established the Beaufort scale of wind speeds to help naval ships estimate the danger of weather conditions to shipping.

The popular perception of the armed forces varied. Without barracks, the army relied on billeting, which was unpopular, as were the taxes to pay for them. The country was always thrilled by accounts of the victories of its army and navy, and as a result the first signs of imperial jingoism can be seen in some of the popular ballads of this period. In contrast, the French were less heavily taxed than the British to pay for their armed forces, but resented it much more. Perhaps Britons had the consolations of victories and a sense of an open government in which criticism of waste was common.

The use of press gangs, often seen in films, was relatively rare, largely because volunteers were plentiful, but two-thirds of recruits were rejected as unsuitable, usually because of poor physique. The need for better-trained troops led to the formation of the Portsmouth Naval Academy in 1733 and the Woolwich Academy in 1741, the latter formed for 'instructing the people of its Military branch to form good Officers of Artillery and perfect Engineers'. In time an officer class grew up, as in other professions, in which generations from the same families entered the army and navy.

During the eighteenth century the cultural expressions of patriotism and empire emerged. The Union Jack, which had been developed as a naval flag in the seventeenth century, was designated as the flag of the United Kingdom after the Act of Union in 1707, and in 1801 the addition of the cross of St Patrick gave the Union Jack its modern form. Unlike most foreign countries, Britain had a flag that symbolized the nation rather than that of its ruling dynasty. The display of the flag on uniforms, above buildings and on ships demonstrated national pride. 'God Save the King' also emerged in the eighteenth century. It was written by a Scot, James Oswald (1711–69), and performed to celebrate Admiral Vernon's victory in 1739 at Porto Bello during the war with Spain. It became popular as a loyalist tune during the 1745 Jacobite rebellion and thereafter became the national anthem through an informal acceptance of its sentiments. In 1754 James Thomson's (1700–48) tune 'Rule Britannia', which he had composed in 1740, was included in an entertainment called *The Masque of Alfred*. It was a confident and popular expression of British naval superiority. Britannia, who had appeared on coins as early as 1665, was also becoming a popular embodiment of the nation and of maritime dominance. Said to be modelled on one of Charles II's mistresses, the image of Britannia as a woman ruler, with trident and shield, became an idealized counterpart of John Bull, who was often depicted in coarser forms.

Slavery
Any discussion of the expansion of Britain's empire cannot ignore the issue of slavery and the slave trade. Slavery was integral to Britain's growth as an imperial and commercial power. Between 1718 and 1775, 50,000 British convicts were sent to work in the West Indies and North America as indentured servants. But, between 1691 and 1779, British ships transported 2,141,900 slaves from African ports to the Caribbean and North America. The French added a further 1,015,000, and the Portuguese and Spaniards also developed their own slave trades. The character of some North American colonies was dramatically changed as a consequence: in 1700,

there were 20,000 slaves in North America; by 1763 this had risen to 300,000. Small islands such as Montserrat were also changed. In 1678, 40 per cent of the population was non-white, by 1730, 80 per cent of the population was black. Slavery was occasionally experienced closer to home. In the first half of the eighteenth century Algerian pirates operated in the English Channel and sporadically captured Britons for sale as slaves.

The supply of slaves relied heavily on circumstances in Africa. The warring Kongo and Luanda nations sold prisoners of war as slaves to British traders. Droughts and famines also led to the growth of slavery among African peoples. Equipped with new means to obtain slaves, such as muskets, African traders were able to bring more slaves to the Atlantic traders. The growth of African states such as the Asante also increased the supplies of slaves.

The slave trade was very important for British shipping. In the nine years after 1750, 1,909 slave ships departed from Liverpool, 869 from London and 624 from Bristol. There were also smaller slaving ports, such as Poole, Lancaster and Whitehaven, which were used by smaller traders. Huge profits could be made from the so-called triangular trade, which was made possible by an Act of 1698, removing the monopoly of the Royal African Company in the sale of slaves. In some cases, individual ship owners sent gunpowder or other goods to West Africa, carried slaves from West Africa to the Caribbean and then imported products, often rum or sugar, back to Britain. On its own, the slave trade was risky and uneven in its profitability. Perhaps this is why the majority of British and Dutch ships only made one slave trade voyage.

The trade fell away sharply by the mid-eighteenth century. Bristol saw a decline from the 1730s and Whitehaven largely abandoned the trade in the 1760s. Thereafter, Liverpool dominated slavery, by 1801 controlling 79 per cent of the trade, worth over £1 million a year. In all, Liverpool ships transported over a million slaves. Liverpool merchants formed strong connections with West African slavers, and developed a banking infrastructure with agents in London and the Caribbean. Many Liverpool traders offered shares in their slave ships: Robert Bostock and John Tomlinson, for example, sold numerous shares in their expeditions. What made the triangular trade attractive was that the empty slave vessels in the Caribbean had the choice of a range of products to import to Britain and could choose the most profitable cargoes from sugar, timber, rum and dyestuffs.

The slave trade supplied labour to the commercial ventures that witnessed the most significant growth in the eighteenth century. European annual consumption of coffee grew from 2 million to 120 million pounds (1–55 million kg), chocolate consumption rose from 2 million to 13 million pounds (1–6 million kg) and tobacco from 50 million to 125 million pounds (23–57 million kg). British sugar consumption grew twenty-fold, while rum consumption rose from 200 gallons (900 litres) to 2 million gallons (9 million litres) by the third quarter of the century. These were the products on which the slave trade was built. Few Britons realized that their coffee, cocoa, tobacco or rum was reliant on such human misery. But even after abolition, British businesses benefited from slavery. As late as the 1840s it was discovered that Birmingham manufacturers were still making collars and shackles for slaves

As in other arenas of history, such as Jews in the Holocaust, the trend of seeing slaves as the passive recipients of a brutal and exploitative historical process must be tempered with the slaves' own rejection of the slave trade in uprisings. Slave rebellions happened throughout the eighteenth century. There were uprisings in New York in 1712 and 1741, and the Stono rebellion in Carolina in 1739, and at various times across South America, the Caribbean and Africa.

Paradoxically, some slave merchants were generous domestic philanthropists. Edward Colston, the Bristol slaver, founded local schools and apprenticeships and on occasion gave the whole profit from his ships to charity. It was said that he had not married because when he had earned enough to ask a woman to marry him, he impulsively gave it all to a destitute mother whose child he saw on the steps of a church. Richard Reynolds, also a Bristol slaver, gave all his profits to charity. On one occasion, finding that he had not used up all his profit, Reynolds wrote to a friend in London asking him for suggestions on how to spend his money charitably. The compassion they felt for their fellow Britons was strangely lacking in their feelings towards the people who were the source of their wealth.

The moral economy of slavery was bleak. It was marked by kidnapping, brutality, exposure to disease and the commodification of people as cargo. Slaves were packed into the holds of ships like luggage. The loss of life on the ocean and sales of slaves all made it abhorrent. About 20 per cent of slaves died during transportation across the Atlantic in these inhumane conditions below decks where disease was rife. Once in the Caribbean or North America, slave work was lethally harsh. The fact that some African slaves were supplied by fellow Africans within their own continent has been used to argue for a limitation of the white 'guilt' for the slave trade. Perhaps, in comparison with the totality of African slavery in human history, white slave traders may not have exploited the continent more than others, but their culpability remains.

Slavery was as much subject to religious ambiguity as other aspects of empire, and from the earliest time there were opponents. In 1750 Horace Walpole (1717–97) voted in the Commons against the slave trade, which he denounced. The Church of England, which received Codrington College in Barbados as a bequest, found itself the owner of slaves who were branded as Church property. There were concerns as to whether slaves could earn their freedom by converting to Christianity, and consequently the governor of Barbados prevented the Quakers from converting slaves. Nevertheless, it is easy to overstate the Church's responsibility and guilt. In 1729, Bishop Edmund Gibson (1669–1748) of London sought to improve the lot of slaves in the colonies, and tried to persuade owners to instruct them in Christianity. He also used missionaries to distribute his printed letters on the subject to slave owners in the colonies. Moreover, Anglicans and Methodists were united in their campaigns from the mid-eighteenth century to abolish the slave trade. This sort of paradox ran through many institutions. The Church of England's inheritance of the Codrington estate impugned its reputation, yet Bishop Keppel of Exeter was the first man to ordain a black man in 1765 at the Chapel Royal in London. In 1772 the courts ruled that slavery was not permitted in England on the grounds that slavery had no legal basis in common law. When in 1807 the slave trade was outlawed entirely, Bishop Beilby Porteus, the son of a Virginia plantation and slave owner, denounced the trade as 'the most execrable and inhuman traffic that ever disgraced the Christian world'.

In considering the past we cannot forget present values and, when we look at slavery, the brutality of our own past is a reproach. The same may be said of the government's casual racism towards indigenous peoples in the colonies. In chartering colonies, deciding boundaries and concluding peace treaties, colonial powers – notably Britain – treated the indigenous populations as if they did not exist. Or at least as if they would always acquiesce in decisions made by European powers. The same may be said of victorious colonial powers in their treatment of the defeated. In 1775 the whole French population of Nova Scotia was evicted as a risk to British security. The same happened to the French in Pondicherry in 1761. Many Spanish settlers left Florida of their own volition in 1763, after it was ceded by the Treaty of Paris to the British – and the British left when the colony was returned to Spain.

5

GOVERNING EIGHTEENTH-CENTURY BRITAIN, 1714–1815

The Hanoverian Succession

By the Act of Succession of 1701, on the death of Queen Anne in 1714 the throne passed to her nearest Protestant relative. This proved to be George, Elector of Hanover, the great-grandson of James I. George I's arrival in London in September 1714 brought a very different style of government to Britain. Unlike Queen Anne, George was an absolute ruler in Hanover, and unused to the parliamentary system of government. Consequently he sometimes chafed at the restrictions of a constitutional monarchy. He spoke English badly and tended to use German or French with his ministers. He rarely ate in public, as monarchs were expected to do, preferring to eat and spend time with one of his two mistresses, Melusine von der Schulenburg and Louise de Kérouaille, nicknamed 'the Maypole' and 'the Elephant' for their oddly contrasting figures. Nevertheless, George was shrewd and intelligent; he deferred to his ministers on domestic issues but insisted on playing an important role in foreign policy, in part because he regarded himself as first and foremost ruler of Hanover.

The accession of a new monarch, by tradition, led to an election. This would enable the sovereign to have a government of his own choosing. The election was held at a time when the Tories were in disarray. Their leader, the Jacobite Bolingbroke, joined the Stuarts in France, having ostentatiously bought theatre tickets in London to throw people off his scent. The Tories were associated with Jacobitism and resistance to George's succession. On his arrival, George I had appointed a Whig ministry, under Lord Townshend (1674–1738) and James Stanhope, so it was no surprise that, armed with government resources, the Whigs won the following election with a majority of 150 seats. The new Whig ministry impeached Bolingbroke, who took up residence at the court of the Old Pretender, the son of James II.

Although the Jacobites had lost an important opportunity when Queen Anne died, they eventually organized a challenge to George I. Taking advantage of the popular dislike of George's Hanoverian retinue, the Earl of Mar (1675–1732) left London and led a rebellion in Scotland to bring the Old Pretender to the throne. It was poorly managed and the rebels had only lukewarm support from France. After initial successes at Perth, and an indecisive battle at Sheriffmuir, the rebellion petered out. Coordinated risings in Wales, Devon and Cornwall were forestalled by swift government action. The Pretender arrived late in the day and without the expected French reinforcements. This led his advisers to argue in favour of abandoning the rising before the rebels had even engaged with the royal army commanded by the Duke of Argyll (1680–1743). Without much confidence, the Jacobites pressed on into England, but were defeated at the Battle of Preston in November 1715. The Pretender, dejected and depressed, left for France after only three months in Scotland, leaving his supporters to be hunted down. The Hanoverian regime had survived its first crisis.

In the wake of the rising of 1715, the government passed a series of laws that aimed to prevent another rebellion in Scotland.

The Disarming Act and the Clan Act outlawed ownership of any weapon in Scotland and sought to erode traditional clan loyalty. Garrisons were built at Fort William, Inverness and Ruthven to secure the Scottish Highlands. General George Wade (1673–1748) also built roads across Scotland to make the Highlands more accessible for the military, and he founded the Black Watch as a militia to control them. The leaders of the rebellion were executed, but the majority of the defeated rebels were pardoned and allowed to return to their homes.

The Jacobite rising showed the government the danger of Britain's isolation in Europe following the Treaty of Utrecht in 1713. In consequence, British foreign policy, directed by James Stanhope (1673–1721), focused on finding allies in Europe. In June 1715 Stanhope used his friendship with the Holy Roman Emperor Charles VI to sign an agreement to permit the building of fortresses in the Netherlands, to form a defensive barrier against France. In the same year, an agreement enabled the resumption of the British trading relationship with Spain. This was followed in 1716 with treaties with the Dutch and Austrians recognizing the legitimacy of the Hanoverian succession.

After 1717 George I's Hanoverian territory was threatened in the Great Northern War, in which an alliance of Demark, Russia, Poland and Prussia attacked Sweden. With the agreement of Stanhope, the Royal Navy then attacked first Sweden and then Russia in defence of Hanover. This action produced unfavourable comments and repercussions in Britain, where the King's Hanoverian advisers were regarded as too influential.

The Whig government gradually became divided by serious tensions. The dominance of Stanhope in foreign affairs caused friction with Townshend and his brother-in-law, Robert Walpole, while Lord Sunderland was frustrated by both the dominance of Stanhope and Townshend and the lack of radicalism in the government's agenda. There was further tension caused by the King's furious disagreement with the Prince of

Wales, which led to the Prince's exclusion from the court. Sunderland used the opportunity to convince the King that Townshend and Walpole were supporting the Prince of Wales, and on returning from a visit to Hanover in 1716, the King dismissed them both. Unexpectedly, other leading ministers resigned in sympathy with them. This split in the Whigs was important because it focused the dissident Whigs on the issue of the King's Hanoverian advisers. When, in 1720, there was a series of defeats in the Commons, the Whig factions agreed to reunite, and forced the King to dismiss his advisers, who were sent back to Hanover.

The summer of 1720 witnessed a major financial problem for the Whig ministry, although it had developed some time earlier, caused by the costly wars of William III's and Queen Anne's reigns. The South Sea Company had taken over the national debt and issued a series of stock offers to finance it. The fiction underlying the company's stock was that there were huge riches to be earned in the South Seas and, to attract more and more investors, the South Sea Company was secretly – and illegally – paying attractive dividends out of the investment capital. Clearly the company could not continue to pay dividends in this way, but in the short term, as people wanted a good return on their investments, the share price soared.

By the summer of 1720 shares in the South Sea Company had risen by over 1000 per cent, and had done so with official collusion. The government also protected the South Sea Company with a law which required all competitors to hold a royal charter, and this was withheld from other companies. Astonishingly, the South Sea Company also developed a scheme to enable eager investors to borrow money from the company in order to buy its own shares. This was one of the features that ensured financial disaster for many investors as they had bought worthless shares and accumulated large debts to do so.

Few saw the truth of the situation, although Isaac Newton, when asked to estimate the future rise of the share value, replied that he could not calculate the madness of people. Ironically, Newton himself was to lose substantial sums in the company. The 'South Sea Bubble' clearly could not continue and burst in the summer of 1720, bringing financial ruin to thousands of investors, great and small. A few investors made enormous profits, including Thomas Guy (1644–1724), who later founded Guy's Hospital with his fortune. Jonathan Swift wrote of Exchange Alley, the place where the stock exchange had witnessed extraordinary scenes as the bubble rose and then collapsed:

> There is a gulf where thousands fell
> There all the bold adventurers came
> A narrow sound, though deep as hell
> 'Change Alley is the dreadful name.

Leading figures in society, including the King, were implicated in the bubble. It was claimed that ministers had taken bribes to ensure the complicity of the court. It was a scandal that would have damaged the country had the truth been known. Only the brilliant defence of both the government and court by Walpole prevented a widespread investigation. Those blamed were principally company officials rather than senior figures in the government. Within two years, both Stanhope and Sunderland died, leaving the leadership of the Whigs to Walpole.

Walpole's Dominance
Walpole's command of politics lasted for two decades, and he succeeded in sidelining any competitors from office. For this reason, and because he became indispensable to successive kings, he is often thought of as the first prime minister, but critics have called his period in power a 'Venetian oligarchy', because he managed Parliament by the skilful use of patronage in a way usually associated with the doges of Venice. Walpole systematically excluded Tories from power in government or as lords lieutenant or magistrates; he bribed MPs and peers

with government funds and jobs. He also chose to remain in the House of Commons, where government patronage was most effective, rather than accept a peerage. Walpole also used Secret Service money in increasing amounts to win elections, and the sixteen representative Scottish peers were chosen from a government list. Episcopal votes in the House of Lords were also significant and some bishops were selected, at least in part, for their Whig inclinations. Walpole was also a smooth manager of people. He only once lost his temper in a council meeting and immediately adjourned it, declaring that no man was fit for business when he had a 'ruffled temper'. He also spread his largesse and patronage, saying, 'there is enough pasture for all the sheep.'

There was a whiff of corruption in the period and Walpole presided over a regime in which wheels were well oiled. In 1718 it emerged that the estate of the executed Jacobite Lord Derwentwater (1689–1716) had been bought by the agents responsible for the sale for a scandalously low sum. In 1725 the lord chancellor, Lord Macclesfield (1667–1732), was found guilty of selling judgeships and was impeached. In 1731 the Charitable Corporation, originally intended to provide loans to the poor at low rates, collapsed when it became clear that the directors had committed fraud and gambled with the charity's money. In 1722 a newspaper noted that Walpole had granted government posts to two of his sons, two brothers and a brother-in-law.

In 1721 Walpole faced a Jacobite plot to take power for the Stuarts, led by Bishop Francis Atterbury of Rochester. The discovery of the Atterbury plot revealed that Jacobites had communicated in secret ciphers, although the evidence was not strong enough for a criminal trial. Consequently Bishop Atterbury was tried before the House of Lords on a bill of 'pains and penalties', found guilty and exiled. A key element in the trial was the evidence of the Revd Edward Willes, 'the King's decypherer', that he had deciphered codes that showed Atterbury's treason. Walpole's effective stage-management of the trial, and his orchestration of newspaper coverage during it, also showed a remarkable political skill.

Walpole's political success was built on a policy of peace and low taxes, which assured him strong support in the Commons. In addition, Lord Townshend ensured that alliances with Prussia and Russia kept Britain free of expensive European entanglements. After a brief hiatus on the accession of George II, in 1727, when the new King made his own choice of first minister, Walpole had gained the support of Queen Caroline, George II's wife, and this gave him a key supporter at court. As a result he returned to power within a few days. George II was the first Prince of Wales to succeed his father since 1625; the pattern of turbulent and irregular successions of 1649–1714 had at last been broken.

At the height of his power, Walpole was thought to be so indispensable to the country that a number of people took out insurance policies on his life. However, he could not take the King's support for granted. Walpole told the courtier Lord John Hervey (1696–1743) of his tactics in managing the King. He said:

Nothing can be done ... but by degrees; should I tell either the King or the Queen what I propose to bring them to six months hence, I could never succeed. Step by step I can carry them perhaps [on] the road I wish.

Despite the developing importance of the Cabinet and Parliament, the monarch played a very active part in the government. Ministers had to ensure that the King was as supportive as the Commons. Walpole felt that, as he took the brunt of the opposition in the Commons, he was the senior partner in the government. His relationship with Lord Townshend was less easy after Lady Townshend, Walpole's sister, died in 1726. Since Townshend's area of influence was foreign policy, he was forced to resign in 1730 when it was discovered that France was rebuilding defences at Dunkirk in violation of a treaty. Walpole now assumed responsibility for foreign policy also, and further heightened his standing.

From the early 1730s, however, there were strains in Walpole's ability to manage the finances of the country, and consequently strains on his control of the House of Commons. Walpole knew that land taxes had to be kept low to ensure the support of the many independent landed MPs. In 1733 Walpole was forced to turn to excise duties on wine, tobacco and other commodities to pay for a reduction in the land tax. It was a misjudgement, which led to an outcry among merchants, shopkeepers and the poor, demonstrating the new power of the press to express popular concern. Those who had been excluded from the government by Walpole also joined the opposition to the excise scheme. Initially he had the backing of the King, but when his majority in the Commons collapsed and it seemed that the army would not support the measure, the King forced Walpole to back down. In humiliation, the scheme was abandoned. There was similar unrest in 1736 over a tax on gin. In Edinburgh the Porteus Riots of the same year had their origins in popular unrest at the hanging of smugglers.

Walpole also faced a problem with his natural electoral supporters, the Protestant Dissenters. Because he was dependent on bishops' votes in the Lords, Walpole had to try to keep Anglicans and Dissenters happy at the same time. In 1736 he proposed a bill that would exempt the Quakers from paying tithes to the Church, because they were not members of it. This would have solved a long-standing problem of repeated Quaker imprisonment for refusal to pay tithes. Though the bill was popular with dissenting voters, the bishops in the Lords refused to pass it, and again Walpole had to back down. These setbacks showed that, while he was politically skilled, Walpole had to ensure that many competing interests were balanced, and this was not always easy. What Jonathan Swift called his 'somersaults on a tightrope' were more and more difficult to pull off.

In the late 1730s, especially after the death of Queen Caroline in 1737, Walpole's grip on power faltered. He sought to restore the rights of merchants to trade with the Spanish colonies in America, but it was clear that Spain only grudgingly allowed this. Spain also continued to chafe at the loss of Gibraltar under the Peace of Utrecht in 1713. British merchant ships did not help the situation by attempting widespread evasion of Spanish customs payments. The Spanish responded by stopping, searching and impounding British ships. The culmination of this was the War of Jenkins' Ear in 1739.

It was in foreign policy that Walpole's end came. When Maria Theresa succeeded her father as ruler of the Holy Roman Empire, Prussia, followed by France, Spain and Bavaria, sought to dismember the empire. As an ally of Maria Theresa, Walpole came to her aid, but he had not bargained for George II's determination to protect Hanover from Prussian advances. The King concluded a neutrality agreement in 1741, and as elector of Hanover voted for the French candidate to succeed as Holy Roman Emperor. This made a mockery of Walpole's support for Maria Theresa, and at the general election in 1741 Walpole's ministry retained only a small majority. A group of MPs, called the 'Patriots', who felt that foreign policy was too much dominated by Hanoverian interests, organized themselves against Walpole. After some close votes in the Commons, in January 1742 the borough seat of Chippenham was lost to the opposition in a by-election. This wiped out Walpole's majority and he resigned. The end of Walpole's parliamentary career demonstrated that a minister without a majority in the Commons could not remain in office.

Walpole, the master of corruption, died three years later, and to the surprise of all he left debts of £40,000. Nevertheless Walpole had helped the transformation of Britain from a country of rebellions and revolutions to one of constitutional rule. He disliked the political trials of an earlier generation and refused to prosecute opponents. He also believed in a balanced constitution in which the government did not seek dictatorial powers. While he tried to control the press, he also endured vicious press attacks. The most scandalous of these was the print of 1737, 'The Festival of the Golden Rump'. This showed George II as a satyr standing on an altar and breaking wind, with Queen Caroline preparing to inject him with an enema, with Walpole in attendance. Behind them stood the mob looking for patronage.

On Walpole's resignation his colleague, the Duke of Newcastle, who had developed remarkable skills in managing government patronage, remained in office because he was prepared to go along with George II's policy in Europe. His younger brother Henry Pelham (1694–1754) joined the government, as did Lord Carteret (1690–1763), who had been Walpole's main rival, under the nominal leadership of William Pulteney (1684–1764). Pelham was the first politician to refer to the country's annual accounts as the 'budget' and his management of government finance restored the national debt to a sound footing. Foreign affairs continued to dominate politics, as the Spanish war was subsumed into the Europe-wide War of Austrian Succession in which Britain and Austria faced France and Prussia. The war became a series of over-lapping conflicts which, in the American colonies, saw France and Britain engage in what is known as 'King George's War'. Carteret was largely regarded as a failure in directing the war and in foreign policy, and resigned in 1745. He left the government in the hands of the Pelhams.

Jacobites and Empire

The War of Austrian Succession was the backdrop to French support for the Jacobite Rebellion of 1745. After an abortive invasion attempt earlier in the year, in July 1745, Prince Charles Edward Stuart (1720–88, also known as Bonnie Prince Charlie or the Young Pretender), son of the Old Pretender, raised a rebellion in Scotland, encouraged by the defeat of the British army at the Battle of Fontenoy in May. Within three months, the Prince's rebel army defeated Sir John Cope and Hanoverian forces at Prestonpans. Soon after, they took possession of Edinburgh. Hoping that the continental military campaigns had weakened English defences, the rebels moved into England; they bypassed General Wade's forces in Newcastle and reached Manchester in November and Derby a month later. The support for the Prince was equivocal. The diarist John Byrom noted that when he was far distant from Manchester everyone talked of Prince Charles Edward as 'the Pretender', but they referred to him as 'the Prince' when he was a few miles from the town. Despite their successes, in Derby the Prince's advisers pointed out that with only a small force of 5,000 men they could not contemplate marching on London.

In London there was some consternation but little panic. Even when the Pretender reached Derby, Horace Walpole wrote 'we fear them no longer', although he was anxious that the French might invade; Britain had only a small standing army and was ill-prepared for an invasion, so British troops in Ostend were recalled to join the defence. Popular loyalty to George II was strong. London weavers offered to form a regiment of 1,000 men, and a group of lawyers, led by the lord chief justice, formed a lifeguard for the royal family at St James' Palace.

Despite the absence of panic, the rebellion unsettled the government and the City of London. During the emergency a run on the Bank of England had been so serious that the directors of the bank had ordered clerks to count the money they paid out deliberately slowly, and to recheck their calculations so as to slow down withdrawals. Agents of the bank were placed in the queues to delay the process further. When they had made withdrawals the agents joined the queue again to pay the money back, as an ostentatious show of confidence in the bank. When the bank seemed as if it might collapse, the patriotic financier Sampson Gideon (1699–1762) gave every penny he had, including the proceeds of a mortgage on his house, to save it.

The Jacobite army retreated from Derby, and this deterred coordinated French invasion plans, and when the rebel army got back to Scotland, it started to lose large numbers from desertions. In April 1746 the British army under George III's son, the Duke of Cumberland (1721–65), reached Scotland, where they found that the Jacobite army had now shrunk significantly. Nevertheless, the bloody Battle of Culloden – in which Highland Jacobite troops with swords charged the British cannon – saw the slaughter of over 1,000 rebels in less than thirty minutes. Culloden showed what a fluke Prestonpans had been: swords rarely won over guns. Altogether 4,000 rebels were killed or injured, and Cumberland earned the nickname 'the Butcher'. The British army lost only 350 men. At the end of the battle, Prince Charles Edward abandoned his army in tears, and fled to France disguised as a maid.

The Duke of Cumberland returned to London in triumph and was feted as a hero. Handel dedicated the oratorio *Judas Maccabaeus* to him. Only the leading Jacobite lords were executed. The aged Lord Balmerino died on the block saying, 'if I had a thousand lives, I would lay them all down here in the same cause.' But he was in a minority in this sentiment: in all, 120 Jacobites were hanged (including 38 British army deserters and 24 civilians from Manchester) and 3,000 were transported.

After the rebellion was defeated, the government was determined to prevent further Jacobite risings. To do so, there was a two-pronged strategy. In Scotland, the policy was to disarm the clans and to outlaw clan military service – a strategy that had failed thirty years before. In practice, this became an all-out war on clan culture, including the proscription of tartan and the removal of sovereign powers from clan chiefs. Highland regiments were formed to defend Scotland, and Fort George built near Inverness.

The second of the government's policies was to exclude Prince Charles Edward from France, which it achieved in 1748; he moved to Italy instead. Despite a planned plot in 1749, Jacobite hopes were extinguished and by 1766, when the Old Pretender died, even the Holy See saw the reality of the situation and refused to recognize Charles Edward as the rightful heir to the three kingdoms. Jacobitism lived on as a sentimental and literary movement. It was particularly strong in the romantic novels of Sir Walter Scott in the first decades of the nineteenth century, but politically it was dead.

After the 1745 rising, George II learned the limits of his constitutional power when he appointed Lord Carteret to the government. Henry Pelham and the Duke of Newcastle resigned, taking with them a large body of ministers. The King was forced to concede and Pelham returned to power. Pelham then constructed a 'broad bottom' administration, including as many of the Whig factions as possible in order to command a majority in Parliament. After a resounding victory in the 1747 election, Pelham felt strong enough to conclude the Seven Years War.

Pelham realized that it would be almost impossible for Britain to beat France and Prussia in continental Europe. He was content with the naval mastery Britain had established during the war. In addition, the rising cost of the conflict, and a bad harvest in 1747, created a financial imperative to seek a peace settlement. The Peace of Aix-la-Chapelle of 1748 was recognition that the other European powers were similarly exhausted. The concluding of the peace also allowed the expenditure on the army and navy to be reduced.

One feature of British politics in the eighteenth century was the serial disagreements between the kings and their heirs: George I fell out with his son; George II fell out with his son, Frederick, Prince of Wales, and George III had more than half a dozen sons with whom he fell out. Henry Pelham was fortunate that the division between George II and Frederick, which had divided both society and politicians, was ended by the Prince's early death in 1751. Frederick had established Leicester House, his London home, as a formidable source of opposition to the King and his ministers. After his death there was no major source of opposition to Pelham, but he died in 1754, to be succeeded by his brother, the Duke of Newcastle.

In the same year Britain was facing problems abroad. In North America, the French began to expand west into the Ohio valley, despite an American defence led by a young George Washington (1732–99). The British fell back on a blockade of French Canadian ports to prevent supplies reaching the forts that the French built on the Ohio. In Europe, Britain formed an alliance with Prussia. Two years later, when the Seven Years War broke out, Britain and Prussia faced war against France, Austria and Russia.

The death of Pelham had created a ministry in which Newcastle had the money and patronage to form a government, but he lacked the skills to direct policy; however, these skills were possessed by William Pitt (1708–78, later known as Pitt the Elder). Britain's loss of Minorca to France in 1756, and setbacks in India, led to the fall of Newcastle. The obvious solution was the formation of a new ministry in which William Pitt, in concert with Newcastle, directed the war. To begin with, the war went badly, with Hanover surrendering to the French. But Pitt's revitalization of the navy bore fruit in 1759, 'the year of three victories'; Horace Walpole wrote of the year:

> Instead of the glorious and ever-memorable year 1759, as the newspapers call it, I call it this ever-warm and victorious year. We have not had more conquest than fine weather: one would think we had plundered East and West Indies of sunshine. Our bells are worn threadbare with ringing for victories

Pitt had raised sufficient money for the war, and by 1759 the government had built the armed forces up to 90,000 troops and 85,000 sailors.

George III, Reform and America

George II died in 1760, and was succeeded by his 24-year-old grandson, George III. George III was the first Hanoverian king to be born in England; he was also the first king for a long time who closely identified himself with England and Englishness. He liked the English countryside and farming, and was soon nicknamed 'Farmer George'. He collected paintings, especially by Gainsborough, and enjoyed English music. In 1761 he bought the Duke of Buckingham's London home, Buckingham House, for his library and gradually developed it into Buckingham Palace. He was also responsible for the present system of funding the monarchy. In 1761 he gave the royal estates of the Duchy of Lancaster to the state, and accepted an allowance (known as the Civil List) from the government. It was a deal that later monarchs might have regretted since the Duchy of Lancaster income is much higher than the Civil List payments to the monarch.

The new King did not countenance the continuation of the Seven Years War, which Pitt strongly supported. Instead, George III placed his confidence in Lord Bute (1713–92), who had been a supporter of his father and close to his mother – too close, some gossiped. Bute exercised great influence over the King and, when he persuaded him to prevent an attack on Spain, Pitt resigned. Bute became prime minister and concluded the Peace of Paris in 1762, which ended the Seven Years War.

George III felt that his grandfather had been dominated by his ministers, and he was determined not to repeat the relationship. His concept of monarchy as being above politics and party was derived from Bolingbroke's essay, written for his father, entitled *On the Idea of a Patriot King* (1738). But George III's choice of Bute as a confidant and adviser was a poor one. By 1763 Bute became unpopular and resigned, leaving the King politically isolated. With the collapse of the Jacobite threat in 1745, the association of the Tories with treason and disloyalty dissolved. The 1760s therefore were a period of realignment in politics, in which the gentry and landed classes found themselves returning to support the Tories.

After the departure of Bute, George III faced a dilemma. He could not contemplate the return of Pitt, while the old Whig ministers were discredited, and there was not yet a viable alternative in the Tories. The King was forced to ask George Grenville to form a government. Grenville was a terrible bore, who, said George III, 'when he has wearied me for two hours, he looks at his watch to see if he may not tire me for an hour more'. It was Grenville's ministry that passed the Stamp Act – which imposed a tax on the American colonies – and that was to initiate the prosecution of John Wilkes' journal *The North Briton*.

Grenville's ministry lasted until 1765, when the King replaced him with the young Whig Lord Rockingham. Rockingham reversed Grenville's foolhardy policies towards America, but he quickly lost the King's confidence and was dismissed a year later. George III had no choice but to turn to the leading Whig, William Pitt, who with the Duke of Grafton (1735–1811), and later Lord North, formed a government. Dr Johnson made a good point when he said that Walpole was a minister chosen by the King and given to the people, whereas Pitt was a minister chosen by the people and given to the King.

Part of Pitt's reputation and standing came from his frightening stare. One of his colleagues was heard to seek the Speaker's protection when Pitt glared at him in the Commons, and both the solicitor-general and the lord chief justice admitted to being terrified by him. In order to retain power, especially in the short-lived ministries of the 1760s, bribes and patronage were increasingly used with less finesse than they had under Walpole and radical politicians soon expressed their concerns.

In 1763 John Wilkes, the radical journalist-turned-politician (he was MP for Aylesbury), accused the King of lying when he had praised the Peace of Paris. Wilkes published this allegation in issue 45 (a significant number redolent with Jacobite meaning) of his news journal, the *North Briton*. The title *North Briton* was itself a wry reference to the fact that Wilkes believed the King was dominated by the influence of the Scotsman Bute. Under a general warrant, which did not specify a charge, Wilkes and forty-nine others were arrested and imprisoned in the Tower of London. He claimed privilege as a Member of Parliament and was released. Wilkes also successfully challenged the legality of the general warrant, and used his courtroom appearance to raise the issue of the corruption of Parliament. Wilkes expressed the views of many ordinary people: Thomas Turner, the Sussex shopkeeper, wrote in his diary of Wilkes' *North Briton*, 'I really think they breathe forth such a spirit of liberty, that it is an extreme good paper.'

Wilkes was forced to flee abroad in 1764. He had been censured in Parliament for publishing a pornographic parody of Pope's *Essay on Man*, and a writ was issued for his arrest. He was also obliged to give up his seat as an MP. Four years later, Wilkes returned to London to stand for Parliament and, after failing to be elected in the City of London, was elected for Middlesex. His supporters were riotous and either tore passing coaches to pieces or insisted on scrawling their slogan 'Wilkes and Liberty' on them. The London-trained bands of volunteers were ineffective, and troops from the Tower had to be called to quieten the city. Wilkes surrendered himself to the court and was sentenced to two years' imprisonment and a fine of £1,000. Outside the court, his supporters chanted 'Wilkes and Liberty!' and troops were forced to open fire, which led to seven deaths.

Despite Wilkes' election in 1768, the Commons refused to admit him as a member because he had been an outlaw when elected. Wilkes stood for the Middlesex constituency three more times, and on each occasion the Commons refused to admit him. On one attempt, in 1769, his supporter, the young Whig Charles James Fox, made such an impressive speech in the Commons that an artist in the gallery tore off part of his shirt to use as a canvas to sketch the scene. The phrase 'Wilkes and Liberty' was now widely adopted as a general cry of those who wanted serious reform of the political system.

Wilkes' followers formed the Society for the Supporters of the Bill of Rights, which pressed for parliamentary reform. The society argued that new towns ought to be represented in Parliament, and MPs removed from rotten boroughs (where there were very few voters – in some cases fewer than six). In the wake of Wilkes' campaign, other radicals pressed for change. Major John Cartwright (1740–1824), who became an important figure in the campaign for reform, published *Take your Choice* (1776). This called for all men to have the right to vote, a secret ballot, general elections each year and equal electoral districts. He later formed the Society for Constitutional Information, which promoted Thomas Paine's *Rights of Man*. There was also the Association Movement in the late 1770s and early 1780s, which petitioned the Commons for parliamentary reform.

In 1770 Wilkes was elected a City alderman and in 1774 he was made lord mayor of London; finally, on his re-election to Parliament for Middlesex, he was admitted to the Commons. Wilkes also successfully championed the right of journalists to report the debates in the House; debates had previously been secret, with journalists regularly punished for reporting what was said. He had managed to show that popular resistance to the government and the Commons could ultimately be successful.

The issuing of general warrants and incursions into the freedom of the press were much reduced after Wilkes' victories. Wilkes was always something of a charlatan and a self-publicist: when, as an MP, he was asked to give up Commons time in which he had planned to make a speech to make way for government business, he replied he could not as he had already sent a copy of the speech to the newspapers. Wilkes continued to be a thorn in the side of successive governments, and supported the American colonists in their opposition to British rule. By the 1780s, however, he had become an establishment figure, commanding the militia against popular agitation in the Gordon Riots and condemning the French Revolution.

In 1770, when Lord North became prime minister, Wilkes' call for reform was joined by other voices, including those of the Irishman Edmund Burke and the Whig Charles James Fox.

Burke had already established himself as a thinker, as well as a politician. In his work on aesthetics, *A Philosophical Enquiry into the Origin of Our Ideas of the Sublime and Beautiful* (1757), he argued that beauty was derived from divine structures in nature. In 1770 he published *Thoughts on the Present Discontents*, which claimed that the King was being manipulated by a secret cabal, led by Bute. Burke also espoused the popular agitation arising from parliamentary reformers, American colonists and popular opposition to the government.

Important politician though he was, Burke was nicknamed the 'dinner bell of the Commons' because he was such a dull speaker that he emptied the House when he stood up. But in 1775 his speech on conciliation of the American colonists was said by Charles James Fox, himself an eloquent speaker, to be such that all MPs should read it. The radical Whig Fox was also to be a prominent politician for the next forty years, though his love of horse racing and writing history distracted him from politics. He was described by Lady Hester Stanhope as looking like the dissolute landlord of a pub, although as a young man he was best known for flashy waistcoats and scarlet-heeled shoes.

Much of Lord North's time and attention was taken up in managing colonial problems. Attempts to resolve the demarcation line between the East India Company's commercial role in India and the government's foreign policy there against the French had been attempted in 1767 and 1769. But in 1773, when the Company asked for financial aid, the government's solution was the Regulating Act, which gave the government oversight of the Company without taking control entirely. This compromise was a step on the road to Pitt's India Act of 1784, which gave control of the Company to a board, on which the government was represented, and appointed a governor general for the colony of Bengal.

It was to help boost the East India Company's finances that Indian tea was exported to North America. This undercut American merchants, including John Hancock, who was a vocal critic of British colonial policy. These cheap imports and the Tea Act tax of 1773 were the immediate cause of the Boston Tea Party. Throughout the period of agitation in America, successive British governments responded to the Americans as a parent towards its child – with some conciliation, but failing to take complaints seriously. After the Boston Tea Party the city was punished by an Act to close the port. Royal control over the Massachusetts government was also strengthened.

As events moved towards a colonial conflict in America, Lord North refused to assume direct responsibility for the war, and Lord George Germain, the secretary of state, did not have the skill or support to prosecute a successful campaign. Moreover, some of North's colleagues were uneasy about the government's policy. Fox left his Treasury post, ostensibly because he disagreed with the government's refusal to publish Commons debates, but really because of his disquiet at North's leadership. North famously sent Fox a letter on his dismissal which curtly read: 'His Majesty has thought proper to order a new Commission of the Treasury to be made out, on which I do not see your name.'

North's policy towards North America commanded general, though not complete, support in Britain. Samuel Johnson pointed out the inconsistencies in the colonists' position. He said the American colonists wanted all the rights and privileges of the English without any of the responsibilities. He also pointed out the irony that what he called 'the loudest yelps for liberty' came from those who were the colonial slave owners.

It proved impossible for the Royal Navy to blockade the whole length of the American coast. Nevertheless the loss of the American colonies was not inevitable; as late as March 1776 the American Congress rejected a motion that blamed George III for the problems of the rebellion. By July, however, citizens in New York City pulled down the statute of the King at Bowling Green. There were some military successes in 1775–6, but a year later Britain's armed forces proved unable to outwit

Washington, culminating in the British surrender at Saratoga. Thereafter, the diplomatic position meant Britain faced over-whelming odds. France formed an alliance with the American colonists in 1776, Spain joined the war against Britain in 1778 and two years later Russia, Holland and other European nations refused to accept British inspection of their neutral cargoes. In 1781 a joint Franco-American army forced the British commander-in-chief, Lord Cornwallis (1738–1805), to surrender at Yorktown. The war had collapsed. Lord North himself said, 'Oh my God, it's all over!'

The psychological impact of the defeat in North America in Britain was cataclysmic. It was obvious that the government had not been successful and this weakened its moral authority. Moreover, the cost of the war, and the higher taxes to pay for it, also led to widespread disturbance. In 1780 popular unrest was directed at Catholics. An Act of 1778 had removed some of the penalties on Catholics, partly in an attempt to recruit them into the army during the American war. The government was convinced that, as Charles O'Connor (1710–91), founder of the Irish Catholic Committee, said in 1786, 'we are all become good Protestants in politics'. But in 1780 the Protestant Association was set up by the unbalanced Lord George Gordon (1751–93) to repeal this legislation. It produced hysterical anti-Catholic propaganda, claiming that, once in the army, Catholics would support their co-religionists in France and Spain and ruin Britain.

Starting in Scotland, a wave of unrest swept through the country in the summer of 1780, culminating in a 'No Popery' riot in London in June. Catholic chapels were attacked and Newgate Gaol was demolished by the mob. Lord George Gordon led a demonstration of 40,000 people to the Commons and forced his way in to present a petition to demand repeal of the Catholic Relief Act. In the end, the army had to be called out to suppress the disorder. Karl Philipp Moritz, a visiting Prussian, noted that more rioters were found dead near empty brandy casks than had died from bullets.

At the same time, agitation from the dominant Anglo-Irish Protestant aristocracy and gentry against the withdrawal of troops from Ireland to fight in North America led to demands for greater Irish autonomy. The Anglo-Irish leaders wanted freedom from the constraints on Irish politics imposed by control from Westminster and the Privy Council. In the face of all this unrest and the defeat at Yorktown, Lord North resigned in 1782. The King was also affected by the loss of America and offered to abdicate and go to Hanover. This was not a serious option, but the change to Britain's empire was significant. With the loss of America, the character of the empire changed to one in which Britain's colonies were increasingly populated by native people who were not of European descent, and many were not Christian.

Pitt and Revolution

Lord North's resignation forced George III, against his preference, to appoint Rockingham as prime minister. He presided over a loose Whig coalition dominated by Charles James Fox and Lord Shelburne (1737–1805). Fox had gravely offended the King by his opposition to the Royal Marriages Act of 1772, which handed authority over royal marriages to the monarch (it is a law that remains in force today). The King also resented Fox's criticism of the American war. Shelburne had equally caused offence over demands that the King agree to recognize the independence of the United States of America. The new government lasted long enough to consent to the demands of the Irish Protestants for greater home rule, and to pass widespread changes to the patronage system. These included debarring government contractors from sitting as MPs, removing the right to vote from Treasury officers and limiting the powers of crown patronage. Rockingham, the only uniting force between Fox and Shelburne, died in July 1782. Fox subsequently refused to serve in a government led by Shelburne, so he split the Whigs by going into opposition against Shelburne.

Shelburne's ministry lasted from July 1782 to March 1783, but he negotiated the Treaty of Paris, the culmination of a strategy to separate the Americans and the French. In this treaty Britain gave formal recognition to the independence of the thirteen American colonies, while the United States was given control over the lands between the Appalachians and the Mississippi. Besides some minor concessions to France and Spain, Britain maintained the rest of the empire. Fortunately, a naval victory by Admiral George Rodney (1719–92) in 1782 secured the West Indies for Britain. Despite the wisdom of the Paris settlement, political factionalism brought Shelburne down. Fox's dislike of Shelburne led him to oppose the government, and North was outraged by the Paris treaty. When North and Fox joined forces, Shelburne was forced to resign, despite retaining the confidence of the King.

There was a brief interlude, during which the King, appalled at North's betrayal of his principles, endured a coalition of Fox and North, under the nominal premiership of the Duke of Portland (1738–1809). When Fox's attempt to resolve the issue of the East India Company's relationship with the government failed, in autumn 1783, the King took his chance and sacked the ministry. He turned to the moderate reformer, the 24-year-old William Pitt, son of the earlier premier, who became Britain's youngest prime minister. As a popular satire put it:

A sight to make surrounding nations stare
Three kingdoms trusted to a schoolboy's care.

Despite his youth, Pitt was a conscientious hard worker; he needed only three hours' sleep a night and started work before breakfast. He dominated politics for over thirty years. His ability was shown in his early years as prime minister. He was head of a minority government, facing the Fox–North majority coalition in the Commons, but he held his nerve, spoke ably in the Commons and conducted the business of government well enough for some independent MPs to switch their support to him. Pitt was capable of brilliant performances in the Commons, although many of his best phrases are now overlooked. Among these was, in 1783, his important claim that: 'necessity is the plea for every infringement of human freedom. It is the argument of tyrants; it is the creed of slaves.'

By March 1784 Pitt had succeeded in building a majority, and the King dissolved Parliament to hold a general election, which Pitt won with a resounding 120-seat majority in the Commons. His ability was also shown in his management of the King by consistently being sensitive to the Crown's interests. Pitt also advanced cabinet government by insisting on being the sole intermediary between the King and the Cabinet, and refusing to allow individual ministers access to the King without his agreement. Pitt's chilly personality did not endear him to many, however: Sir Nathaniel Wraxhall said of him 'if not repulsive [he] was cold, stiff and without suavity'. But, Pitt had an iron will. In 1786 he had a tumour removed from his face without anaesthetic and without being tied down, telling the surgeon he would stay still throughout.

Pitt showed that he had not entirely abandoned his reforming instincts by introducing a bill, in 1785, to remove representation from thirty-six rotten boroughs. These were boroughs that during the Middle Ages had justified representation in the Commons, but the population had declined to the point that they usually contained only a few voters. They were now controlled by a single patron who nominated the MP. The thirty-six seats were redistributed to London and the larger counties. Pitt was also responsible for establishing the Sinking Fund, a mechanism that allowed surplus money from taxation to be invested to create a sum big enough to pay off the national debt. This was part of a larger financial project which simplified taxes and reduced evasion of excise duty. Pitt also negotiated the Triple Alliance with Prussia and Holland to contain French ambitions in Europe and across the globe.

Pitt was adept at promoting good relations with Britain's erstwhile colonies in North America. In 1785, John Adams was received as the first United States ambassador in Britain. This improving relationship also bore fruit for British colonies in the West Indies by enabling them to resume trade with America, especially in grain, fish and timber. However, Britain now treated American ships as foreign under the Navigation Acts, and insisted that British ships carry goods to and from the United States. It was a decade before the government allowed American ships to transport goods from the West Indies to American ports.

It was good fortune that Pitt was in power when, in 1787, George III suffered his first attack of ill health. It has often been assumed that George III suffered from insanity, but recent research suggests it was possibly a blood disorder called porphyria. The King was unwell for four months, and it was unclear how the government should be conducted. Unlike most European monarchies, Britain had not seen a king disabled by ill health since the reign of Henry VI in the fifteenth century. What made the crisis so serious was that the King's eldest son, George, Prince of Wales, was a playboy and a supporter of Fox. He would, if appointed regent, probably have sacked Pitt in favour of Fox. Parliament spent such a long time debating the legal issues surrounding a regency bill that the King had recovered before it was passed. However, the King's health remained fragile and he suffered from further serious bouts of illness in 1804 and from 1810 until his death.

With the King's support, Pitt easily won the 1790 general election. In 1791 he introduced the Constitutional Act, which divided Quebec into Upper and Lower Canada. Upper Canada, the area furthest west, adopted English institutions and law; this benefited the 'empire loyalists' who had moved to Canada after the American War of Independence. Lower Canada remained French in institutions, including seigneurial land tenure and the Catholic Church. Each colony was granted representative government. This was a sensible and prescient measure that both detached Canada from the United States and also from closer links with France.

The Strains of War

The foresight of the Constitutional Act was seen in 1793, when revolutionary France declared war on Britain, in an attempt to create a revolution in Britain too. Pitt's response was to prosecute a war with limited aims. These included the defence of British interests and possessions, but did not include the restoration of the monarchy in France. In doing so, Pitt expanded Britain's alliances with Prussia and Holland to include Austria and Spain.

Some in Britain had welcomed the French Revolution. Fox, for example, greeted the storming of the Bastille with the claim of 'how much the greatest event that has happened in the world and how much the best'. The Revolution Society, which had been founded to celebrate the centenary of the Glorious Revolution in 1688, praised the French Revolution for adopting British ideas.

The revolution was initially viewed as a triumph of reason and equality over tradition and privilege. In such a perspective it seemed thoroughly acceptable. But in 1790 Edmund Burke sounded a warning in his *Reflections on the Revolution in France*. Burke argued that the French Revolution would lead to chaos, violence and tyranny. The *Reflections* sold extremely well; Robert Dodsley (1704–64) earned a fortune from the 18,000 copies he printed. In writing his *Reflections*, Burke broke with his radical background and with Charles James Fox, and argued for defence of the status quo in Britain. Burke was answered by the radical Thomas Paine in *The Rights of Man* (1791). Paine disparaged Burke's reverence for institutions, which, he said, were founded on past inequalities and despotism. He argued that for social and governmental institutions to be legitimate they had to be founded on the protection of the rights and dignity of men.

But the French Revolution moved from the principle of liberty to terror and Robespierre's Jacobin regime. Like Burke, many in Britain reacted to it by turning to greater conservatism. In particular, the move to secularize France shocked the Church of England. Some bishops even closed down Sunday schools for fear that they might spread literacy, which they thought was dangerous. Once Britain was at war with France, patriotism seemed to favour those who rejected the revolutionary ideas of the French.

These responses to the French Revolution were played out in British politics. Besides Burke, the majority of the Whigs, including Portland and Lords Fitzwilliam (1748–1833) and Carlisle (1748–1825), also supported Pitt during the war, and George III became a renewed symbol of patriotic pride. Fox was marginalized to become the leader of a radical Whig rump that was no threat to Pitt's ministry. Pitt also felt that the demands for further parliamentary reform were a dangerous distraction and refused to consider more widespread reforms. Pitt was in part responding to anxieties that events from abroad were threatening Britain. The French made three attempts to invade Britain in the 1790s. The invasion through Wales in 1797 collapsed in near farce as a group of women rounded up the invasion force. But in 1798 the French General Humbert invaded Mayo in Ireland and it took two weeks for the army to defeat the attempt. In response, the government built Martello towers (named after Mortella in Genoa where they were first used) in the English Channel to defend the coast, reformed the militia and extended the militia system to Scotland and Ireland.

Faced with external threats, the government did not respond positively to domestic campaigns for change. In 1794 Pitt suspended the Habeas Corpus Act to permit the imprisonment without trial of people suspected of political agitation. A year later, the Treasonable Practices Act defined treason to include words as well as acts, and the Seditious Meetings Act outlawed any meeting of more than fifty people without a licence. These measures were directed at Jacobin Clubs, which supported some of the French Revolution's principles, and at the London Corresponding Society, a working-class organization that championed the reform of Parliament.

Charles James Fox opposed these restrictive measures in the Commons. He argued that if the government left no room for demonstrations and legitimate complaint it risked violence and force. In fact, prosecutions under these Acts were low, lower than the number of rebels charged after the 1715 and 1745 risings. More serious were naval mutinies at Spithead and Nore, caused by the fact that able seamen's pay had not risen since 1653. These were swiftly dealt with, in part because the government could not afford to alienate the navy during a war.

As the cost of the French war grew, Pitt was forced to extend the Sinking Fund and raise taxation. This included the introduction of income tax, as a temporary measure – though one which was reintroduced in the nineteenth century. There were also restrictions on the exchange of gold for banknotes. Food riots and naval mutinies in 1799 led the government to more repressive measures, including the dissolution of radical societies and the passage of the Combination Acts. These outlawed groups of working men combining to demand higher wages, and were the origin of the ban on trades unions. Moreover, the need for naval recruits forced Pitt to agree a quota system whereby each county was required to sign up to provide a set number of seamen.

Coinciding with the French war were problems in Ireland, where Wolfe Tone now sought independence from Britain, and there were fears that Ireland would provide a back door into Britain for the French. Pitt sent Lord Cornwallis to quieten the island and his solution was a Union of Britain and Ireland, like the Act of 1707 with Scotland. A consequence of such an Act would be a union of the British and Irish parliaments. Like Scotland, Ireland would be represented in the new parliament in Westminster.

The Act of Union came into effect in 1801 and granted Ireland 100 seats in the Commons, together with representative Irish peers and bishops in the Lords. Lubricated with generous bribes to the Irish Parliament, the measure passed into law and the new United Kingdom Parliament met in 1801.

Pitt wanted to ease the Union's acceptance in Ireland by making concessions to the Catholics. This included granting Catholics some political rights. When, in February 1801, Pitt was unable to get George III's agreement to these concessions – on the grounds that they violated his coronation oath – he resigned and was succeeded by Henry Addington (1757–1844).

Addington's two-year premiership coincided with a hiatus in the war with France. The brief Peace of Amiens of 1802 allowed Napoleon time to rebuild his army and navy following a series of British victories. But Addington saw that Napoleon was simply marshalling his forces and in 1803 declared war again on France. Addington's direction of the war was unimpressive and he resigned in 1804, making way for Pitt's return. Pitt's management of the war ensured Britain was part of the new alliance of Russia, Sweden and Austria against Napoleon. Although there were defeats on land at Austerlitz and Ulm in 1805, Horatio Nelson's (1758–1805) resounding victory at Trafalgar ensured that the Royal Navy retained naval superiority until the end of the war.

What made Trafalgar such an important victory was that Nelson broke from orthodox naval tactics. He used two lines of ships to cut into the French and Spanish fleet. It enabled the British ships to deploy much greater firepower against the joint Franco-Spanish navy. It was also a victory that captured the popular imagination. From Nelson's rousing signal 'England Expects that Every Man this Day Will Do his Duty', to his heroic death on the quarterdeck of HMS *Victory*, Trafalgar boosted patriotic pride. Broadsheets, newspapers, prints, poems and sermons celebrated the victory. With the French navy destroyed as a threat, the Royal Navy was able to neutralize the challenge from smaller navies and from Napoleon's menace of an invasion. The French attempt to impose an economic 'continental system' that was closed to British goods was also ended by the victory. William Pitt only survived Nelson by three months, dying in January 1806. His health was broken by the stresses of the demands of office and by excessive consumption of port. His debts were paid by the nation.

It is a measure of Pitt's ability that his ministry could only be replaced by a 'Ministry of all the Talents'. This was a coalition of Whigs, led by Fox and Grenville, who were joined by Tories such as Addington (who had become Viscount Sidmouth). Only George Canning (1770–1827), a charismatic leading Tory, but also a divisive figure, refused to serve in the administration. Perhaps its greatest achievement – in the absence of a peace settlement with France – was its abolition of the slave trade in 1807. Since 1772, when a judicial ruling made slavery illegal in Britain, the slave trade in the colonies had been under growing pressure. An abolition campaign was led by William Wilberforce (1759–1833), supported by many members of the Church of England, Quakers and Methodists.

The Society for Effecting the Abolition of the Slave Trade was founded in 1787 and was successful in distributing materials that portrayed the evils of the trade. Thomas Clarkson, who had planned to be an Anglican cleric, was especially active in spreading information about the trade's horrors. Josiah Wedgwood's support for the campaign was encapsulated in his design of an emblem for the campaign: a slave in chains kneeling to pray for freedom with the powerful phrase 'Am I not a man and a brother?' Medallions with the image were widely sold and worn. Parliament was bombarded with petitions, and annual bills were presented to outlaw the trade. These were supported by a report of the Privy Council in 1789. Even William Pitt was convinced of the justice of the cause. But in 1788 supporters of the slave trade pointed out that hundreds of Liverpool ships, 7,000 sailors and £13 million worth of domestic and colonial business relied on the trade. When a compromise was proposed, Fox rejected it, saying he neither felt nor wished to feel 'anything like moderation on the subject'.

In 1790 a select committee was set up to review proposed legislation to abolish slavery, but a proposal was narrowly defeated in 1793. Thereafter the French war distracted attention from the parliamentary campaign. The campaign was revived in 1804 and a bill passed the Commons but was too late in the session to go to the Lords. Only when the maritime lawyer James Stephens suggested a clever ruse was the deadlock broken. Stephens' suggestion was to outlaw the trade by British subjects in British ships. Wilberforce maintained a silence so as not to reveal how damaging such a bill would be to the slave trade, and it passed, almost unnoticed, in 1806. After the general election of 1806, Grenville introduced the Abolition Bill in the Lords, to clear its final hurdle and by March 1807 it had passed into law. Abolition of slavery throughout the empire had to wait until 1834, but a blow for political morality had been struck.

What is much less well known is the work of the Particular Service, a small naval squadron established to prevent the slave trade. For sixty years the service stopped ships of all nations to search for slaves and free them, work that cost the lives of 17,000 sailors. It was responsible for freeing 160,000 slaves – not least because its sailors were paid a bounty for the slaves they freed. The squadron regularly brought Britain close to diplomatic conflict with Spain, Portugal, France and the US when it stopped foreign ships. It also led some illicit slavers to throw their human cargo overboard when a British naval mast came too close for comfort.

The Ministry of all the Talents broke up in 1807 over the grumbling issue of Catholic Emancipation, which sought to relieve Catholics of all the penal laws passed since the reign of Elizabeth I. Pitt's former colleagues formed a government under the Duke of Portland, which included able Tories, such as Lord Liverpool (1770–1828), George Canning and Lord Castlereagh (1769–1822). Unfortunately, the ministry was bedevilled by divisions, especially between Canning and Castlereagh, who loathed each other. Canning and Castlereagh even fought a duel with pistols in 1809 (Canning missed, but Castlereagh wounded him in the thigh). Under Portland, the war against Napoleon in Europe went badly, but Wellington's brilliant leadership during the Peninsular War, designed to evict the French from Spain, proved successful. On Portland's death in 1809, Spencer Percival (1762–1812) succeeded him as prime minister. Percival had Castlereagh's support, but this meant that Canning went into opposition. Canning refused 'to play second fiddle'.

Spencer Percival's ministry was also dogged with problems. The King's illness returned in 1810 and became permanent; his son George was appointed Prince Regent. The King was housed at Windsor, where he became blind and deaf. The Peninsular War came under sustained political attack and, though Percival defended it, the direction of the war was a cause of concern.

As mechanization of industry became more widespread to meet the economic demands of industrialization and the war, those workers thrown out of work damaged machines in what became known as Luddite unrest, named after a fictional leader of the machine wreckers, Ned Ludd. The disturbances were so widespread that Percival was forced to concede a Commons inquiry to investigate the violence. In May 1812 Percival became the only British prime minister to be assassinated. He was shot in the lobby outside the Commons by John Bellingham, who was later discovered to be insane.

Percival was succeeded as prime minister by Lord Liverpool, who held office until 1827, making him Britain's longest serving prime minister since Walpole. Liverpool was able to bring Canning back into the government, and also appointed able men such as Wellington, Robert Peel (1788–1850) and William Huskisson (1770–1830) to office. As is so often the case today, longevity as prime minister was due in part to his ability to hold disparate colleagues together. Liverpool did this by a clever practice of concessions that maintained equilibrium between them.

Liverpool's most pressing problems were the war with Napoleon and, in June 1812, a war with the United States. The

War of 1812, as it is known, was largely an American response to a British blockade of the US in an attempt to disrupt French trade. The US was also exasperated that Native Americans were given refuge in Canada and often re-equipped with British arms. The American declaration of war was followed by an attempt to invade Canada, which the British repulsed – even driving the Americans back beyond Detroit, which the British captured. With most troops tied up in Europe, Britain could do little other than hold back repeated American attempts to invade Canada. In August 1814, however, a Royal Naval contingent invaded Chesapeake Bay, occupied Washington DC and burnt the president's house (some accounts hold that the 'White House' got its name from the whitewash applied to it after the British burnt it). By this point, however, the costs of the war exhausted both sides. It cost Britain £25 million, and the US economy was badly hit as the blockade cut deeply into the country's agricultural exports.

In December 1814, both sides agreed the Treaty of Ghent, in which Britain abandoned its US land demands and the boundaries between the US and Canada were reinstated. Britain did not make any concessions about the blockade or the impressments of Americans into the Royal Navy as it was clear that the Napoleonic war was ending. Although rarely remembered today, the war was important in securing the boundary between the US and Canada. Psychologically this turned Americans towards its western boundary, rather than expansion northwards.

The war with Napoleon was eventually brought to a successful conclusion in 1815. By 1813, Wellington's efforts in the Peninsular War had ejected the French from Spain. Although Napoleon was victorious at the Battle of Dresden, the Battle of Leipzig three months later forced the French army to retreat behind the French border. The allied forces maintained their momentum and entered Paris in March 1814. Louis XVIII, Louis XVI's brother, was restored as king. At the Treaty of Fontainebleau in April 1814 Napoleon was exiled to the Mediterranean island of Elba. Technically, Napoleon was the sovereign on Elba but he was required to remain there. In March 1815 he escaped, returned to France, and recalled a quarter of a million of his old troops to his flag. After defeating the Prussians at Ligny in June 1815, he was defeated at Waterloo two days later. The Battle of Waterloo was one of the great military engagements in history. The fighting took most of the day and saw the destruction of the British heavy cavalry and the collapse of the French infantry. Only the arrival, late in the day, of the Prussian troops under Marshall Blücher ensured an allied victory. In the days that followed, teeth were extracted from the 30,000 corpses, and 'Waterloo teeth' populated dentures well into the nineteenth century. In the wake of the victory and the end of the war, Wellington was made a duke and Liverpool was granted the Order of the Garter by a grateful nation.

The war was formally concluded by the Congress of Vienna, which lasted seven months between 1815 and 1816. It was perhaps the largest settlement of European boundaries, which had been disrupted and redrawn repeatedly during the two decades of the French wars. Britain's aims were largely achieved by Lord Castlereagh's negotiations. He sought the creation of the Netherlands as a strong kingdom to the north of France. He also aimed to consolidate Britain's empire, which he did with the formal acquisition of Cape Colony in southern Africa, Tobago, Ceylon and a protectorate over the Ionian Islands and the Seychelles.

6

THE TRANSFORMATION OF
BRITAIN'S ECONOMY

The year 1776 was an important one for Britain in many respects. The events in America drew attention away from two important events at home that were dramatically influencing the economy of Britain. In that year the Scotsman James Watt (1736–1819) finally manufactured his own design of steam engine. It had been a long struggle for Watt, who had suffered from ill health and frequent headaches as a child, but proved to be a quick learner. He had trained as an instrument maker, though his interests inclined towards natural philosophy. He made and sold quadrants, compasses, burning-glasses and microscopes, and had a keen interest in pottery manufacture. His desire to become an engineer had been thwarted by the Glasgow Guild of Hammermen, who objected that he had not served the required apprenticeship. He was rescued from disaster by a kindly professor at Glasgow University, who offered him space in his workshop. From 1762 Watt tried out different designs for a steam engine, in an attempt to eliminate the defects of the existing engines.

In 1763 Watt saw a great opportunity when the university planned to repair its Newcomen steam engine. Watt experimented with it at the same time as he repaired it. As we will see later, this – together with his later partnership with the manufacturer Matthew Boulton (1728–1809) – put Watt on the road to his great invention. In March 1776, Watt installed a perfected engine in the Bloomfield colliery in Tipton and, a month later, another at John Wilkinson's ironworks in Willey, Shropshire. He charged the purchasers of his engines a fee and also a percentage of the fuel savings they made, guaranteeing them some efficiency savings as well as giving Watt two sources of income. Boulton and Watt also insisted on visits to their customers to ensure their machines were correctly assembled. Their machines were sold to almost 500 companies, but although Watt was granted extensions to patents, his designs were widely copied. People found the Boulton and Watt machines fascinating. In the 1770s, Boulton's Soho factory was a place that tourists visited to watch steam engines at work.

In the same year, Richard Arkwright's (1733–92) new factory at Birkacre, Lancashire, was burnt down by rioting textile workers who objected to the lower rates of pay he offered. Arkwright was the son of a tailor and had begun work as a wig maker and barber, and even drew teeth. His Birkacre factory was the first in the Chorley area, and contained his new water frame as well as a number of other mechanized processes. The mill, which had previously employed 400 workers, now needed far fewer and was only prepared to pay them lower wages.

The burning of Arkwright's factory in October 1776 was not the first such action. Months earlier, there had been riots by textile workers in Shepton Mallet in Somerset and they had submitted a petition to Parliament against mechanization. The riot at Birkacre caused Arkwright to abandon his lease on the mill. He even installed a cannon to guard another mill at Cromford against the possibility of rioting textile workers.

When petitioned by workers distressed by the decline in jobs and wages, the Commons showed its support for mechanization rather than for the workers. These two events in the same year that Britain was losing her American colonies were symptoms of a rapidly changing economy.

The Problem with the 'Industrial Revolution'

Like the British Empire, Britain's role as the first industrial nation has become less fashionable in the last half-century. Industrialization has appeared to be problematic in the years since the end of the Second World War. As the first industrial nation, Britain encountered the problems of economic decline and industrial decay, and the social problems arising from them, before other nations. Just as Britain seemed to have reconciled itself to being an economy focused on high technology and financial services, 'globalization' once again seemed to make industry a dirty word. Patriotic pride in being the first industrial nation has fallen into decline.

The decline has been encouraged by historians' and economists' inability to explain why Britain alone saw an industrial revolution, and straightforward explanations of why Britain was 'the first industrial nation' are much sought after. There was no single equation, combination of factors or general theory to explain Britain's economic growth. As a result, explanations for Britain's industrialization are untidy, complex and less satisfying. They include social and economic factors, but they also involve political factors such as the growth of political stability, diplomatic factors such as engagement with other countries in war and trade, intellectual factors such as the development of new ideas in science and technology, and religious factors such as the way in which work was valued by some religious denominations – what has been called the 'Protestant work ethic'. It is equally important to recognize that the economy before the industrial revolution was not stagnant. In fact the pre-industrial British economy was perhaps the most dynamic in Europe and had experienced considerable change and growth for many years. At the heart of the industrial revolution certainly lay new attitudes to work, underpinned by three main changes: the use of machines to undertake repetitive, laborious work that people could not do in sufficient quantities; the use of machines to replace animals as a source of power and to convert heat into work; and the exploitation of raw materials, especially minerals, in replacing animal and vegetable materials.

It is common to regard the industrial revolution as something that happened in large factories in the growing towns and cities of the north of England; in fact, of course, industrial products and processes also had a significant effect on rural life. The countryside was gradually prey to all sorts of agricultural and technological advance. Iron and steel tools spread across the country and railways passed through fields. Rural life was part of the industrial revolution by virtue of being a consumer of it – made possible by improved transport. The spread of industrialization was also uneven over time and irregular in geographical extent. The agricultural revolution that coincided with growing industrialization was far more geographically widespread. While the numbers of people in Britain during the eighteenth century who earned their living directly from the land halved, their experiences were as dramatically changed as those of their relatives and countrymen who went off to the towns. The inter-relationship between agricultural and industrial development can be seen in the increase of food to feed the growing towns, which made products to improve agricultural productivity.

In thinking about the industrial revolution, cause and effect sometimes become confused. Were population growth and mobility, complex financial systems, changes in agriculture to boost food production, better transportation, exploitation of coal and iron, entrepreneurship, technological advance and invention, new tastes for luxury, and diversity of goods causes or effects of industrialization? How much were intangible and immeasurable elements – religious attitudes, political stability and social optimism – a cause or a facilitating feature of the industrialization? Sometimes the Latin maxim *post hoc ergo propter hoc* (before this, therefore caused this) trips up historians, who occasionally assume that if something came before something else it probably caused it.

It is easy to assume that the industrial revolution was a uniformly progressive and improving process. While this was rarely the case in economic terms, it was certainly not in personal and social terms. For the men, women and children in industrial Britain, life was as hard and gruelling, and in many cases more so, as it had been under the rural economy of the Middle Ages. William Blake's (1757–1827) reference to 'dark Satanic mills' in the hymn 'Jerusalem' suggests that not all contemporaries saw industrialization in terms of improvement and progress. By the nineteenth century factory reform was necessary to mitigate the worst features of an employment system that consumed people as readily as it did coal or iron ore.

The Agricultural Revolution.

The dominance of agriculture in 1700 did not just rest on the fact that it employed 80 per cent of the population. Farming and rents were also the principal source of income for the great landed families. The Church's income was derived from tithes, and the government's in part from land tax. Land ownership gave the nobility and gentry their security and status. It was associated with offices such as those of magistrate, high sheriff and lord lieutenant. As we have seen, ownership of land was an aspiration for many merchants; even slave traders, such as William Beckford, used their money to buy landed estates.

'Land' meant many things: it included rich lowland pastures and deficient upland soils, poorly drained boggy moors and acid or depleted soils, as well as fertile arable loam, forests and mountains. This variety meant that agriculture in Britain was a collection of small local economies rather than a single rural economic system. What determined the character of agriculture in a region was whether animals could be reared or crops grown, whether sold for profit or sustenance, traded locally, or transported further afield. Most agriculture operated on an annual seasonal cycle with sowing, lambing or calving, harvesting and ploughing establishing the calendar, lore and customs of rural society.

There were much longer agricultural cycles too. Timber for houses, shipbuilding, furniture making and for use in all manner of wooden articles operated on cycles of many decades. Consequently, trades such as shipbuilding required an enormous investment of money. HMS *Victory*, built between 1759 and 1765, used wood from 6,000 trees that had been felled fourteen years earlier, and cost over £62,000 (over £50 million in today's values). Thirty miles (48 km) of rope were required to hold the ship together and rig its sails, and the construction relied on imports of such items as masts from Norway. But shipbuilding was a changing occupation that was affected by the growth in the economy.

Shipbuilding at Cardigan is an example of this growth. The port was well placed, close to a supply of Welsh oak and with a traditional fishing industry. In the 1740s about 1,000 ships operated in Cardigan Bay. In one night in 1745 over 1.3 million herring were landed in Aberystwyth. As ships found and exploited the huge herring shoals in the mid-eighteenth century, they needed a much larger capacity. For a time, Cardigan specialized in the manufacture of ships with removable decks that could carry cereals and stone as well as fish. Its first bank, founded in 1762, was the Banc y Llong, the 'ship bank'. But the larger ships of 300 tons or more, which were increasingly in demand, could not get over the sandbanks near the quay in Cardigan. In its last days, at the end of the eighteenth century, Cardigan made ships that were too big for its own quay and which then worked the fishing industry out of Newquay, Swansea and other deeper ports.

Wood was such an important commodity in this period that people regarded the planting of trees as a patriotic duty, and the Royal Society of Arts offered prizes and medals for developing forestry and for new techniques in woodland cultivation. In iron-making areas coppices were regulated to enable charcoal to be made and to ensure the growth of new trees. There was a sixteen-year cycle to remove wood for charcoal and allow new growth to develop; demand for wood could be unpredictable, however. Oak, which hardened when dried of sap and tightened so as to lock timber frames together, could last for centuries, but, as the 1666 Great Fire of London showed, timber frames could be destroyed in a few hours, creating an urgent demand for wood, not easily satisfied immediately. Forestry linked much agricultural production to the wider economy. From the 1730s, when large quantities of mahogany were imported, wood was also part of the global economy.

The green shoots of the agricultural revolution began to emerge during the Commonwealth of the 1650s, when there was what has been called the 'yeoman's agricultural revolution'. This was a growth in the productivity of small farmers, especially in corn yield, using the open field system. But it is also clear that the fullest form of the agricultural revolution, including the use of new technology, did not really begin until the first half of the eighteenth century. In places such as Norfolk the county's yield of wheat, barley and oats remained unchanged from 1300 to 1700, but between 1700 and 1850 there was a two-and-a-half-fold increase. In Scotland, lowland agriculture did not experience significant changes until the final quarter of the eighteenth century.

Between 1650 and 1750 a number of important changes took place in agriculture that enabled land productivity to grow. There were new techniques and practices, such as new fodder crops, new crop rotation, watering of meadows by means of channels, better livestock breeds – including Southdowns and Leicester sheep and Dishley cattle with more intensive rearing – and new machinery. The most significant was Jethro Tull's (1674–1741) seed drill.

Tull had trained as a lawyer and learned a range of agricultural techniques while in Europe recovering from tuberculosis.

In 1701 he designed a seed drill that sowed each seed to a pre-set depth and covered it with soil. This replaced inefficient broadcast sowing that required workers to scatter seeds on to the land, hoping they would germinate – and only a third grew.

Andrew Meikle's (1719–1811) mechanized threshing machine, invented in 1784, did the work of many labourers. His invention was a five-flail threshing machine driven by water, extracting corn from the harvest in a matter of hours rather than the days of laborious work that it had previously taken. A later modification threshed in a revolving drum. Meikle's machine was so widely copied, despite a patent, that he fell into poverty and was only saved by £1,500 raised by his friends.

As a result of these new methods and machines there was a dramatic increase in agricultural productivity. By the 1740s, when there was population growth, food production met this increased demand, with enough for there to be a surplus for the export of grain, and for gin to be made from it. This increase in productivity occurred across all measures: the raw figures of farm output, the area of land under cultivation, the productivity per acre and the productivity from each labourer. The rate of agricultural production was also achieved by a declining percentage of workers. But this increase in agricultural production did not prevent starvation among the poor in Britain from time to time.

The growing productivity of land was complemented by the growth of the area under cultivation, and the sown arable area nearly doubled. This was partly due to land reclamation: fens, marshes, heathland, moors and woodland were reclaimed, often for high intensity arable cultivation. Drainage was also vitally important in bringing new land under cultivation. The drainage of land in Lincolnshire, Norfolk, Suffolk and Cambridgeshire between the 1720s and 1770s brought tens of thousands of acres into use.

The amount of land lying unproductively fallow also fell significantly. This was a consequence of the introduction of root crops, especially turnips, which not only replaced the practice of leaving fallow, but also produced fodder for cattle. They were championed by Viscount 'Turnip' Townshend, who had retired from politics in 1730 to devote his life to his Norfolk estates. Drawing on experiences as ambassador to The Hague, he developed the four-crop 'Norfolk rotation' of turnips, barley, clover and wheat. This method meant farmers did not have to leave the land fallow but rotated field use over four years. Townshend also enclosed, reclaimed and improved his land, using manure and marl. Turnips and clover were especially effective on heathland in Norfolk and Cambridgeshire because they prevented exhaustion of soil nutrients. Townsend was thus able to offer long-term leases as an incentive to his tenants to improve land. It was said that he increased his income by £9,000 a year by these methods. Alexander Pope said Townshend became quite obsessed with turnips and could hardly talk to visitors about anything else. In Wales, Thomas Pryse of Gogerddan in Cardiganshire also adopted turnips from the 1740s.

Farming also dramatically improved the nitrogen levels in soil, which boosted productivity. This nitrogen came from new land released for cultivation, from better manuring of land (including the use of seaweed and human excrement), better drainage and the reduction of acid soils by the addition of lime and marl. But, most of all, clover improved the nitrogen in soil. In this period, clover seems to have increased the volume of nitrogen returned to soil by up to 60 per cent.

The output of agricultural labourers also increased. This was due in part to the growth of larger farms, which required fewer specialist workers. For example, a small dairy farm needed a cowman and a herdsman, but a big dairy farm, four times larger, might need only a cowman and two herdsmen. It was also due to new inventions. The Rotherham plough, which had a strong triangular frame and an iron mould-board, was invented by Joseph Foljambe of Eastwood, near Rotherham, and patented by him in 1730. It was a much sturdier plough than traditional models and could be made cheaply. It was easily pulled and needed only one horse and a ploughman instead of teams of horses and ploughmen. The Rotherham plough was sold and used in most part of the country and became the main form of plough in Norfolk by the 1760s, remaining in use in Britain until the introduction of large tractor-pulled ploughs. Improvements in the size of scythes also enabled fewer men to harvest corn. Generally better diets improved the energy levels and consequently the output of each worker. Men were also replaced by horses, with a 63 per cent increase in the number used on farms. Much of this worsened the lot of the labourer, whose livelihood was looking increasingly insecure. Labour contracts, which had previously been annual 'hirings', were reduced to monthly or weekly contracts.

Many of these improvements were spread through farming books and guides. Experiments in agriculture were disseminated in such works as Richard Bradley's three-volume work, *A General Treatise of Husbandry and Gardening, Containing Such Observations and Experiments as are New and Useful for the Improvement of Land: With an Account of Such Extraordinary Invention and Natural Productions as May Help the Ingenious in their Studies and Promote Universal Learning*, published in 1723. Lord Kames' *The Gentleman Farmer: Being an Attempt to Improve Agriculture by Subjecting it to the Test of Rational Principles* of 1776 was also popular and influential.

Such self-help guides covered an astonishing array of subjects. In 1698 John Worlidge published *The Compleat Bee-Master*, showing how to keep bees for honey. Other guides gave information about grasses, breeds of cattle and sheep and even soil improvement. Many farmers wrote their own manuscript 'farm books', documenting experiments and improvements they had garnered from elsewhere.

There also grew up a new profession of land agent or manager, as larger estates and farms needed more planning and management. Edward Laurence's *The Duty of a Steward to his Lord, Represented Under Several Plain and Distinct Articles; Wherein May be Seen the Indirect Practices of Several Stewards, Tending to Lessen, and Several Methods Likely to Improve Their Lords Estates* of 1727 showed how significant this role could be in agriculture on large estates. By 1808 the study of soil had also become more developed when the Revd William Lewis Rham, vicar of Winkfield, Berkshire, published a scientific essay on soil analysis and its connection to increased yield in the *Agricultural Society Journal.*

In Scotland the Society of Improvers was founded in 1723. It had the aim of spreading new methods of agriculture, in particular the development of larger farms and land drainage. In Wales, Thomas Johnes' *A Cardiganshire Landlord's Advice to his Tenants* of 1800, published in English and Welsh, was influential. It provided advice on how to drain land, improve ploughing and adopt new techniques such as crop rotation and growing turnips.

Agriculture was not an exclusively male bastion. Anne Evans, who inherited the Highmead estate in south Cardiganshire in the 1770s, was said to know more about agriculture than any man and turned her estate into a renowned dairy farm.

The agricultural revolution also saw the intensification of specialization in production. In Norfolk, for example, there was intensive mixed husbandry based on wheat and stall feeding of cattle on oats. In Shropshire, Hertfordshire and the Midlands there were specialist dairying and cattle fattening farms.

The enclosure of land produced larger farms which were progressive and tended to adopt crop innovations. On enclosed farms, wheat yields rose only marginally, but barley and oat yields shot up by 40 per cent and 78 per cent respectively. Two-thirds of all land enclosures were complete by 1700. During the eighteenth century landowners turned away from negotiating enclosure agreements with yeoman farmers and tenants to forcing enclosure through by Act of Parliament. This often ignored local opposition and caused resentment at the loss of tenancies, which sometimes boiled over into violence. In Galloway in 1724, enclosure led peasants to take direct action, knocking down dry-stone walls before troops were called in to restore order.

In Ireland, where the Catholic majority already resented paying tithes, enclosure made matters worse. From the 1760s the Whiteboys developed as a secret organization of peasants determined to prevent enclosure. They resorted to deliberate crippling of cattle as they saw livestock as the reason most landlords wanted to enclose land. Their activity was most intense around Cork, where a Catholic priest, Nicholas Sheehy (1728–66), encouraged their activities until he was arrested for sedition. There were soon so many enclosure bills in Britain that a general Act was passed in 1801 to try to simplify the procedure and save parliamentary time. In Surrey alone, there had been 101 enclosure bills in the eighteenth century, although half of these failed due to lack of time or petitions from opponents.

Enclosure produced two major changes in the landscape: first, it looked entirely different; there were no longer large open spaces, as the now-familiar pattern of fields and hedgerows grew up. Between 1650 and 1800, 220,000 miles (350,000 km) of hawthorn hedging were planted to enclose fields. Secondly, intensive farming required fewer labourers, and villages became depopulated as farm labourers left, often to seek work in the growing industrial towns. By 1773 there was an investigation by the government, which feared the loss of tenant farmers and labourers to the towns. Customs officers were required to report the destination of emigrants, and by 1833 the Passenger Act limited emigration in an attempt to retain labour for farmers and mill owners.

John Byng's tours of England in the 1780s recorded mordant criticism of landowners. Byng saw that enclosures depopulated villages, raised rents and made itinerant labourers out of farm servants. When common lands were enclosed, the rights to raise ducks, geese, sheep and cattle on them and to collect firewood were swept away. Consequently workers became dependent on their wages alone. Even gleaning – the practice of women and children gathering in the 'left-overs' of the harvests near hedgerows and on the margins of land – was discouraged and sometimes prevented by new bylaws.

It is clear that widespread resistance to enclosure was far more common than is often assumed. The poet John Clare had witnessed enclosures in his home parish of Helpstone and felt that they swept away a whole community that relied on the common land and all manner of rural customs and folk practices. He wrote in 'The Tragedy of the Enclosures':

> There once were lanes in nature's freedom dropt,
> There once were paths where every valley wound –
> Inclosure came and every path was stopt;
> Each tyrant fix'd his sign where paths were found,
> To hunt a trespass now who cross'd the ground.
> Justice is made to speak as they command;
> The highway now must be each stinted bound:
> Inclosure thou art a curse upon the land,
> And tasteless was the wretch who thy existence plann'd.

By 1800, Britain was unique in having only 30–35 per cent of its workforce employed in agriculture. A fall in grain prices might have hit agriculture badly if there had not also been a growth in productivity. From the 1740s there was also a population growth that boosted demand for food and stabilized prices. After this, though, there was significant price inflation fuelled by high demand for food and some short-term shortages. For small farmers who did not innovate, these factors caused serious problems. By the end of the century the Napoleonic war caused a further significant hike in food prices. A quarter of a ton of wheat, which cost 45 shillings in 1789, rose to 84 shillings in 1800 and 102 shillings in 1814. Rents, even in Ireland and Scotland, rose by 90 per cent. For the labourers who had to buy food and pay rents, these price increases caused serious problems.

Transport Revolution

Sooner or later, most agricultural produce had to make its way to market. In the case of livestock this was often undertaken by drovers herding cattle, sheep, geese and turkeys to London from as far afield as Yorkshire, Scotland and Wales. In the 1690s, roads carried huge quantities of food to London: 87,500 cattle, 600,000 sheep, 150,000 pigs and countless thousands of turkeys each year. Dry goods were usually carried by teams of packhorses and wagons. Drovers' roads and wagon routes converged on London, since cross-country roads were poorly developed. Merchants as far distant as Sheffield sent their goods to London to be distributed across the country. In 1690, there were 350 packhorse and wagon services each week on routes from London. In the following fifteen years these services grew by 25 per cent. They were fairly slow. It took over five days for a team of packhorses or wagons to travel from London to Exeter, Manchester or Newcastle and over a week for them to go beyond these cities.

Partly in response to the need for better transport, the eighteenth century witnessed the most remarkable expansion of the road system. In 1663 an Act of Parliament allowed a stretch of the Great North Road between Hertford and Huntingdon to be repaired. Tolls were charged on the new road to pay for the repairs, and the roads paid for in this way were privatized into the ownership of trusts. Generally the repair of roads was the responsibility of the individual parishes through which they passed. Consequently, road repairs were frequently neglected. In 1698 Celia Fiennes noted in her journal that roads were often full of holes – in some places these were so deep that people drowned in the potholes in roads. But, from the Restoration, new toll roads, sanctioned by Act of Parliament, were set up. They were called turnpike roads because a 'turnpike' or pole was held across the road and lifted when the traveller had paid a toll.

As the century went on, more and more travellers, merchants and traders saw the benefits of better roads. Between 1689 and 1729 there were eighty-one turnpike Acts, although a number of the trusts to manage these roads failed. This was partly because the trustees could not always raise the capital to build the roads, and because some trusts had been over-optimistic in their estimates of road traffic and the income did not cover the road-building costs. By 1730 about half of the major roads leaving London were toll roads, and from 1729 there were turnpike trusts in Ireland also. Protests against the charges of turnpike roads became a problem especially in Wales in the late eighteenth century.

In the second half of the eighteenth century the number of turnpike roads grew dramatically. In the twenty years after 1760 Britain's turnpike road network grew from 5,000 miles (8,000 km) to 25,000 miles (40,000 km). This huge growth in road building was an example of centralized planning twinned with private enterprise. Between 1760 and 1774 there were over 400 Acts of Parliament, until in 1773 a general Turnpike Act was passed.

As road conditions improved, so did the speed of travel. In the 1750s stage coaches achieved an average speed of 5 miles (8 km) per hour; by the 1790s this had risen to almost 7 miles (11 km) per hour. By contrast, news of the fall of the Bastille spread at just 4 miles (6 km) per hour across most of France. By the end of the century, on the London to Bristol route, average speeds rose to 8 miles (13 km) per hour and between London and Birmingham to 15 miles (24 km) per hour. In August 1784, helped by firm summer roads, a mail coach made the journey from London to Bristol in a single day, albeit needing fourteen changes of horses. These speeds were helped by the introduction of iron and steel springs to replace leather straps as the form of suspension on coaches. Faster speeds required more horses. A stagecoach which went 200 miles (320 km) in six days needed eighteen horses; whereas a coach that travelled the distance in two days needed seventy horses.

In 1754 a Manchester newspaper advertisement reported: 'however incredible it may appear, this coach will actually arrive in London four days after leaving Manchester'. Gradually coach services reached the furthest parts of the country. By 1760 the first coach service from London to Falmouth began. The frequency of services also rose by the 1780s; during the summer season, there were sixteen coaches going from London to Bath each week. Coaches also got larger: in 1775 most stagecoaches could accommodate eight passengers inside and ten on top. Along coaching routes the ancient inns that served coaches were joined by new larger inns. But the experience of stagecoach passengers was not good: travellers staying overnight often had to share beds; employees in inns frequently found themselves sharing a bed with a travelling stranger from the stagecoach. Then, as now, people grumbled about public transport. In 1743 the *London Magazine* published an article on 'the miseries of the Stage Coach', which focused on the smell, dirt, discomfort of travel and the vulgarity and bad manners of fellow travellers.

Wagon and coach wheels also improved significantly. Iron ties held wooden wheels together and in the mid-eighteenth century cast-iron wheels coped with much longer distances and faster speeds. An Act of 1753 outlawed wheel rims narrower than 9 inches (23 cm), which were the cause of deep and dangerous ruts on roads. Some turnpike trusts offered discounts to very wide-wheeled vehicles, which acted as road-rollers and maintained road surfaces. Roads served a political as well as a commercial purpose. The pacification of the Highlands was achieved in part by moving troops relatively quickly along new roads. Between 1726 and 1738, 250 miles (400 km) of roads had been built in Scotland for military purposes. The foremost military road builder, General Wade, even claimed that roads had a civilizing effect. By 1820 John McAdam (1756–1836) developed roads that had stones of a uniform size and a binding of tar or stones on top that was especially strong.

Better roads also meant that horses could haul larger loads. By the end of the eighteenth century a single horse could haul loads as heavy as 1,400 pounds (3,000 kg) and more. John Wesley, the founder of Methodism, who criss-crossed Britain in his determination to spread evangelical religion, was only able to travel so extensively because of the dramatic improvement in roads in the second half of the century. Post boys also used the new roads to carry the post, but in 1772 the American Quaker John Woolman was so shocked at the brutal treatment of post boys and their horses that he advised friends not to use the postal system.

Roads were not the only means of transport to grow in this period. In 1688, Gregory King estimated that 8,000 families were engaged in trade by land, but only 2,000 in trade by sea. Coastal transport grew only slowly during the early eighteenth century. Between 1709 and 1730 the tonnage carried by coastal shipping rose just 13 per cent, from 97,000 tons to 110,000 tons; much of this growth was due to larger ships. The largest ports in the early eighteenth century were the east coast ports serving London: Scarborough, Sunderland, Newcastle, Great Yarmouth, King's Lynn and Whitby. These carried commodities such as coal from the Durham coalfields. But, gradually, ocean trading ports were developing. Bristol's development began in the fifteenth century. In 1712 Bristol's Sea Mills were constructed and in 1715 Liverpool's docks were started.

Inland water traffic came to be dominated by canals, which were also to grow significantly in the eighteenth century. The reason was simple: a packhorse could carry 2 or 3 hundred-weight (100 or 150 kg), a wagon and a team of horses could cope with perhaps 30 hundredweight (1,500 kg), but a fully laden canal barge drawn by a single horse could transport 600 hundredweight (30,000 kg). Consequently, heavy and bulky goods could be carried much more cheaply by canal. The canals were also a natural extension of the river systems, spreading the advantages of existing estuary trade further inland. Some of the first canals were built to advance the benefits of river and estuary trade further inland: the Mersey, Ouse, Trent, Severn and Avon canals were all of this sort. In 1757, the Sankey Brook Canal from St Helens to Liverpool extended a natural stream. Similar improvement could be achieved by dredging and straightening rivers, as happened along the length of the Thames.

Use of canals did not require great technological advance since a single horse could draw a laden barge. The first canal in Britain was built near Exeter in 1560. But the scale of canal building changed significantly in our period. From 1660 to 1725 there were thirty-four Acts of Parliament permitting the compulsory purchase of land for canals, and the extent of canals grew from 685 miles (1,100 km) to 1,160 miles (1,900 km). They were not cheap to build, however; a canal in the eighteenth century cost about £5,000 a mile. But they could produce a good yield: the Oxford Canal Company produced a dividend of 30 per cent for a number of years.

In time, building canals became more ambitious. By 1761 James Brindley (1716–72), a diabetic and self-taught engineer, built a 7-mile (11-km) underground canal from the Duke of Bridgewater's colliery at Worsley to Manchester. Brindley had studied the art of canal building as a millwright and had learned how to cut channels to bring water power to mills. His Bridgewater Canal included an aqueduct over the river Irwell that attracted many visitors and sightseers. The Bridgewater Canal led the price of coal to drop by a half. The huge increase in the tonnage of coal carried meant that the Duke's profits from the Worsley colliery rose from £406 in 1760 to £48,000 in 1803, and gave Manchester a greater supply of coal for its factories. In other towns such as Newbury and Guildford the growth of canals damaged local economies as the towns were now bypassed.

'Canal mania' was competitive but resulted in as many failures as successes. There was the Worcester Bar in Birmingham, where the channels of the competing Worcester and Birmingham Canal and the Birmingham Canal Navigation

Company were just 7 feet (2 m) apart, but goods had to be trans-shipped between the two because the companies could not agree to link them. There was technical innovation, and some canal technology was as impressive as that of later railways. The Bingley flight of five locks, which connected Leeds and Liverpool, carried boats up 60 feet (20 m). It opened in 1771 at a ceremony attended by a crowd of 30,000, who marvelled at the technology. But, like all the economic changes, canals attracted opposition. Josiah Wedgwood, who made good use of them, reported in 1783 that he had heard of threats to destroy canals.

By 1810 Britain had the most widespread and well-developed transport system in the world. There were 30,000 miles (48,000 km) of turnpike roads, 2,125 miles (3,400 km) of navigable river and over 2,000 miles (3,600 km) of canals. In comparison, France, a much larger country, had 4,000 miles (7,200 km) of navigable rivers but only 600 miles (965 km) of canals. Britain also had 1,500 miles (2,400 km) of horse-drawn railways. These railways, like those in Newcastle, where horse-drawn trucks ran along wooden rails carrying coal from mines to coastal barges, pointed the way to the next great transport change. The first iron railway was built at Whitehaven as early as 1738.

Industrialization
Coal and iron lay at the heart of the industrial revolution. Before the eighteenth century, smelting to extract iron from its ore required charcoal. This meant that iron works had to be near forests where charcoal could be made. But between 1709 and 1711 Abraham Darby (1678–1717) began to use coke rather than charcoal to extract iron. Darby's second ironworks in Coalbrookdale had the capacity to make 12 tons of iron a week. His iron for casting was superior to others and could make much thinner, and therefore cheaper, pots and kettles and in much larger quantities. By the mid-eighteenth century, Darby's son, and later his grandson, were able to supply bar

iron for small forges. This made it possible for his iron to be used across the country by small manufacturers as well as in bulk by large cast-iron works. From 1780, pig iron production (named from the moulds in which they were formed) in Britain doubled every eight years.

Darby's works showed the value of coal for manufacturing as well as for fuel. Its abundance in Britain meant that extraction was relatively easy. For the most part, coal before the second half of the eighteenth century was quarried. It was largely dug out of pits near the surface. The earliest coalmines in Yorkshire were only 300 feet (100 m) deep, and much deeper coal were not able to be extracted. By 1770, 6.5 million tons of coal was mined annually. Forty-five years later, this had risen to 16 million tons. This increase was partly due to the use of wooden pit props to work deeper mines, initially on Tyneside, which went down to 1,000 feet (300 m).

The principal problem for deep mines was the air supply and explosive coal gas. The lamp invented by the chemist Humphry Davy (1778–1829) contained a very fine mesh, which allowed air to feed the flame but kept out 'firedamp' gas, thus enabling light to be taken into deep mines. Davy was a brilliant inventor. As a young man he had experimented with nitrous oxide, to create laughing gas, and even disabled himself in an explosion during an experiment. He was a popular lecturer and after-dinner speaker (who often just put a clean shirt over his dirty one on the way from his laboratory to a dinner). He earned £1,000 a year from his inventions, became president of the Royal Society and was made a baronet in 1818.

In due course, steam engines were used to pump fresh air into mines. This allowed mines to go even deeper. By the early nineteenth century, coal was being mined in Newcastle and Tyneside, Durham, South Yorkshire, the Midlands and South Wales as well as in smaller pits in Cornwall, Gloucestershire, Somerset, Cumbria and Kent. The importance of coal can be seen in the mathematics of its energy: when burnt, coal produced 400 times more energy than it took to extract, and only a sixth of its value was used in its transport. Knowledge of coal deposits became important. In 1822 Britain's first geological map was printed, showing the location of coal seams. In the same year, France's first rudimentary geological survey was only just beginning.

Iron, of course, was not the only metal important to the industrial revolution. In South Wales copper mining was as prevalent as iron smelting. By 1796 there were twenty-five furnaces in South Wales, of which three were in Dowlais. The copper from South Wales was used, among other things, to plate the bottoms of naval vessels. As barnacles did not grow on copper, this gave British battleships a manoeuvrability that was invaluable, as demonstrated at the Battle of Trafalgar,.

In 1776 the American Quaker Jabez Maud Fisher visited the Swansea valley. He recorded that the Forest copper works 'vomit out vast clouds of thick smoak, which, curling as they rise, mount up to the clouds'. Elsewhere in Wales, Lord Powis had exploited reserves of lead on his Montgomeryshire estate since 1692. In the twenty years after 1725 he earned £140,000 in profits. But iron dominated so many small and cheap goods that it was the most widely used metal. Its manufacture was growing in Scotland too, where by 1761 the ironworks at Falkirk employed over 600 workers.

The way in which iron, coal and steam connected can be seen in the work of John Wilkinson (1728–1808). Wilkinson was the son of a Nonconformist ironmaster who had been educated in Lancashire and had seen Abraham Darby's works in action in Coalbrookdale. In the 1750s, in Willey, he established a blast furnace and within twenty years he was one of the first ironmasters to introduce a steam engine to power his furnace. The Willey works became famous for making iron in quantities large enough to cast into cylinders. Some of these were used for cannons but, by the end of the 1770s, they were also being used by Boulton and Watt in the manufacture of their own steam engines. This allowed Boulton and Watt to make engines large enough to power steam hammers and rolling mills. In turn, Wilkinson used both of these at his expanding mills. Wilkinson's technique for boring cannons from solid metal involved rotating the gun barrel rather than the bore cutter. Patented in 1774, this method produced cannons that were less likely to explode, and were more accurate. The navy sought to overthrow Wilkinson's patent on the grounds of national interest, fearing a monopoly on the invention.

Wilkinson invested in coal and ore mines in France and Cornwall. All of these also bought Boulton and Watt steam engines. By 1796 Wilkinson's huge furnaces produced an eighth of the nation's iron. He expanded into making iron canal barges for heavy transport and even owned a number of banks. He invested in canals, including the Flint Coal Canal, the Shropshire Canal, the Shrewsbury Canal and the Glamorgan Canal. At his country estate, in Grange Sands, he employed steam engines to drain useless moorland, and limed the soil to make an attractive estate.

Steam engines were a vitally important factor in the industrial revolution. A number of steam engines had been developed at the end of the seventeenth century. John Evelyn saw one in use in tin mines Cornwall in 1702, pumping water from the mines. Thomas Newcomen's (1664–1729) 'atmospheric engine' of 1712 was the first machine to harness steam in a reliable mechanical fashion. It was by no means snag-free; it relied on split-second timing by a 'plug man' to open the valves that emptied the cylinder, and the use of cooling to operate the engine meant that it had a cycle of only twelve pumps a minute. Nevertheless, it was the principal steam engine in Britain for almost seventy years, being used in Coalbrookdale and numerous factories and collieries. By 1733 there were about 100 Newcomen engines in use in Britain, five of them in Ayrshire. This compared with eighty water mills left in Lancashire, Derbyshire and Nottinghamshire in 1788. Gradually, refinements made Newcomen's steam engine more effective. For example, John Smeaton made larger versions of it, Richard Arkwright invented the wheel for driving machinery and James Pickard added the use of a crankshaft. But, as has been seen, it was James Watt who advanced the technology dramatically.

Watt realized that 80 per cent of the steam in a Newcomen engine was wasted when the cylinder was cooled. He introduced the condenser, which enabled the steam to cool outside the cylinder and therefore did not require the whole engine cylinder to be cooled. This also meant that steam could be used to push the piston up and down, thereby increasing the rotations to many more than twelve a minute. Watt's first attempt at building a new engine was made in 1769, but it was a further seven years before his partnership with Matthew Boulton enabled an effective engine to be patented and made on an industrial scale.

Thereafter, for more than a quarter of a century, the Boulton and Watt engine dominated the industrial scene, and by 1784 the 'sun and planets' gearing mechanism had also been patented and the refinements of the steam engine for future use was complete. In 1781 Matthew Boulton said that the people of Manchester, Birmingham and London were 'steam mill mad'.

The steam engine provided the power for the most important industry of the industrial revolution: textiles. The significance of the textile industry was not simply its potential to make cheap clothes and export them, but it exemplified an industry in which almost every process became mechanized. From the carding and spinning of raw wool into yarn, to weaving on mechanized looms, the processes of making woollen and cotton cloth was moved from the small scale of spinning wheels and handlooms in workers' homes to vast mills churning out huge quantities of cloth.

The period witnessed a torrent of inventiveness that improved this mass production of textiles. John Kay's (1704–80) flying shuttle (1733) enabled looms to be much wider and made it possible for weavers to work much faster. As a youth Kay was apprenticed to a maker of weaving reeds but left after a month, having learned all he could from him. It took some time for Kay's shuttle to be perfected, and the claims that his shuttle multiplied many times the speed of a weaver may have been exaggerated. Nevertheless, Kay's invention was so useful that he charged factory owners an annual fee for its use. He spent much of his time fighting copies of his invention, at one point suing fifty-two woollen weavers of Rossendale.

Lewis Paul's rolling spinning machine (1738) and carding machine (1748) moved domestic processes on to a much bigger scale. James Hargreaves' spinning jenny (1764) made an eight-fold increase in a worker's output of spun woollen thread, and it could be worked as easily by children as adults. He made the prototype from a piece of wood using a pocket knife. The invention was a response to Kay's shuttle, which had increased weavers' output and so created a demand for more thread.

Richard Arkwright's water frame (1771) harnessed looms to water power and enabled huge increases in production, and of stronger and more evenly woven cloth. Poverty forced Arkwright to share his patents with partners who invested in them and, like Kay, in a long series of court cases he was also forced to sue to defend his patents and to prevent copiers of his designs. Samuel Crompton combined the principles of the jenny and Arkwright's water frame in his mule, while the Revd Edmund Cartwright's power loom (1784) used drive shafts to power multiple looms. Cartwright had invented his power loom because Manchester mill owners said they needed bigger, faster looms to cope with the volume of spun wool and cotton made by Arkwright's spinning machine. Cartwright's power loom attracted a petition of 50,000 unemployed weavers against it, but in 1808 Cartwright was voted £10,000 in gratitude by the House of Commons for inventing such a useful device.

The whole face of industries such as weaving was changed by mechanization. Within less than two generations, domestic weaving had been largely extinguished as a commercial enterprise. The value of the output of woven cotton grew from £4 million in 1783 to £15 million in 1803.

Exports of cotton textiles rose in value from £11,000 in 1740 to £28 million in 1820, when there were more than 900 cotton mills. The number of woollen broadcloth pieces produced in West Yorkshire between 1727 and 1815 rose from 29,000 to 330,000. In Scotland the older linen industry – though it doubled output between 1740 and 1780 – also gave way to cotton; in the west of Scotland, the linen producer David Dale converted his business to cotton production in the 1780s. Even Ireland had a burst of activity in cotton production, although this was in decline by 1820.

The textile industry was an example to others in the mechanization of industrial processes of production, the use of water and steam power, the division of labour and increasing organization of work into large factory units. The United States quickly adopted textile technology and ideas from Britain. The American Jedediah Strutt took Arkwright's factory technology to America, and Eli Whitney's cotton gin was modelled on British technology. Textile manufacture was also used as a model by British businessmen, such as Josiah Wedgwood in the pottery industry. His Staffordshire pottery factories introduced mechanization into the manufacture of earthenware, 80 per cent of which was exported. In 1746 the brass factory at Warmley in south Gloucestershire had developed into an integrated mill, where raw ores went in at one end and brass wire, pans and other goods emerged at the other, with all the production processes taking place in a single factory.

Factories became the principal unit of manufacture. In Richard Arkwright's Derwent and Cromford works, canals, wharves and seven-storey factories were built, with housing for workers nearby. Robert Owen's (1771–1858) New Lanark mills on the Clyde housed 200 families from the Isle of Skye to work in them, and Owen often made inducements to people to come to his mills rather than emigrating to the US. He paid reasonable wages, refused to employ children younger than ten in the factory, and provided a free school, with a nursery for under-fives. There were also evening classes for adults. Despite the scepticism of his opponents, Robert Owen's business was very successful, and his factory productivity outstripped his competitors'.

The Consumer Revolution.

The industrial, transport and agricultural revolutions changed life in Britain. Breakfast, for example, took on a form recognizable today. Higher food production meant eggs, bacon and bread were in surplus and available in local grocers' shops. Cups, saucers, knives, plates and pans were cheaper and more widely available. Coffee and tea were imported for sale: the consumption of tea rose from 54,600 pounds (25,000 kg) in 1706 to 2.3 million pounds (1 million kg) in 1750 (although there were large parts of the country in which tea and coffee were rare before the end of the eighteenth century, such as Somerset and Cumberland). All these goods were transported across the country; many were imported from abroad. A whole meal culture was born and a higher calorie intake was effected.

The ingenuity of people seemed to bloom: in the 1720s, 89 patents were sealed, but by the 1760s this rose to 205 and by the 1790s to 647. Dean Josiah Tucker said that the English home contained all manner of conveniences, such as furniture, carpets, screens, windows, curtains, chamber bells, brass locks and fire fenders, that were hardly seen in continental homes.

At the heart, and the start, of the consumer revolution was an appetite for goods. As the economist Dudley North (1641–91) wrote in 1691:

The main spur to trade, or rather to industry and ingenuity, is the exorbitant appetites of men which they will take pains to gratifie, and so be disposed to work, when nothing else will incline them to it; for did men content themselves with bare necessities we should have a poorer world.

Consumption shifted from necessities to include luxuries. This shift was fuelled, in part, by a sense that items handmade locally and domestically were no longer as desirable as those made by specialist manufacturers. Plates, for example, made by unskilled hands from local clay, could not compare with porcelain or china or even slipware – often made very cheaply – from specialist potteries and manufacturers. Walls were no longer seen bare; they were covered in wallpaper or even silk, tapestry and occasionally wainscoting.

'Emulative consumption' – consuming goods in imitation of your social superiors – was identified as a trend in the economy in the late seventeenth century; but in the eighteenth century it became a core element in economic growth. Josiah Wedgwood knew how important emulation was. In the 1770s he created very expensive vases that could only be bought by the very wealthy. Once he had sold enough of these, he introduced a cheaper line in imitation of these vases for sale to the middle classes – he made a fortune by using such techniques. The growth of luxuries was not only the case in durables; the same was true of food. The consumption of imported food items grew dramatically in this period. The figures for the Port of London showed that in 1663 only 16.3 per cent of its trade was imported; by 1800 this had risen to 34.9 per cent – and this in a period in which general food consumption was rising.

In the eighteenth century, more than at any earlier period in British history, people began to endow their purchases with meaning and value. An example can be seen in the life of Elizabeth Shackleton, the daughter of a London draper, who married a Lancashire landowner. As a wealthy widow, Elizabeth managed her own estate and, like many contemporaries, she categorized possessions into her 'best' and everyday items. They became accessories in managing her household and servants. Linen, for example, was purchased, checked, sorted, rotated and stored by servants who understood these duties. Visitors were shown new items that were displayed for them: china, table-cloths, even furniture were exhibited to impress callers. This display of the latest and best was central to consumption and to the sense of 'politeness' that characterized the eighteenth century.

The social rituals of tea drinking enabled Elizabeth Shackleton to use and display her sugar tongs and bowls in front of friends and relations. For more intimate friends, there were rings, tokens and trinkets. She purchased pictures and furniture with an eye to ornamenting her home in a particular style, while developing social pretensions based on fashionable food and clothes. By following fashions in London newspapers, she was able to bring them to Lancashire. Less fashionable items, such as domestic utensils, could be bought locally. All of this suggested that Elizabeth Shackleton found meaning in the social rituals and vanities of consumption.

It would be rash to suggest that all people gave themselves up to consumption without thought. For some, and especially those with roots in the Puritan ideas of the previous century, consumption could be troubling. The Welsh evangelical Howell Harris, for example, when visiting London in 1744, was anxious whether he should spend his money on tea. He feared abusing God's generosity. It was only when he found his fellow Methodist George Whitefield (1714–70) drinking tea that he overcame his scruples. Similarly, Quakers were conspicuous in not buying the bright new fabrics and consumer goods of the eighteenth century. There were other expressions of dislike of consumption: in 1677, anticipating legislation by 330 years, the Mayor of Norwich ordered that 'no person do take tobacco in the streets by day or by night'. This was partly from fear of fires but also dislike of the smell. Ten years later, tobacco was also banned from the city corporation meetings in Norwich.

Urban Revolutions

The eighteenth century was a period of rapid urbanization. In 1700, 17 per cent of the population lived in towns of more than 2,000 people. By 1800 this had risen to 27.5 per cent, and the population was rising. In 1700 London had a population of 500,000 – more than all the other English towns put together. There were only five towns with more than 10,000 people in

1700, but by 1800 there were twenty-seven. In 1700 Norwich was the second largest city in the country; a century later it was Liverpool. Deep ports accommodating bigger ships won out in competition with smaller ports: Plymouth replaced Exeter; Liverpool replaced north-western ports such as Lancaster; and the deep water ports of Sunderland, Tynemouth and South Shields, which exported coal, beat their southerly rivals such as Whitby.

Much urban growth was evolutionary and part of the longer-term processes of the gentrification of towns. In London, this was seen in the development of the West End of London, where aristocratic estates were built in Mayfair, St James', Piccadilly, Soho and Covent Garden. In other cases, urban development was planned and achieved by a step-change of regeneration. This happened in Warwick after a fire in 1694 and was effected by an Act of Parliament. Similar investment occurred in many towns and cities such as Bath, Glasgow and Dublin. In these towns, squares were laid out surrounded by elegant brick buildings, and containing attractive gardens. In such towns, which were sometimes spas, the range of facilities of an 'urbane' life were built. These included theatres, assembly rooms, pleasure gardens, art galleries, parks, coffee houses, race courses, market squares and churches. In many towns, street lighting was introduced to make streets safer and more usable.

Across the country there were 800 markets and 3,200 fairs. Some of these were the equivalent of national department stores. The annual Stourbridge Fair, near Cambridge (which had been chartered in the sixteenth century but had been held as early as the reign of King John) lasted for a full month from the end of August. Traders brought goods to it from all over the country including Yorkshire and Manchester cloth, Hereford hops and fruit, Lincolnshire wool, Birmingham brass and iron goods, Sheffield cutlery, Nottingham lace and Leicester glass. There were book and paper stalls and even scientific instruments for sale. Defoe said the Stourbridge Fair was bigger than the great markets at Leipzig, Frankfurt and Nuremburg. Consequently, the concession of a stall at the fair was very expensive: in 1668 one booth on a lease of twenty-one years cost 50 shillings a year. When the fair had to be cancelled because of the plague in 1665 there were damaging economic consequences. But such fairs were gradually bypassed by growing canal and road traffic that enabled shops in towns to stock goods all year round. As one German visitor noted in 1782, every person in London who owned or rented a house or even a room, set up a sign selling some product or service. Each of these was supplied by road or canal. Gradually wholesale and retail selling were becoming separate. By the end of the eighteenth century, Stourbridge Fair lasted only a fortnight and by the middle of the nineteenth century it had become an entertainment rather than a commercial fair.

Fairs and market stalls were gradually replaced by shops that could satisfy the growing demand for local and national produce and maintain a large stock. In Bath, from the 1720s bow-fronted windows were used to display goods to the public. In 1745 the Bath Corporation began to clear stall places to make way for more shops, although in Norwich, throughout the eighteenth century, the city council allocated part of the market place to 'petty chapman' and 'pitching pence' payers who gave a penny to the council for the right to stand and sell their wares.

At the start of this period shops were few and shopkeepers relied on annual visits to fairs or London to buy their stock. The shopkeepers of Lancaster, for example, rode to London together to obtain their stock over a two-week period. Gradually the number of shops grew, and an important factor in their growth were pattern cards. Wholesalers sent out pattern cards for clothes, furnishings and other items so that consumers could buy them to order through the shops. In some trades these quickly replaced commercial travellers.

Some manufacturers, such as Matthew Boulton and Josiah Wedgwood, set up exclusive sale rooms in London and other cities in which people could see their goods before they bought them. It was a short time before these sale rooms became shops. Initially such shops were only available to the wealthy and sometimes even by appointment. The number of shops grew dramatically in the first half of the eighteenth century, from about 50,000 in 1688 to 162,000 in 1759, when the government even considered imposing a tax on shops. In Bath, shops quickly adopted promotional techniques, including sales of old stock and advertising new fashions.

Supplying shops were networks of wholesalers. In the 1770s the Association of London Tea Dealers was established, ostensibly to prevent the evasion of duty on tea, but it also acted as a cartel to ensure that prices were not affected by competition. Wholesale drapers tended also to cooperate to keep prices up. Tea as a commodity sold in shops ballooned. By 1784 there were large numbers of tea dealers in many towns. Colchester had 179, Birmingham 342, Portsmouth 140 and Cambridge 174. Of course such shops represented a spectrum, from the fashionable and expensive tea dealers to the backstreet sellers. In Edinburgh the leading grocer and tea merchant, William Fettes, made a fortune with which Fettes College was later endowed.

The principal competitors of the new shopkeepers were traditional hawkers, who sold all manner of goods in the streets. During the eighteenth century there was growing pressure on Parliament from shopkeepers to restrict their numbers and to take away the licences of hawkers when they undercut the shops. In some towns the mayor and corporation joined in petitions against hawkers. The effect was significant and between 1723 and 1785 the numbers of hawkers halved. However, they remained widely used in rural areas where there was insufficient demand to justify setting up a shop.

One aspect of the growth of shops was a decline in haggling and the adoption of set prices. Whereas in 1660 haggling was common with street vendors and at fairs, by the end of the eighteenth century it was much rarer. In part this was due to the use of advertising, catalogues and price lists which indicated prices to customers. Market stalls tended to continue to permit haggling, and it remained more prevalent in drapery than, for example, in grocery shops; but, by 1838, when Emerson Bainbridge set up Britain's first department store in Newcastle, he insisted that all prices were fixed and haggling was not permitted. By 1850 Bainbridge's store had twenty-three departments under one roof, covering clothing, drapery, dry goods, shoes, hats, jewellery, furniture and leather goods.

The Industrial City

London exerted a strong economic influence over the rest of Britain in this period. It was the major supplier of financial services such as banking, insurance and investment. It was also the focus of government regulation of the economy. Even then it was a grumble of the provinces that the government cared little for them and their economic needs. London was also the principal source of news and of fashions in clothing, food, literature and most other cultural forms. There was some suspicion of London in other areas. In 1800 a Manchester publication, *The New Cheats of London Exposed*, warned young people of the numerous 'cheats, frauds, villainies, artifices, tricks, seductions, stratagems, impositions and deceptions' that they would meet in London. The title page included the verse:

> Herein are shewn the various feats
> Of Whores, Rogues and other Cheats
> Here Youths are taught those snares to shun
> By which too many are undone.

London's manufacturing continued to grow in the second half of the eighteenth century, but it did not reach the extraordinary levels achieved by other British towns.

A dramatic example of rapid urbanization is Leeds. In the early eighteenth century Leeds was a market town. Its principal trade was textiles, supplied by sheep on the pasture in the nearby upland dales. There was a ready supply of water for processing the wool, and some rivers provided access for the finished cloth to towns such as Goole and Hull. In the eighteenth century, coal from mines to the south supplied the steam power that enabled cloth-making to become a large-scale industrial, rather than a small-scale domestic, process. The growth of cloth sales was reflected in the need for three new cloth halls built in 1711, 1775 and in the nineteenth century. Leeds also had other industries that took advantage of steam power, including potteries and linen manufacturing. Iron working had been undertaken in the area since the Middle Ages, but coal and coke made iron smelting much easier. Foundries and iron workshops were introduced into the town in the 1780s.

To help the industries in Leeds, the corporation provided street lighting, which was oil fired from 1775, and gas fired from 1819. The corporation widened bridges to ease road traffic and their spans were also widened so that bigger boats could enter the town. Local woodland was felled to enable turnpike roads to be constructed to the town from the north and south. The river Aire was made navigable by the start of the eighteenth century, and Leeds was also connected to Liverpool by a canal begun in 1770. A railway brought coal from Middleton colliery into Leeds in 1759, but this was horse drawn until a static steam engine was built to haul trucks in the early nineteenth century.

Leeds developed all the features of a large town. By 1754 it had two newspapers, an infirmary was founded in 1767, a second in 1771, and a theatre was opened in 1795. Schools were built and a number of boarding schools and day schools were established for the growing middle-class occupants of the suburbs around the town. Medieval buildings were steadily cleared and replaced by new mills and civic buildings. Open spaces in the town were also built on. As the town grew, the parish church of Leeds added chapels in each new district. By the nineteenth century there were twelve chapels, and the vicar of Leeds often oversaw a staff of more than a dozen curates.

The principal problem for Leeds was overcrowding as more people came looking for work. The medieval layout of the town was organized around burgage tenements. These were strips of land with a house fronting on to the main streets. As more housing was needed, people built houses in their gardens and provided access to them through alleys, and sometimes even tunnels under the frontage house. These tenement houses quickly became overcrowded.

In some yards, as these tenements were known, more and more buildings were squeezed in. In Boot and Shoe Yard in 1795 there were twenty-two separate homes and by 1839, there were thirty-four; since these homes could accommodate ten people, epidemic diseases grew dramatically. Children were forced to work alongside adults in appalling conditions; in 1785 there were more than 600 boys employed by chimney-sweeps to climb up chimneys to clean them.

Towns were not only places of growth and development, some were decaying and in decline. Frome, Glastonbury and Wells in Somerset declined in relative importance because of the decrease in the wool trade. In other cases, towns and cities that had been important were eclipsed by industrial towns. This happened to many cathedral cities, which were also reduced in relative importance. In Rye in Sussex, the decline of the silk trade and the silting-up of the estuary which the town relied on meant that by the second half of the eighteenth century the principal economic activity of the town was smuggling, as many of its residents drifted away to work elsewhere. Other ports, such as Harwich, suffered from the development of larger naval ports and the demand for deep water docks. It declined from a busy and active town when Defoe visited it in the early eighteenth century to one with just four sea captains by the end of the century.

Towns were also the focus of discontent and violence. In times of hardship there was more scope for unrest. Food riots occurred in Newcastle in 1740 and Belfast in 1756 and in a number of towns in 1766. The Taunton election of 1754, fought out over more than six months was the occasion for repeated riots, fuelled by poverty among textile workers.

There is often an assumption that urbanization broke up communities. The popular image is of the rural poor taken out of their village community and lost in the urban masses – and this probably did happen in some cases. But there is also some evidence that new communities in the big industrial towns were quickly formed and that people often developed strong bonds even in the squalor of new towns.

Factory Working

In *The Compleat English Tradesman* of 1724 Daniel Defoe wrote that to follow a trade and not to enjoy it was like slavery. For the worker drawn to towns to work in factories by the prospect of employment, especially when their own work had been taken by machines, industrialization was close to enslavement. In 1791 Robert Sadler of Chippenham published a poem entitled *The Discarded Spinster; or, a Plea for the Poor, on the Impolicy of Spinning Jennies*. The purpose of the poem was to counter the view that everyone had benefited from mechanization. Sadler wanted to:

> give language to their sorrows, and by that means, introduce their distresses to the knowledge of those who, possessed of power, perhaps only need the knowledge to inspire them with the will to relieve [them].

By dispossessing the poor who had skills and independence, Britain was squandering its resources and reducing people to brutes. The experience of industrialization was also examined in 1794 in *Social Observations on the Loss of Woollen Spinning as a Cottage Industry*. In it, the different impact of economic change on men and women was described. Combers could sometimes turn to other work, but their wives and daughters could rarely find other jobs. A woman with four or five children who could previously work alongside her carding wool was consigned to destitution. Even where there was work for women and children it was at starvation wages.

The same author then visited a number of textile factories in which he saw combing machines and the spinning jenny working. One child had to take flakes of combed wool and put them in as many as fifty bobbins as well as turning crank handles; working in this way, a child did the work of 100 cottage workers. The children, mainly girls, were supervised by men. Sometimes parents objected to this, but hunger forced them to hand their girls into the hands of older men. The girls may have been 'neat and orderly', but herding them without their parents and only supervised by rough men would, he feared, produce 'a dissolute race of poor' children. The author worried not only about morals but about the children's health and hygiene. Workers were without pride in their work, he argued, without a sense of independence and security, without sunlight and fresh air, without the natural order of parents supervising them and without a sense of the natural cycle of seasons and life spans.

In factories, time became a commodity in a way that it had not been in the pre-industrial economy. More and more people owned and carried watches. In 1797 it was estimated that clock makers had bought enough metal to make between 400,000 and 800,000 watches and clocks. New attitudes to time led to a clash of cultures, in which customary work patterns that focused on seasonal daylight gave way to mill rules with highly regulated time. Bells rang to indicate the start and finish of the day's work. Punctuality was expected and lateness was met with fines and punishments.

Education, especially in Methodist schools, emphasized the importance of good time-keeping. Wesley emphasized the 'husbandry of time' and time 'thrift', and evangelicals such as Hannah More stressed the benefits of 'early rising'. Time could be manipulated: in the 1830s, evidence to Michael Sadler's

(1780–1835) House of Commons committee on factory conditions included the claim that factory owners rigged their bells
to ring early for the start of the day and late at the end of the
day. There were said to be cases of factory clocks being rigged
by weighting the mechanism. Timekeeping was only one habit
demanded by an industrial economy; there were others.
'Commercial schools', which taught the skills required by
businesses, were becoming popular; between 1770 and 1789,
eight were opened in Derby alone.

The uprooting of people had an unsettling effect on religion
too. The Church of England tried to keep abreast of the
burgeoning industrial towns. In the huge Lancashire parish of
Whalley, the twelve chapelries grew from a population of
13,000 in 1720 to just under 50,000 by the end of the century. In
Whalley the Church of England was effective in building new
large churches, reseating existing churches and adding galleries
and aisles. But it was an enormous struggle, which relied on
public funding through church rates, private endowments and
the church's own collections for other parishes. There were
twenty such projects in Whalley during the eighteenth century.
By 1778 there were also five Methodist meeting-houses in
Whalley, though most supplemented rather than replaced
church services.

Not all parishes could keep up. Consequently, in a number
of northern industrial parishes, parsons complained of misbehaviour, absence from church services, indifference to religion
and inattention to religious principles.

In some industrial parishes, despite extraordinary efforts,
the Church and its clergy were overwhelmed by the unprecedented demographic upheaval. Elsewhere, Nonconformist
churches were similarly swamped. What was happening was
that industrialization was making clear what had been the case
since 1689: Anglicanism may have been the national Church
but its membership was voluntary. Moreover, in some parishes,
the national Church was only one denomination among many.
People might buy their china from Dresden, or Wedgwood or

from a local pottery; they could similarly worship where they chose, although there remained legal restrictions on Catholics.

By 1790 the regional pattern of the industrial revolution had been established. Population growth was focused on the north of England and South Wales. Between 1800 and 1850 income tax yield from Yorkshire rose by 23 per cent, and population trebled in Lancashire, Yorkshire, Cheshire and South Wales. Nineteen out of the twenty fastest growing towns in the eighteenth century were near coalfields.

The population growth had also altered the demography of the country, in stark contrast with today's demography: in 1800 the English population was very young, with 55 per cent of people below 25 years of age.

Britain's economy in 1800 had undergone exceptional changes, making it the first industrial economy of the modern era. Although the forces that achieved these changes had been building for some time, the pace of economic development was breath-taking. No sectors of life were unchanged by the industrial economy, and few people failed to experience both the benefits and the disadvantages of such unprecedented economic growth. It changed the physical environment, it provided an abundance of new manufactured products and altered the nature of work. Once the industrial genie was out of the bottle it could not be put back; Britain's society was changed for ever.

7

CHALLENGING THE ESTABLISHMENT

Historical trends such as the rise of Britain to world power, the economic changes of the period and the growth of political stability are sometimes seen as smooth and unchaotic developments that happened without challenge and dispute. Of course change is not like that: it is often resisted and relies on disagreement and criticism. James Watt's invention of the modern steam engine, for example, rested on his recognition of the shortcomings of Newcomen's engine. Much of life in Britain in this period was influenced by those who attacked politics and authority or resisted the existing order. Some people opposed the changes we have traced, or caused change by their own challenge to the established way of things.

Where did such challenges and resistance come from? In the 1720s Voltaire concluded that Britain had something that was unique in Europe: diversity of religion and a degree of religious tolerance. In Britain, unlike much of the rest of Europe, people could legally worship as Quakers, Baptists, Presbyterians or Anglicans, and there were many varieties of each. The

Toleration Act enabled people to hold different beliefs. In many Nonconformist churches members made their own choice of minister and organized the worship themselves. This inculcated egalitarian views and promoted a desire for greater self-determination. While there was widespread, and sometimes hysterical, anti-Catholic feeling in Britain, for the most part there was also forbearance of different opinions and beliefs. In the early eighteenth century there was much concern about how much the Church, or any religious group, could shackle consciences. This led to resistance to any who tried to force people to hold a particular set of beliefs. This chafing at control over religious beliefs drew on ideas of liberty and the freedom that the British had earned from tyrants – in the guise of Charles I and James II. It was this freedom that some people had in mind as they defied the establishment.

The Jacobite Challenge to the State

In the first half of the eighteenth century the principal challenge to the authority and stability of the British State was Jacobitism. Jacobites were the supporters of James II and the exiled Stuart dynasty in France, who aimed to win back the throne from first William III, then Queen Anne, George I and George II. They cast long shadows over politics from 1689 to 1750. The succession of Anne in 1702 and George I in 1714 happened against a backdrop of anxiety and suspense. Would there be a military challenge to the succession?

Jacobitism flavoured politics with the heady mixture of spies, plots, secret codes, clandestine gatherings and rumours of rebellion. People close to the centre of power were thought to be treasonous Jacobites. Even John Anstis, Queen Anne's Garter King at Arms, was suspected of being a Jacobite. In 1710 it was estimated that as many as 50 of the 330 Tory MPs were Jacobites. To some, there seemed a real possibility that there might be a second Stuart restoration. In retrospect, the Jacobite leaders, James II, his son the Old Pretender and grandson the Young Pretender and many of their leading supporters, were inept and lacked both resolve and self-possession. But this was only apparent when they had repeatedly bungled and mismanaged their attempts to regain the throne.

From the perspective of a Hanoverian supporter between 1702 and 1750, Jacobites represented a real and imminent danger. The threat was one reason why patronage formed such an important feature of government and society in the eighteenth century. Patrons could be assured of loyalty when they had personal knowledge of an appointee.

The attempts to assassinate William III in the 1690s, the rising of 1715, the plots of 1718, the treason of Bishop Atterbury of Rochester, the support of the French court and the rising of 1745 meant most politicians had to keep one eye on the Jacobite threat. Military dispositions also had to accommodate the need to respond to threats of invasion. Some disaffected politicians, such as the Earl of Mar, turned to Jacobitism when they were disappointed in offers of office. Others hedged their bets by keeping open the lines of communication with the Stuart court in France. The Duke of Marlborough, despite holding office under Queen Anne and George I, maintained a life-long contact with the exiled court.

The possibility that the Old Pretender might renounce Catholicism even intrigued Queen Anne with the possibility that she might be succeeded by her brother (despite the 'bedpan' rumours), rather than her Hanoverian cousins. But the Old Pretender clung to his Catholicism and consequently Queen Anne stuck to the plan for the Hanoverian succession.

What made Jacobitism especially dangerous was its religious component. The Non-jurors, those Anglicans – including the Archbishop of Canterbury – who left their offices in 1689 rather than abandon James II, gave Jacobitism a respectable theological base. They claimed that James II had not stopped being king in 1689 simply because he had left the country, and that people who had abandoned James had committed a sin. They had sworn oaths of allegiance to James that could not be abandoned when it was inconvenient. Non-jurors showed that Jacobitism was not the political arm of the Catholic Church because it had a legitimate Protestant identity. Consequently, the division between those politicians who embraced the Glorious Revolution and those who – openly or secretly – remained loyal to James were much more worrying. The issue was not simply whether James II or William III was the more effective military leader. It was, rather, whether it was sinful to rise up against a legitimate ruler? Was the duty of the subject simply to obey the king? Might those who had 'sinned' in the revolution of 1688 have lost their chance of salvation? Time and again, churchmen returned to these questions, until, by 1714, they represented some of the principal national anxieties.

The works of some of the most popular writers, Defoe, Swift, Addison, Pope and Steele, were shot through with references to the threats from Jacobites and the legitimacy of the Hanoverian succession. Most were written from a pro-Hanoverian perspective, but nevertheless revealed a tension and anxiety about the Jacobite threat. These concerns were compounded by the Hanoverian succession of a Protestant king, George I. In front of King George there were many princes more closely related to Queen Anne, but they were excluded from the throne because they were Catholics.

Like all systems when threatened from outside, the establishment demonized Jacobites, Catholics and their French hosts. Leading Jacobite rebels were treated harshly: in 1696, 1716, 1723 and 1746 the dismembered bodies of Jacobite traitors were displayed on Temple Bar, the Tower of London and London Bridge. But politicians also knew that, up and down the country, yeomen, drunken mobs, Oxford academics and others were fined, flogged and occasionally imprisoned for their public support for James II, his son and grandson. Periodically, magistrates, lords lieutenant, militia officers and even bishops were ordered to search homes for arms and confiscate horses from suspected Jacobites to safeguard the State. There was strong intellectual support for Jacobitism from Oxford University, whose Toryism merged into Jacobitism. Oxford even sheltered some notable open and crypto-Jacobites. In some areas, Jacobites adopted the veneer of respectability. In eighteenth-century Wales, the Society of Sea Serjeants – a regular meeting of gentry held in the ports of south-west Wales – became a Tory Jacobite club. Members had a portrait of the Pretender inside the lids of their snuff boxes (in time, though, the society became a recreational one that admitted women and banned swearing).

In later years, Jacobitism took on romantic overtones but, between 1707 and 1750, some in Scotland saw it as a way to show their opposition to the Act of Union. Gaelic and the clan system became cultural expressions of Jacobitism, and persecuted Episcopalians often supplied supporters for the cause. During the rising of 1715, however, apart from a couple of small uprisings in Northumberland and Lancashire, the country remained quiet. The rebels had promises of support from Wales, Staffordshire, Worcestershire and Derbyshire that never materialized. Jacobitism also framed Britain's relationship with Ireland, which, since the defeat of James II at the Battle of the Boyne, was always tense. Scotland and Ireland seemed to increase the surface area for Jacobite attacks. It gave an added impetus to the State's need to encourage and support the Protestant settlers and landowners in Ireland.

Jacobitism's decline after 1745 was intensified by the success of Britain in foreign wars against the French, eventually forcing the Pretender out of France. But the fecklessness of Charles Edward Stuart in offending his British supporters also dried up funds, and the failure of even the papacy to recognize him as the rightful king in 1766 hammered nails to the Jacobite coffin. The stability of the Hanoverian regime, together with the childlessness of both Charles Edward Stuart, who died in 1788, and his brother Cardinal Henry Stuart (1725–1807) ended any chance of a restoration of the Stuarts. The defeat of the Jacobite challenge showed that nothing had consolidated the Hanoverian regime more than time. By the succession of

George IV in 1820 no one gave any thought to the possibility of a challenge to the throne.

Crime

Crime and disorder were the greatest challenges to Britain's civil peace. As in many periods of British history, there was a perception that these were rising and urgently needed to be dealt with. In the fifty years after 1688 one of the greatest fears was that there was a rising tide of immorality and sin. In the 1690s the Societies for the Reformation of Manners organized vigilante patrols and undertook private prosecutions of prostitutes and other immoral behaviour. Sin was as great a concern as crime, and the distinction between them was only gradually beginning to emerge.

Fear of crime led to a gradual increase in penalties and restrictions on legal loopholes. The 'benefit of clergy' – which was originally a means of ensuring that clergy were judged by each other rather than by laymen – had become a way of reducing the numbers of criminals punished with the death penalty. By the Restoration, any layman could claim benefit of clergy if they could read or recite Psalm 51. Such a convict was branded to prevent a second claim, but was relieved of the threat of the noose. From 1692 the benefit of clergy had become such a fiction that women claimants did not even have to recite the psalm. It became a way for judges to relieve a minor criminal of a disproportionate death sentence. In some cases laws – such as those tightening penalties for theft – excluded clergy from their terms to prevent anyone claiming the benefit. Besides the erosion of the benefit of clergy, the law increasingly imposed the death penalty for relatively minor offences.

Although there was a growth in the number of capital offences, juries and judges were reluctant to use the death penalty, except in the most serious cases. In Ireland this was very common, especially where indigenous Catholic juries decided cases in which the prosecutors were Protestant and

English. Across Britain at the end of the sixteenth century, about a quarter of capital felons were hanged (the rest were pardoned or reprieved); by the start of the eighteenth century this had fallen to a tenth. Sometimes there were technical ways of avoiding the death penalty, such as amending the value given to goods stolen to bring it below the threshold for capital punishment. Even where a sentence of execution was passed, pardons were common, especially for women and those with dependants. In Wales, a convict sentenced to flogging, who had the sympathy of the community, was sometimes given a ritual flogging, with the whip smeared with false blood; one example of such a case was an elderly pauper who had stolen some peat for fuel. So in Britain at the start of this period there was the paradox of fierce penalties in law, but rare use of them in the courts. But this was to change dramatically.

In 1688 there were 50 offences that could be punished by the death penalty, by 1765 this had risen to 160 and by 1815 to 225. This 'bloody code' started in 1697 with death as the penalty for forging the seal of the Bank of England. But the Black Act of 1723 alone created fifty capital crimes. It was prompted by the 'Blacks' of Waltham in Hampshire, who were poachers and thieves who disguised themselves with blackened faces. Poaching had been common for years, and the London venison markets relied on such activities, although a law of 1670 only permitted people with an income over £100 a year to kill game. The 'Blacks' had been active from 1710, and the offer of rewards for their capture or identification were ineffective. By 1719 the 'Blacks' were engaging in organized criminal poaching with bands of a dozen or more men stripping the Bishop of Winchester's parks at Farnham and Waltham of deer. The 'Blacks' were increasingly violent, killing a number of gamekeepers, and threatening anyone who was likely to expose or act against them. The outrage at their activities led the government to make cattle maiming, destruction of saplings, damaging fishponds, extortion, poaching and blackmail liable to the death penalty. By 1723 the government was also intolerant of lawlessness. The trial of Bishop Atterbury for treason had created a sense of anxiety that 'Blacks' might become politicized by the Jacobites, in spite of their declared support for Protestantism and the Hanoverian regime.

In part, the growth of the numbers of capital offences was a consequence of English common law, which contained few specific definitions of crimes. Consequently, as new offences were defined in law, more criminal offences came into being. This resulted in many laws, each of which outlawed a particular crime with its own penalties, in sharp contrast to those countries that had an organized criminal code of laws. Growth of capital crimes may also reflect how the law protected the interests of property. This extended far down the ranks of society; Old Bailey proceedings show that plaintiffs often included artisans, shopkeepers and journeymen as well as the landed classes. In Essex, for example, a fifth of all prosecutions were brought by the labouring classes.

The nature of crime and punishment rested on the assumption that most people were law-abiding so there was little need or provision for the detection of crime. Prosecution was the responsibility of the landed classes and deterrence was critical to buttress the inner morality and honesty of the masses, as was the encouragement of the individual willingness to prosecute criminals. In 1693, for example, a reward of £40 was introduced by law to anyone who apprehended and successfully prosecuted highway robbers. This was later extended to burglary. Besides the usual rewards, there was a premium for criminals convicted in the parish of Charing Cross. In 1699, the government also permitted an additional inducement in the form of excusing a prosecutor from holding burdensome parish offices, such as overseer of the poor or surveyor of highways.

In time, these rewards encouraged the efforts of professional 'thief-takers', the most notorious of whom was Jonathan Wild (1683–1725). From 1713 Wild built a lucrative career catching thieves and sending them to the gallows. Wild claimed to have helped convict over sixty criminals, and frequently asserted that he had 'recovered' stolen property when apprehending criminals – in fact he had arranged for the theft of the property himself. He had a network of informers, and from his ledgers the term 'double cross' is derived since he put a cross against the name of his informers and two crosses against those who had given him false information or misled him.

Despite suspicions of Wild, the Privy Council sometimes consulted him on the perceived rise in crime. He glamorized himself with the nickname the 'thief-taker general'. As a result of his pursuit of the hero-villain Jack Sheppard (1702–24), Wild himself became unpopular and in 1725 he was hanged for theft and involvement in a gaol break. Wild's great achievement was in making crime newsworthy and a source of media hysteria. Throughout his time as a thief-taker, he ensured that the newspapers followed his exploits and fuelled fear of theft by lurid accounts of the activities of the criminals he then captured. *Jackson's Oxford Journal* carried all sorts of stories that focused on crime: rewards for stolen goods, accounts of thefts and murders, descriptions of criminals at large and accounts of trials and of executions. Crime could be found everywhere.

Elsewhere in Britain, detection of crime was haphazard. In Ireland there was the additional problem that, under a law of 1715, only Protestants could qualify as parish constables; there were so few of them that the office was often left unfilled. Parish constables, helped by watchmen – and in London the city marshal and beadles – were responsible for keeping the peace. Watchmen were established in the reign of Charles II and were nicknamed 'charleys'. Constables were supposed to be chosen from householders in rotation, but the wealthy often paid deputies to act for them. In many parishes in London, Watch Acts replaced the householders' duty to act as constables. In these parishes a tax was raised to pay the watchmen.

By the 1780s most parishes in the capital had a watch system with regular patrols of the streets, but it was not a solution to crime. In 1796 Patrick Colquhoun (1745–1820), a London magistrate, described the watchmen as largely ineffective. They were old men 'often feeble and almost half-starved from the limited allowance they receive'. There were occasional ad hoc solutions, as when John Fielding (1721–80), the blind magistrate (nicknamed 'the Beak') formed the Bow Street runners, an early police force. The runners were formed in 1749 with rights that reached to 4 miles beyond the City of London. The runners were an experiment funded by the government, but eventually they had to raise money from rewards. Fielding was said to be able to identify 3,000 criminals from the sound of their voices. His runners circulated a *Police Gazette*, which listed descriptions of criminals. In time, the *Police Gazette* won a wide readership for its lurid accounts of crimes.

One feature of the early nineteenth century that is familiar today was a growing sense that young people were especially prone to commit crime, and the phrase 'juvenile delinquent' was coined in 1810. Mary Carpenter (1807–77), who had worked in 'ragged schools' in Bristol, published *Reformatory Schools for the Children of the Perishing and Dangerous Classes and for Juvenile Offenders* in 1815. She described the almost feral behaviour of some young criminals, but was convinced that they could be reformed through education. She was influential in persuading the government to make provision for reform schools in the 1854 Youthful Offenders Act. However, accounts of delinquent youths were widespread; newspapers, and especially those in large cities such as Manchester, regularly featured accounts of youth crime. Especially shocking were accounts of gangs of knife-wielding 'scuttlers' who organized muggings and thefts. In consequence, fear of young people and knife crime was an important feature of nineteenth-century Britain.

As in many periods, popular opinion of the level of crime was at odds with the evidence of criminality. Local studies of Kent, Cheshire, Sussex and Surrey after 1688 showed that numbers of serious crimes, such as homicide, seemed to drop significantly. Property crime fell more sharply, while civil disputes were also in decline. Historians have suggested that this represented both a drop in criminality and a reluctance to prosecute it. Possibly the 'bloody code' and the economic growth of the period had some impact on criminality. But popular opinion was that crime was on the rise, partly due to the fact that accounts of crime in newspapers largely came from London, which was by no means representative of the rest of the country. Nevertheless, the perception affected all classes. Even George II deplored the rise in murder and theft in his speech at the opening of Parliament in 1753.

There were, of course, occasional 'crime waves'. In the 1690s, there was a series of audacious highway robberies. In 1691 there was the theft of £2,500 from the Worcester wagon that was carrying tax yields, and a year later £15,000 from another tax wagon. Rewards were offered and proclamations made, but in the years up to the 1720s highway robbery was a major problem. There also seems to have been a correlation between increases in crime and severe winters or poor harvests, and also when troops returned from wars. In 1697, when the army was demobilized after the Treaty of Ryswick, guardhouses were built from Kensington to Westminster to protect travellers from thieving ex-soldiers.

Crime was sometimes glamorized. Dick Turpin (c.1705–39), for example, was hailed as a popular hero despite his activities as a highwayman and a murderer. His unlikely claim to have ridden from London to York in fifteen hours thrilled the readers of his exploits. So did his speech before his execution and the bravado with which – it was said – he threw himself off the gallows to his death. Thereafter, Turpin was portrayed in ballads, theatricals and chapbooks as a popular hero.

Smuggling was sometimes regarded as a 'legitimate crime'. Despite repeated anti-smuggling laws passed in 1698, 1717, 1721 and 1745, smuggling was seen as justifiable evasion of burdensome taxes. Consequently, it was a practice in which some communities colluded with criminals. In the years 1710 to

1720, the Mayfield Gang, led by Gabriel Tomkins, brought together Sussex farmers who smuggled wool to France and excise smugglers who brought back liquor to sell. With magistrates and gaolers in their pay, or sympathetic to them, the gang did not fear the law. By 1717, the Mayfield Gang, together with the Hawkhurst and Groombridge Gangs, dominated most of the Sussex coast. In 1720 there was even a pitched battle between the Mayfield Gang and excise officers. Despite his claim to have smuggled 11 tons of tea and coffee in a single year, Tomkins eventually became an exciseman – a case of the poacher turning gamekeeper that was fairly common in the eighteenth century.

Looting of wrecks on the coasts was similarly regarded as a customary right, rather than a crime. In the Napoleonic wars, Commander James Gardner recalled seeing 300 residents of Hastings looting a boat that had run aground. Such legitimate pickings could be abused; in Cornwall, there were stories of local people luring ships on to rocks so as to loot them of their cargoes. In 1736 the Smuggling Act, seeking to clamp down on smugglers, ended the right to bear arms by making it grounds for arrest. This was a feature of British law that did not enter the US.

Punishment

Deterrence and detection of crime were increasingly problematic, and so was punishment. Popular moral works, such as the *Newgate Calendar*, a widely read series of the confessions and thoughts of criminals as they awaited death in Newgate Gaol, emphasized the terror of the law and the penitence of those who had been convicted. The *Calendar* presented the law as just and unchallengeable. Assize sermons, preached in each town as the assize judges arrived to hear the cases, also highlighted the importance of punishment and its divine origins. In 1752 the Murder Act laid down that a murderer's corpse might be either permanently hung in chains or sold for dissection. This provision was designed as a moral deterrent.

Punishment was the only solution for those who would not listen to the inner voice of God or their consciences or the external voice of magistrates and clergy. The problem was that punishments, including the pillory and executions, were often occasions for popular celebration and drunkenness, so the deterrent effect for spectators was often diluted by the 'entertainment' of watching a criminal hang from the gibbet. In London, the hangings at Tyburn were even known as 'Paddington Fairs'.

Minor criminal offences were dealt with by the magistrates at the petty sessions or, more formally, at the quarter sessions. Serious offences would be handed over to the assizes to be heard by judges on circuits around the country. Stocks, whipping, the pillory, fines and imprisonment were the main punishments. The bridewells, houses of correction or gaols, were intended to be a 'short, sharp shock' rather than for longer periods of imprisonment. For the most part, they 'corrected' poverty, idleness and prostitution. In London, in the 1690s, about 900 people served terms of imprisonment annually, rising to 1,300 in the 1720s. The majority of these were women, which suggests that prisons were used as a means of social control. It also suggests that women's transgressions were regarded as more serious than men's. About 60 per cent of prisoners were debtors, and there was an element of extortion in the imprisonment of a debtor until debts were paid.

In 1729 James Oglethorpe (1696–1785) chaired a House of Commons committee to inquire into the state of gaols. The reports on conditions in the Fleet, Marshalsea and Westminster gaols were horrifying. The wardens paid money to obtain their jobs and therefore needed to recoup it from their prisoners. They did so by charging fees for every possible provision, including bedding, food and nursing. The prisoner, or his relatives, paid up because the alternative was to sleep naked in stone-floored dungeons, shackled with irons and prey to every illness carried by fellow prisoners, especially cholera, which killed half its victims.

Wealthier prisoners could rent separate chambers or apartments, called 'sponging houses'. The warden of the Fleet Prison earned nearly £3,000 a year from the 382 prisoners. The evidence heard by the committee was so shocking that the prisons were condemned as 'barbarous and cruel' in a unanimous resolution of the House of Commons. A Prison Reform Act in 1729 released many debtors from the threat of imprisonment and regulated the behaviour of gaolers. The warden of the Fleet Prison was even charged with the murder of an inmate. The conditions in most prisons did not improve significantly, though.

In the early years of the eighteenth century two new punishments emerged as standard responses of the criminal justice system: prison and transportation of criminals. Before the first decade of the eighteenth century, imprisonment was a relatively rare punishment. Prison was most often used for religious crimes such as violation of the Act of Uniformity of 1661 or for nobles – who might be consigned to the Tower of London. The poverty of most criminals made fines impractical, and the absence of sufficient gaol accommodation prevented the widespread use of imprisonment outside London. In 1706 a law allowed judges greater discretion in the use of branding with a hot iron as a punishment, but practice showed that branding on the cheek tended to make a criminal unemployable and therefore a charge on the Poor Law. Instead of branding criminals the law permitted them to be sentenced to hard labour in gaols.

The lack of prisons also encouraged the use of transportation of criminals. This had been used in the seventeenth century, and was also adopted as a punishment for religious crimes, such as violation of the Clarendon Code. Transportation was also used for the punishment of a large number of Monmouth rebels. This was principally transportation to work in plantations in the West Indies. In 1718, however, transportation was made more widely available to judges as a punishment. It removed the criminal from Britain, provided labour for the colonies and was more proportionate to some crimes than hanging or the pillory. Transportation for life was rare; sentences of transportation or seven or fourteen years were more common. Jonathan Forward, a London merchant and slave trader, was given the contract to transport convicts to the Americas. By 1776, 50,000 British convicts had been sent across the Atlantic.

Transportation quickly became discredited as a system of justice, however. Criminals awaiting transportation often waited – or were transported – in unseaworthy hulks. From 1787, after the loss of the American colonies, Australia also became a place of transportation. In the 'first fleet', forty-five convicts died on the journey and twenty-two babies were born to women convicts en route. The food was execrable and the convicts' clothing often had to be burnt on arrival to prevent infestations of lice and other vermin from taking over the colonies. The first arrivals lived in chaos. They were unable to construct waterproof huts and the marines got drunk and failed to control the convicts, who often wandered off. But, in time, the transportation and the reception of convicts became better organized. It remained a legal punishment until 1868.

Riot and Disorder
Crime could be a community activity. Riot and disorder were sometimes seen as a legitimate political response to food prices and wage disputes. Economically inspired disorder was a response to diverse concerns: turnpike tolls, enclosures, mechanization, land drainage and profiteering. In 1727, 1757 and 1773 there were riots by impoverished tin miners in Cornwall and in 1727 they raided a grain store in Falmouth. This 'moral economy' of the crowd was seen as a way in which people took direct action to redress the imbalances between the rich and poor and restored equilibrium.

There is some evidence that there was a 'legitimizing notion' behind the actions of many mobs. One cause of this was the erosion of customs that protected the poor. For example, farmers more often tried to sell their corn at a higher price for export, or to dealers, rather than to the community that needed food. This 'forestalling' meant that farmers told local people who wanted to buy corn that it was already sold. In Ireland, this led rioters to seek to prevent food exports, as happened in Dublin and Galway in 1740, Limerick in 1741, Wexford in 1757 and Sligo in 1758. The government repeatedly issued orders requiring markets to display regulations against 'forestallers, badgers, leders, broggers, hucksters etc', but to little effect. The mob therefore saw itself as restoring a legitimate paternalist tradition of feeding local communities before farmers sold corn for a profit. In the Rag Fair riots in East London in 1736 the rioters objected to their wages being undercut by cheaper Irish workers.

Evidence that there was a thoughtful element in these hunger-driven riots and disorder can be seen in a number of cases. Sometimes rioters carefully selected their targets, such as the Albion Mills in Blackfriars, London, in 1791 and the Snow Hill steam mills in Birmingham in 1795. Some rioters were keen to shout their loyalty to 'God and the King', and the mobs could also be restrained in their actions. In 1766, in Gloucester, for example, the mob was polite to the farmers that they were protesting against. In 1795, in both Oxfordshire and Ely, rioters asked magistrates to oversee the forced sale of corn at a fixed price from farmers who were seeking to export their grain for a profit.

Mobs were often led by, and included, women. In 1757, a group of women in Taunton gathered in the market square and,

> by means of their united vociferations and repeated clamours, constrained the farmers to bring down the price [of wheat] to six shillings six pence [from eight shillings six pence a bushel] which the good women were willing to pay.

There was also a religious component to the rioters' mentality. In 1772 a warning issued to the gentlemen of Newbury by a mob included the injunction not to make a god of money but to think of the starvation of the poor and of attaining heaven. And in the Welsh village of Llangrannog in the first half of the nineteenth century anti-tithe agitators held a mock auction, selling the patron of the parish to the devil.

Much economic unrest naturally included a political under-current. In 1725 there were malt tax riots in Glasgow, and this was the occasion for people to express their dislike of the Union with England. Even city officials in Glasgow joined the unrest and were obliged to petition George I to release them from gaol. The Porteous Riots, in Edinburgh in 1736, were an expression of support for smugglers and against the city guard, which was associated with the English.

It was to combat this sort of disorder – and the fear of Jacobite uprisings – that the Riot Act of 1714 was passed. The Act allowed magistrates, mayors or aldermen to declare any group of twelve people or more an illegal assembly. Such a gathering was liable to prosecution and forcible dispersal. Before troops or the militia could disperse people, the relevant passage of the Act was read to the assembly. This was:

> Our Sovereign Lord the King chargeth and commandeth all persons, being assembled, immediately to disperse them-selves, and peaceably to depart to their habitations, or to their lawful business, upon the pains contained in the act made in the first year of King George, for preventing tumults and riotous assemblies. God Save the King!

This was known as 'reading the Riot Act'. What made the Act so powerful was that the troops, and anyone assisting the magistrates in dispersing the rioters, were indemnified against any injury or damage to property they caused. It also authorized the death penalty for anyone engaged in such an unlawful assembly if they refused to disperse.

Some single-issue disorders took place, such as the Rebecca Riots: disorders in Wales in the 1830s and 1840s against tolls charged on the turnpike roads. Turnpike toll houses had been destroyed in riots as early as 1734, but by the early nineteenth century, Welsh turnpike trusts charged high tolls and used the money for purposes other than the repair of roads. The cost of tolls placed a serious financial burden on impoverished communities, especially after the poor Welsh harvests of 1837–41. The communities took the law into their own hands: gangs of men, often disguised as women, attacked toll gates. These *merched Beca* (daughters of Rebecca) took their inspiration from Genesis 24: 60 – which included the line 'let thy seed possess the gate of those which hate them' – and were seen as part of the direct action of traditional Welsh justice. The first Rebecca protests broke down toll gates in Carmarthenshire in 1839. Other communities adopted the idea, and Rebecca Riots became widespread. Evidence suggests that rioters did not indiscriminately attack turnpike gates, and the widows who were often toll collectors were left unmolested. Church tithes became a secondary target since clergy were often turnpike trustees. Occasionally these riots led to deaths. After some ring leaders were arrested and transported to Australia, a Royal Commission into the question of toll roads was held and some of the toll gates were removed in 1844.

'Rough Music'

Community disorder could also express popular moral judgements. These protests, marked by the banging of pots and pans, were known as charivari, skimmingtons or 'rough music'; in Wales it was known as *ceffyl pren* (the 'wooden horse'). Such noisy events were intended to embarrass those who had broken the community's norms. They were a combination of mockery, censure, judgement, ostracism, morality, mime and enforcement of patriarchy. In 1790, for example, Alice Evans, the wife of a Shropshire weaver, was subjected to a skimmington for beating her husband in which she was depicted by a man wearing a dress. The men's action was said to be from fear that 'their own spouses might assume the same authority'. In such demonstrations, cuckolds – husbands whose wives had committed adultery – were traditionally depicted wearing horns. In 1731, in Charing Cross, a skimmington was provoked by the marriage of a man in his seventies to a girl of 18; sometimes they were directed at the remarriage of widows and widowers too.

'Rough music' often targeted those who were disliked in the community for other reasons, such as unpopular local officials. In 1800, the Revd Charles Cotterell, rector of Hadley, Hertfordshire, as well as being a magistrate and tax commissioner, was lampooned in verse and a cartoon on his church door. The cartoon showed him saying, 'Oh what a miserable shitting, stinking dogmatic prig of an April fool do I appear.' Occasionally a national figure might be subjected to it, as Bishop Horsley was when he said in the House of Lords in 1791, 'the mass of the people have nothing to do with the laws, but to obey them'. Horsley was burnt in effigy in Rochester, his own cathedral city.

The 'Church and King' mobs also burnt Tom Paine in effigy. These riots, which were principally in Birmingham in 1791–2, were led by activists who opposed the interests of the Dissenters and also sought to counteract what they saw as dangerous French Revolutionary ideas. The rioters, who may have enjoyed the complicity of Anglican gentry and magistrates, targeted the home of Joseph Priestley, the leading Unitarian, whom they regarded as a dangerous threat to the stability of the Church and State.

Challenges to the Sexual Order

The poet Philip Larkin (1922–85) may have claimed that sex was invented in 1963, but our forebears knew of it some time before that. For the most part, sex remained a hidden constant in the lives of people in this period – as it was before and since. But there were occasional challenges to the moral authority of religion and the sexual authority of society at large. Throughout the eighteenth century, in many areas, and in some areas right up to the end of the century, the Church courts regulated moral behaviour. Clergy prosecuted moral offenders in the archdeacon's court (sometime called the 'bawdy court'). Offences tended to be moral transgressions such as fornication (that is unmarried sex) and defamation. If convicted, the offender might be sentenced to a public penance. This involved standing in church, admitting to the offence and promising to reform their behaviour.

In 1776, for example, John Hooper of Luttons Ambo in Yorkshire was required to make a public penance in the parish church for the sin of fornication with Ann Scott. This was typical of the way that Church courts dealt with irregular sexual behaviour. Fornication, adultery, bawdiness and bastardy (giving birth to an illegitimate child) were all dealt with by these courts. Usually a couple caught fornicating were pressed to marry, and women with illegitimate children were persuaded to name and marry the fathers; adultery was often treated with an injunction to stay away from the other party. Other such punishable offences were marital disharmony, failing to keep the Sabbath, drunkenness, swearing and defamation. The purpose of the prosecution was to restore family and parish harmony and the 'natural order of things', to safeguard the moral welfare of the parishioners and to save their souls from damnation. If an offender lapsed they might be excommunicated.

Such ambient sexual transgressions were treated very differently from what were regarded as serious sexual challenges to the natural order of things, such as rape or homosexuality. Rape in the eighteenth century was emerging as a much more serious crime than before: it moved from being treated as a moral transgression of a sexual norm to an assault. Fear of rape grew among middle-class women, with more widespread use of chaperones as protectors. Much domestic sexual violence was probably hidden from view, and rape within marriage was not then an offence in law.

Homosexuality seemed much more worrying because it was perceived as unnatural and thus had overtones of the kind of behaviour associated with witchcraft and mortal sins. While the existence of homosexuality in the Royal Navy, universities, public schools and even in some parts of the court was often ignored (James I, Lord Rochester, William III and Queen Anne were all accused of having same-sex relationships), it was not publicly tolerated. If it emerged too far from the shadows, homosexuality was treated very severely. The Society for the Reformation of Manners organized raids on male brothels, or 'molly houses', in 1698, 1707 and 1726. On the last occasion, when Mother Clap's molly house was raided, constables found men dressed in women's clothes, men engaging in 'marriages' and indecent behaviour in back rooms. Such cases were treated harshly by the law, and the raid on Mother Clap's led to the executions of three men.

Charges of sodomy were rare, not least because of the difficulty of extracting evidence in court. More usually, such cases were treated as assaults, which were easier to prove. Between 1730 and 1830, of 243 cases of the prosecutions of homosexuals, 172 were on charges of assault. The punishment was usually imprisonment or the pillory – which could be a death sentence if the mob threw stones and bricks. There was also a significant amount of homophobic literature, such as *Hell Upon Earth: or the Town in Uproar* of 1729, which denounced homosexuality in London. Homosexuality also caused a wider social anxiety; when Lord Castlereagh became unbalanced and committed suicide in 1822 his demise was marked by a concern that he was about to be exposed as a homosexual.

Lesbianism was never a criminal offence, but could still be pursued in the courts by other means. In 1777 Ann Marrow was prosecuted for fraud for marrying a woman while dressed as a man. In the pillory, she was treated so roughly that she was blinded and left for dead. In such cases, the idea of women enjoying and controlling sex was perhaps the element that troubled the crowd. Yet, when dissociated from sex, lesbian relationships could be treated as charming romantic friendships. Of these, the most celebrated was that of Sarah

Ponsonby (1755–1832) and Lady Eleanor Butler (1739–1829), who eloped in 1778. They set up home together in Llangollen, dressed as men and lived to all intents and purposes as a married couple. Their intellectual pursuits and their charitable work attracted the support of many rich and famous men and women who visited them.

Despite the fact that brothels were relatively common, especially in London, prostitution, whether organized or informal, was treated ambivalently. The availability of 'disorderly women' was widespread, and the word 'whore' became much more commonly used. However, the mob took revenge on prostitutes and brothel keepers. In 1730, when Mother Needham, a well-known brothel keeper, was placed in the pillory, she was pelted to death by the mob. This anger may have reflected men's disquiet that prostitution brought independence for many women, and women's concern that prostitutes' clients were their husbands. Just occasionally prostitution was the path to riches. Lavinia Fenton (1708–60) was sold to a brothel when she was no more than a child, and a client paid £200 for her virginity; in time she took to the stage, and in 1728 ran away with and in 1751 married the (much older) Duke of Bolton, to the scandal of society.

Attitudes to sex in this period were framed in part by the growth of 'politeness', which suggested a greater sympathy by men for the feelings of women. It also led to a greater demand for the perfection and passivity of women and an expectation of sexual numbness, as well as placing a premium on women's reputations and therefore fuelling the growth of defamation suits in Church courts. Marriage in such a polite society was, in the words of Samuel Richardson's (1689–1761) heroine Clarissa, the highest form of friendship. This was a new, affectionate, form of relationship, unlike the property-focused and arranged marriages of previous generations.

As the Church courts declined towards the end of the eighteenth century, moral and sexual offences were regulated by criminal courts and the Poor Law. Workhouses were often the resort of women who could not support themselves during illicit pregnancy or unmarried motherhood. The Magdalen Hospital for Penitent Prostitutes, established in 1758, created a model for the route out of prostitution. There was also a considerable market for moral literature published by the Society for the Propagation of Christian Knowledge (SPCK), including tracts against masturbation and other sexual practices. Folk practices often ran counter to moral precepts: in Wales up to the first half of the eighteenth century there was *priodes fach* ('little wedding'), a sort of trial marriage that allowed cohabitation before the formal solemnization of marriage.

The criminal law was increasingly invoked to regulate brothels and marriages. In an Act of 1752 the prosecution of brothel keepers was made easier. The following year, Lord Hardwicke's Marriage Act prevented poorer men and women from marrying casually for a small fee. The Act required all marriages to be held in churches, in the hours of daylight, and notice to be given by the reading of banns in each of the three weeks leading up to the wedding. The law also set the age at which a couple could marry without parental approval at 21 years. However, the Act did not apply to Scotland, so there emerged the trend of eloping to Gretna Green – just over the Scottish border – where marriages were not regulated by the 1753 Act.

In the second half of the eighteenth century prosecution societies, such as the Society for the Suppression of Vice and the Proclamation Society, resumed vigilante private actions against immorality. The Proclamation Society was established after the publication of George III's proclamation 'For the Encouragement of Piety and Virtue, and for the Preventing and Punishing of Vice, Profaneness and Immorality' in 1787. It was inspired by a fear of atheism and a desire to instil greater moral behaviour, especially in London. The King agreed to make the proclamation at the behest of William Wilberforce, the noted evangelical layman. In 1802 the Society for the

Suppression of Vice became a much more political organization seeking to prosecute radicals and oppose free speech.

By 1857 the Society persuaded Parliament to pass the
Obscene Publications Act and was still going strong in the late
nineteenth century. Nevertheless, there were the first signs of
the emerging liberation of sexual attitudes that came more than
a century after 1850. In 1767, for example, John Wilkes argued
that no one had the right to enquire into an individual's private
amusements if they were not prejudicial to the rest of society.
As early as the 1780s Jeremy Bentham argued that there should
be complete decriminalization of all consenting sexual acts
between adults.

The Challenge to the Constitution: Reform

After 1745, the principal challenge to the State was a growing
demand for political reform that sometimes spilled over into
calls for constitutional change. John Wilkes' campaign
awakened an interest in political reform in Britain that
extended beyond his own interest in being elected. This was
because the Society for the Supporters of the Bill of Rights,
which began as a means to fund Wilkes' campaign, adopted a
wider campaign for reform. It sought more frequent elections,
in the hope that they would make the House of Commons
more responsive to public opinion; lower taxes; and an end to
the corruption of patronage and bribery in the political system.
The supporters of the society were principally merchants and
shopkeepers. These were the commercial forces in society, who
were excluded from the land-oriented political process, but
who were increasingly affluent and educated.

The society focused its activities on petitions to Parliament,
pamphlets and wearing the badges and rings that demonstrated
commitment and membership. It was not just a London-based
campaign; it established local groups in Bristol and Liverpool,
and attracted membership of some leading reformers such as
Josiah Wedgwood. It was closely connected with the London
Corresponding Society formed in 1792, which aimed to draw

together the many local reform societies from all over the country, in places such as Manchester, Nottingham, Derby, Sheffield, Stoke and Tewkesbury, with news and guidance from London. The London Corresponding Society sent handbills to its local associated groups, calling for reforms and organizing petitions. By May 1793, 6,000 signatures had been collected for the first of its petitions.

Also formed in 1792 was Lord Grey's aristocratic Friends of the People, which sought more equal representation and frequent elections. The supporters of political reform had links with the supporters of American colonists and with the campaign to report and publish the proceedings of Parliament. It was also thought that published debates would make the Commons more responsive to popular opinion.

The Society for the Supporters of the Bill of Rights was the model for a number of later societies, one of which was the Society for the Promotion of Constitutional Information, founded by Major John Cartwright, a former naval officer who had fought in the Seven Years War. In 1771 he retired and became a major in the Nottinghamshire militia. His brother was Edmund Cartwright, inventor of the power loom. Drawn to radical causes, having supported the American colonists in their struggle in the 1770s, John Cartwright – alongside Francis Place (1771–1854), Sir Francis Burdett (1770–1844) and William Cobbett – was a radical activist who relentlessly campaigned for the reform of the constitution.

The variety of reform movements in this period can best be seen in the work of two Anglican clergy who supported reform. The first of these was the Revd Christopher Wyvill (1740–1822), rector of Black Notley in Essex. Wyvill had been radicalized by his experiences and education in Cambridge in the 1760s, but had inherited an uncle's estate in Yorkshire. By the late 1770s he was concerned by the catastrophe of the American war and what he saw as the waste and extravagance of the government. He felt that men of property should join in defending the constitution from corruption.

Initially, Wyvill sought changes in economic policy, but soon realized that the problem was more deep-seated. He concluded that only parliamentary reform would improve government, but he was a moderate and gradualist in his approach to reform. He rejected the more radical proposals of Major Cartwright and Thomas Paine; he did not believe in universal suffrage, preferring that the vote should only be restricted to property owners. He also believed that the idea of a secret ballot was unprincipled and that men should be willing to state their electoral preferences publicly. In November 1779 Wyvill called a county meeting in York to petition Parliament for economic and parliamentary reform, and attracted over 600 landowners. The meeting established the Yorkshire Committee, which organized petitions in 1780 and 1783.

Wyvill was adept at using the *York Chronicle* to support his cause. He also successfully spread the model of a county association to landowners in other areas. Wyvill was keen to ensure that radical elements in London did not dominate the campaign for reform. He tried unsuccessfully to interest Rockingham and Fox in his reform proposals, but only Pitt pursued his ideas, and they were defeated in 1783. After this, it was increasingly difficult to keep the Yorkshire Committee together, as factionalism and disagreements grew. Urban radicals drowned out the voices of more moderate landowners, and later the French Revolution made reform seem dangerous to the government. John Cartwright also accused Wyvill of being contemptuous of the working classes. Consequently, Wyvill's own interests returned to economic reform, the abolition of the slave trade and Catholic Emancipation.

If Christopher Wyvill was an 'insider' when it came to the campaign for reform, John Horne Tooke (1736–1812) was not. He was the son of a poulterer and, although he was educated at Westminster and Eton, he was a sizar (that is, a servant who was also a student) at Cambridge. He had been born John Horne but added the surname Tooke after a friend bequeathed him an estate. He certainly inherited a fearlessness from his father, who had once prosecuted the Prince of Wales for nuisance. Horne Tooke wanted to enter the law, but poverty forced him into holy orders and he became the incumbent of New Brentford near London. A social concern for parishioners led him to open a dispensary and to study medicine to help the poor and sick. His real interests, though, lay in radical politics. He was acquainted with the leading thinkers of his day, including Richard Price, David Hume, Voltaire, Laurence Sterne and Adam Smith. By 1764 he supported John Wilkes and was prepared to publish reckless material in *The Petition of an Englishman* of 1765. This accused the King's mother of an illicit affair with Lord Bute and included a map of Kew showing the route Bute took to the royal apartments for assignations.

Horne Tooke's support for Wilkes' repeated election campaigns extended to organizing accommodation for his supporters in his parish, and helping draft petitions. He was also active in the Society of Supporters of the Bill of Rights. In spite of a later rift with Wilkes, Horne Tooke supported his principal causes: annual elections and an end to corruption. His notoriety in London led to the burning of his effigy in 1767. Among the other causes, Horne Tooke espoused were anti-enclosure unrest and the American colonists. His public support in 1777 for a subscription for the victims of the British army at Lexington led to his trial and imprisonment for a year for libel.

Despite this, Horne Tooke was close to William Pitt and joined the Thatched House Tavern petition in 1782, supporting Wyvill and Pitt's modest reform proposals. As Horne Tooke grew older, however, he became more radical. He stood unsuccessfully against Fox in the Westminster election of 1790, and organized the distribution of Thomas Paine's *The Rights of Man* and joined the Friends of the Liberty of the Press, formed at the Crown and Anchor tavern in London in January 1793. Within a year, Horne Tooke was kept under surveillance by the government, and was arrested, but acquitted, on suspicion of supporting an insurrection. He became the grand old man of radical politics, supporting younger men who would carry on the fight for reform in the years to come – Sir Francis Burdett, Francis Place, Jeremy Bentham and William Godwin.

The examples of Wyvill and Horne Tooke show how diverse support for reform was in the second half of the eighteenth century: it extended across a wide spectrum from clergy, aristocrats and landowners to radical republicans and crypto-revolutionaries. Nonetheless, the reform agenda gradually crystallized on the importance of reforming Parliament. This was a persistent issue that would not go away, whatever the responses of the government.

Challenges to the Church

The Church had its own problems; some Anglicans sought to expand its theological boundaries. Since the early years of the eighteenth century there had been tension between High Churchmen, who saw a need to defend the status of the Church and its priesthood, and Low Churchmen, who sought to encourage Dissenters to return to the Church. Low Churchmen also chafed at the restraints the Church placed on their consciences through the Thirty-Nine Articles of faith (the Church's statement of beliefs). All clergymen had to sign the articles, as did students who entered Oxford University and who graduated at Cambridge. Some Low Church clergy, such as Samuel Clarke (1675–1729), the rector of St James' Piccadilly, questioned aspects of the articles and had objections to signing them. In his *Scripture Doctrine of the Trinity* of 1712, Clarke listed all biblical references to the Trinity and concluded it was not a scriptural doctrine. Privately he doubted the full divinity of Christ.

Inspired by Samuel Clarke, Archdeacon Francis Blackburne's *Confessional* of 1766 argued that it was a nonsense to ask clergy to sign articles of faith that could be interpreted in different ways by different people. It was, in any case, argued Blackburne, a restriction on private judgement and sincerity of belief. A similar division affected Dissenters when, at Salter's Hall in 1719, the principal ministers were split. Some supported subscription to articles of belief and others preferred not to have their consciences constrained by what they saw as shackles.

By the summer of 1771 the campaign for freedom from the requirement to subscribe to the Thirty-Nine Articles drew up a petition in the Feathers Tavern in London. This asked Parliament to repeal the need for Anglican clergy to sign the articles. The number of clergy who signed the petition was small, only about 250, but it included some influential clergy, among them Christopher Wyvill and twenty Cambridge fellows (Oxford, the more conservative university, mustered only three). Some significant laymen supported the petition, including Sir George Savile and Lord George Germain as well as Bishops Law of Carlisle and Watson of Llandaff. The petition was rejected by the House of Commons by 217 votes to 71; in 1779 a law relieved Nonconformists of the obligation of subscribing to the Thirty-Nine Articles.

In the wake of the failure of the Feathers Tavern Petition, some notable clergy who doubted the doctrine of the Trinity left the Church. Most had been strongly influenced by Archdeacon Blackburne. They included John Jebb, John Disney, Edward Evanson and Theophilus Lindsey, and they formed a group which agitated for religious freedom. Jebb resigned a living in Suffolk to become a physician; Disney resigned a parish in Lincolnshire to become a political activist and then a Unitarian minister; Evanson left the vicarage of Tewkesbury when he was prosecuted for scruples over the doctrine of the Trinity; and Lindsey, vicar of Catterick, also resigned to become a Unitarian minister.

From the 1770s there were growing demands to repeal the Test Act, which reserved all public offices to members of the Church of England. The demand was on the grounds that the separation of Dissenters from the Church was permanent. Moreover, Dissenters claimed that they had proved their loyalty to the settlement of 1689 and the Hanoverian regime, and consequently they had earned the right to fill public offices. Beginning in 1772, Dissenters made repeated applications to Parliament, calling for the repeal of the Test Act, citing their rights as citizens to religious freedom. A small loosening of the Toleration Act in 1779 did not satisfy them, and their campaign continued to ridicule the Test Act. In 1787 one pamphleteer wrote that, in royal palaces, 'not even a bug can be destroyed ... but by the hallowed hand of a communicant'. It also became clear to ministers that the exclusion of Dissenters from public office in, for example, the Bank of England and the East India Company was no longer in the public interest. Talented Nonconformists were excluded from public office simply on the grounds of religion.

In 1787 a bill for repeal of the Test Act won some support in Parliament, but by the 1790s the government was more in need of Church support than ever and rejected repeal. Fox proposed a repeal of the Test Act in 1790, but that also failed and sparked the 'Church and King' riots in Birmingham. Consequently, Dissenters were now represented as dangerous 'Jacobins' (as revolutionary Frenchmen were known). By 1797 Dissenters admitted that they were further from the repeal of the Test Act than ever, and the challenge was frozen for another twenty years.

Another challenge to the Church came from within. Methodism emerged in the Church of England in the 1730s, when John and Charles Wesley began the Holy Club in Oxford. Its members took communion weekly, held prayer meetings and fasts and visited prisoners in Oxford Gaol. This placed John Wesley in a tradition of High Church Anglicanism that had survived from the seventeenth century. What made Wesley's beliefs distinctive was his claim in 1738 to have been converted, and that salvation depended on conversion to an evangelical faith. Methodists began to preach outside churches and to hold separate meetings from Church services.

Methodists' field and open-air preaching was a particular problem for the Church. It seemed to subvert the whole parish system, and tempted people away from their own churches. Methodism also implicitly impugned the services of the Church by offering an alternative to parish worship. The movement appeared to reject the authority of the bishops, and some, such as Bishops Gibson of London and Lavington of Exeter, were consequently fierce opponents of Methodism. Other bishops welcomed and tolerated it. Methodists continued to worship at their parish churches and met together after services in 'classes', or groups, to pray and hear preachers. As time went on, however, Methodist meetings gradually replaced the weekly parish services – even though John Wesley exhorted his followers not to abandon the Church. In parts of Wales, Methodists and Anglicans continued to worship together well into the nineteenth century.

Wesley's preaching and that of other Methodists such as George Whitefield appealed to folk religion; people were attracted to the emotional power of Methodism, and its call to personal holiness. The Methodist exhortation to rebirth and redemption exerted a compelling pull on the working people of Britain. Some evangelical clergy, like Daniel Rowland (1713–90) in Wales, learned their style of pulpit 'thunder' from Congregational ministers and strongly emphasized sin, punishment and divine retribution. Like the High Church Tractarians a century later, Methodism offered an energy and excitement in its religious appeal. Wesley's sermons also stressed the need for new birth for salvation and justification by faith – it was a doctrine that people were saved by the 'merit of our Lord and Saviour Jesus Christ, by faith, and not for our own works or deservings'.

Methodism's main breach from the Church of England came in 1784, when John Wesley changed his mind about the necessity of ordination by bishops. Without any authority, Wesley ordained clergy who had the power to administer the sacrament; he primarily did this to supply America with Methodist ministers. In effect it was Presbyterian ordination. The action deeply offended the Church, and even Wesley's own brother

Charles, yet John Wesley still claimed to be an Anglican and said that he lived and died a member of the Church of England. By his death in 1791 he had ridden some 700,000 miles (1.1 million km) on preaching tours and had often preached two or three times a day. His publications had earned £20,000 for Methodism, and he had won over 57,000 members and commissioned more than 500 preachers. Most significantly, freed from the costs of a national parish structure, in the nineteenth century Methodism gained ground in some industrial towns of Britain. Though it later fractured into Calvinistic, Wesleyan and other branches, Methodism was to play an important role in the religious life of industrial Britain in the nineteenth century. Even Methodist Sunday schools were feared to be in the hands of the radical supporters of Thomas Paine.

After the death of John Wesley, who had been resolutely conservative and a supporter of the established order, Methodism began to challenge the social order. In 1792 the governing Methodist Conference was strongly influenced by working-class radicalism. Samuel Bradburn, a leading Methodist preacher, claimed that all preachers should support the calls for liberty found in Paine's *Rights of Man*. In the following year political radicals called for Methodism's complete separation from the Church of England. Alexander Kilham, another noted preacher, was a committed republican; although he was later disavowed by the conference, Kilham was influential with Methodists and won widespread support in colliery districts including Tyneside, Cheshire, Staffordshire and Barnsley.

Challenges to the Rational Order

The growing enlightened and rational order of the eighteenth century was countered by the emergence of a Romantic movement in painting, poetry, music, architecture and ideas at the end of the century. Romanticism was also a response to the industrialization and urbanization of Britain. It emphasized imagination, emotion and beauty, and suggested that nature did not need to be tamed as much as experienced in all its raw power. The cool reason of Enlightenment ideas were rejected in favour of demonstrative and passionate expressions of art. These Romantic forms can be found in many fields. The measured, witty and polite poems of Pope, Gay and Gray gave way to the florid passion of William Wordsworth (1770–1850), Percy Shelley (1792–1822) and Lord Byron (1788–1824). The musical elegance and sophistication of Henry Purcell, George Frederick Handel and William Boyce (1711–79) were replaced with the complex virtuosity of George Pinto (1785–1806) and W.S. Bennett (1816–75) and, from the continent, Beethoven and Schubert. In painting, the sociable images of Kneller, Hogarth and Rowlandson were replaced by supernatural, mystical and picturesque works by William Blake, J.M.W. Turner (1775–1851) and John Constable (1776–1837).

In Romantic and Gothic literature, characters took on heroic forms in the works of Sir Walter Scott (1771–1832) and Mary Shelley (1797–1851). Even Jane Austen (1775–1817), who often wrote of domestic issues that were closer to the concerns of the eighteenth century, elevated her male characters into heroes and villains. Austen seemed to combine social realism, derived from eighteenth-century Enlightenment ideas, with a romantic and economic sensibility that captured the imagination of readers then and now. While many of Austen's novels, such as *Sense and Sensibility*, reflected the economic realities of life that would have been familiar to many readers, they also expressed a desire for passionate and fervent relationships.

Britain was open to many stimuli from abroad. Romanticism was derived from German literature and music in the works of Goethe, Schiller and Haydn; French painting in the art of Delacroix and David; French philosophy in the thought of Jean Jacques Rousseau; and later in American literature such as the works of Herman Melville, Edgar Allen Poe and Nathaniel Hawthorne. Even Russian influences from Pushkin and Lermontov brought Romantic ideas to Britain.

While Romanticism is often treated as charming and sentimental, it had a hard edge. Gothic novels were intended to create a sense of horror and fear as well as excitement. Romanticism was also seen by some as a staging post in a decline that led ultimately to fanaticism and insanity. Hannah More, the evangelical writer, feared that romantic and sentimental novels would induce a sense of fantasy among the poor. Some regarded Romanticism as a cause of suicides – and contemporary news coverage gave the impression that this was on the rise.

The heightened emotions of Romanticism could lead to such sensational events as the murder of Martha Ray in 1779. Ray was a singer who became the mistress of Lord Sandwich. She also knew James Hackman, who became besotted with her and asked her to marry him on a number of occasions. It is not clear whether Martha Ray encouraged Hackman, but he became insanely jealous when he suspected she was also seeing Lord Coleraine and killed her at Covent Garden. Lord Sandwich's sorrow at Martha's murder was widely reported, and Hackman blamed an overwhelming unrequited love for her. Equally, John the Painter, an arsonist who set fires in dockyards in Portsmouth and Bristol in 1776–7, was said to have been inspired by the desire for notoriety – a thoroughly Romantic idea. He achieved it, with 20,000 people attending his execution.

Foreign political influences also brought the idea of Romantic nationalism to Britain. Romantics embraced the French Revolution as an idea that promoted French national culture and lore. It also seemed to embody youth and vitality; William Wordsworth later wrote of the Revolution:

Bliss was it in that dawn to be alive
But to be young was very heaven.

The heroic image of 'Marianne' leading the French people in Delacroix's painting of 1830 captured the revolutionary zeal of a heroine urging the republicans to freedom. British Romantics took up the idea of liberty and equality and were especially attracted to the idea of transforming the world into an ideal society. Images of freedom were used on banknotes and coins. William Blake, Percy Shelley and Lord Byron all regarded the Romantic movement as one that supported political rebellion. Romanticism inspired agitators for a number of radical causes, including those against the slave trade and in favour of Irish nationalism.

Similar Romantic nationalism was seen in Poland, the German states, Wales and even in the US. This ideal motivated Lord Byron to fight, and die, in the Greek War of Independence of 1821–9. Byron's poetry spoke of people's yearning to be free and in charge of their own destiny, including the famous lines:

> The mountains look on Marathon –
> And Marathon looks on the sea;
> And musing there an hour alone,
> I dream'd that Greece might yet be free
> For, standing on the Persians' grave,
> I could not deem myself a slave.

Many Romantics, such as Lady Hester Stanhope, who lived in the Lebanon for twenty-seven years from 1812, were aristocrats and wealthy. But ordinary people in Britain were captivated by the often-florid published accounts of the Romantics' lives and exploits. In the 1840s Romanticism inspired the conservative 'Young England' movement of Benjamin Disraeli, which encouraged a nostalgic sense of England as a feudal nation united by the monarchy. By the mid-nineteenth century, Romanticism became a form of wistful longing to return to the values of the medieval period and inspired artists and designers such as Augustus Pugin (1812–52), Thomas Carlyle, John Ruskin (1819–1900) and William Morris (1834–96).

8

CHANGING AND REFORMING BRITAIN

The End of the War

The year 1815 is often seen as a turning point, and in many ways it was. Napoleon was finally defeated, after a decade and a half rampaging across Europe. At the peace settlement in the Congress of Vienna the map of Europe was redrawn. Troops came home and the economy adjusted to peace. These military, diplomatic and economic changes seemed to suggest that everything had changed. Of course it had not.

In Britain, where Napoleon's rule had not reached, social structures and boundaries were unchanged. Much went on as it had before. The parson of Abingdon preached in 1815 that 'we have, as it were, but heard of the war', but few could claim to have been so unaffected. Although the conflict had caused serious problems for Britain, it was more than a decade before significant political and social reforms were introduced. Nevertheless in the immediate post-war period economic and social pressures built up that could not be ignored. Consequently reforms were already underway before the great reforming ministries of the 1830s, so there was not a stark contrast of an 'unreformed' period followed by a reforming one, as is so often suggested.

The final victory over Napoleon came at the Battle of Waterloo, in which 50,000 troops died on all sides; about 10,000 horses were also killed in the battle. It was said that the noise of the battle was so loud it could be heard on the Sussex coast. In the twenty-two years during which Britain had been at war, it had cost the lives of between 200,000 and 250,000 British soldiers and sailors. As a percentage of the country's population, it was far higher than the deaths in the First World War. To pay for the war, the national debt had tripled to £830 million and taxation had quadrupled. There had been other casualties too, including through allegations of corruption in politics. In 1805 Henry Dundas (1742–1811) had been forced from the Admiralty for misappropriation of funds. In 1809, the Duke of York had resigned over rumours that his mistress had taken bribes for the commissions and promotions of army officers. In 1811 George III had finally succumbed to permanent illness and his son George had been made Prince Regent. As a result, the corruption and decay of the old order seemed to have become discredited in the imagination of some. The journalist William Cobbett attacked the regime as one of 'old corruption'.

There was no promise to returning troops of a 'land fit for heroes', and 330,000 demobilized troops and sailors returned, often facing severe poverty. They added to the already serious economic problems of the country. There had been a series of crop failures, and farm workers had also been affected by a wartime rise in rents at a time of a fall in agricultural incomes. In Wales these wages had started to fall in 1813. European farmers, who had been excluded from the market in Britain during the war, were now able to sell their corn to Britain. Some of them did so at desperation prices as their own economies were also suffering. The value of gold declined and interest rates fell as government spending declined sharply.

War industries shut down and workers were thrown out of work. Continental demand for British goods also fell away and competition from abroad was fierce as foreign industries recovered. There was also the cost of maintaining an army of occupation in France, which kept taxes higher than they might have been. Just as in 1945, Britain had won the war but seemed to be losing the peace.

Lord Liverpool, who had succeeded as prime minister in 1812 after Spencer Percival was assassinated, was beset with these concerns. Liverpool had served his political apprenticeship during the troubled ministries of Addington, Portland and Percival, and had been foreign secretary, home secretary and secretary for war, so he was well versed in riding out storms. Liverpool's Tory ministry was dominated by men of the 'middling sort', and sustained by landowners' votes in the Commons. In 1815, faced with falling corn prices, the government passed the Corn Laws. These kept corn prices high for the next thirty years by excluding foreign corn from Britain. Like the European Common Agriculture Policy of 160 years later, the aim of the Corn Laws was to protect farmers by keeping the price of food artificially high so that farm owners maintained their incomes. The poor were its casualties. The Corn Laws would be a millstone round the neck of successive governments in dealing with the poor.

In a bid to ensure the loyalty of the middle classes, income tax, which had been introduced as a temporary measure in 1798, was removed, despite the prime minister's preference to keep it. This made the government more dependent on taxes on goods, which were paid by everyone. The government's finances also faced serious problems; payment of interest on the national debt took half the government's income. In an attempt to control the money supply to restrain inflation, in 1819 the government returned to the gold standard and this deflation intensified the depression.

These were not the only economic problems facing the country. Mechanization in industries such as weaving had replaced handloom weavers with powered looms. In agriculture, threshing machines did the work of many labourers, and the conditions and pay of most workers were low. These circumstances led to violence, machine wrecking and food riots by the starving. The radicals, who argued for wholesale changes to correct these, connected the conditions of the poor with the need for parliamentary reform. All this made ministers worried, particularly the reactionary Home Secretary Lord Sidmouth. These anxious ministers clenched their fists and insisted on maintaining public order. Sidmouth was joined by the reactionary ministers Lord Chancellor Lord Eldon (1751–1838) and Foreign Secretary Lord Castlereagh in demanding a stern response to lawlessness. The flexible but fairly passive Prime Minister Liverpool allowed these ministers to have their way in the first years after the end of the war.

While the government regarded economic policy as its domain, it did not accept that it had a role in relief of poverty. This was the job of the parishes, and the parishes were inundated with the poor, many of whom were demobbed soldiers and sailors. By 1818 the cost of poor relief rose to £18 million – it had been only £4.25 million fifteen years earlier. In Cardiganshire, for example, the cost of the poor rates doubled in the three years after 1816. The Speenhamland system of 'outdoor' relief suddenly seemed a bad idea. A negligent employer could pay starvation wages in the knowledge that the ratepayers would have to make up the wages to a living level.

Revolution and Reform

In such conditions, historians often wonder why Britain did not experience a revolution of the kind that happened in much of Europe in the first half of the nineteenth century. Between 1815 and 1848 France had three revolutions. There were the makings of revolutionary feelings in Britain. The Prince Regent, later King George IV, was enormously unpopular. He was satirized in the press as gluttonous and self-indulgent. At his coronation his wife, Caroline of Brunswick, who had been out of the country for over a decade, returned and was prevented from entering Westminster Abbey in an embarrassing scene. The country was, as today, discomforted by royals who did not behave with decorum. In their subsequent divorce, Caroline became popular, despite evidence that she had been unfaithful to the King.

The government was also unpopular. In 1820 the Cato Street conspiracy planned to murder the Cabinet while it dined at Lord Harrowby's house. It was only foiled at the last moment. Popular unrest occurred in such events as the Spa Fields Riots in London in November and December 1816. In August 1819 the Peterloo Massacre took place in St Peter's Fields, Manchester. The local magistrates had turned mounted militia onto a local protest meeting that was seeking universal suffrage, and was being addressed by the radical Henry 'Orator' Hunt (1773–1835). The militia was ill-organized, poorly commanded and simply cut a swathe through the crowds. Eleven people were killed and 400 injured by the troops. When Hunt was brought to London to stand trial for his role in the Peterloo debacle, he was acclaimed a hero, while prints circulated of sabre-wielding troops slashing at ordinary people.

The reactionary instinct in the government worsened its management of events. The repression by the government reached its peak in the Six Acts, which even the Prime Minister called 'odious'. These granted magistrates almost unlimited powers to search for arms, criminalized the use of arms, restricted the right to bail, required permission to be given for public meetings, increased penalties for authors of anti-government tracts and imposed a tax on newspapers and a bond for editors to prevent the growth of anti-government newspapers.

Explanations of why Britain did not have a revolution in this tense atmosphere are varied. Britain's relatively open social system, which allowed enterprising people to rise through the ranks of society, may have prevented the emergence of a class of talented but frustrated people who turned to revolution. Such an open system also reduced tension compared to closed aristocratic societies, such as pre-Revolutionary France. Conversely, perhaps religion, and especially Methodism, played a highly effective role in teaching people that there was a natural order to society and each person had their place, to which they should resign themselves.

Another important explanation lies in the flexibility of the government in seeing the dangers that faced it. In 1822 Liverpool was able to transform his ministry when Lord Castlereagh committed suicide. In his place as foreign secretary, Liverpool promoted the more liberal George Canning. He also brought in other liberal Tories, such as John Robinson (1782–1859) and William Huskisson. Canning's reputation for liberal Toryism was cemented when he supported the Greek revolt against the Ottoman Empire, guaranteeing Greek independence. Liverpool's new liberal Tory ministry changed the strategy of confrontation with the people to one of amelioration of their problems. In the budgets of 1824 and 1825 the government moved towards free trade, which cut prices and stimulated trade with the colonies. The window tax was also reduced. John Robinson, the new chancellor of the Exchequer, was soon nicknamed 'Prosperity Robinson'. It was originally a sarcastic slur by the journalist William Cobbett, but it soon stuck as the economy picked up. Cobbett also nicknamed Robinson 'Goody Goderich' (when Robinson was created Viscount Goderich), and later Goderich was embarrassed by stories that he broke down in tears when under pressure.

William Huskisson was appointed president of the Board of Trade and succeeded in persuading Tory merchants to accept a gradual freeing of trade and relaxation of protectionist laws. (In 1830 he also gained notoriety as the first person to die in a railway accident, being run over by Robert Stephenson's (1803–59) *Rocket* at the opening of the Liverpool to Manchester railway.) Robinson and Liverpool were lucky that agriculture also experienced an upturn, which reduced some of the worst problems of the poor. But, through the tactic of economic concessions, the government did enough to prevent radical demands for change from boiling over.

It was not just in economic policies that Liverpool's post-1822 Tory government became more liberal. Some ministers, such as Robert Peel, recognized that reform and the maintenance of social order were not in conflict. Robert Peel was the son of a textile manufacturer, and a representative of a new breed of sons of merchants who entered politics. He did not therefore carry the baggage of aristocratic values and was willing to respond flexibly to events as they arose. Peel's reform of prisons and his establishment of the Metropolitan Police in 1829 are examples of such reforms, and earned him a reputation as a pioneering home secretary. Peel's motive in forming the Metropolitan Police was to avoid the need to call on the army so often to restore order. In doing so, Peel drew on his experience of establishing a police force while he was chief secretary for Ireland a decade earlier.

As home secretary, Peel reduced the 278 criminal offences to 8 major criminal statutes; he also removed more than 200 capital offences. Peel's prison reforms were inspired in part by Thomas Fowell's *Inquiry Whether Crime and Misery Are Produced or Prevented by our Present System of Prison Discipline*, published in 1818. Other reforms were more cautious, such as the repeal of the Combinations Acts in 1824, which permitted workers to join trades unions; but the right to strike was denied them in the following year.

Some members of the government also seemed to appreciate that the process of politics was subtly changing. In 1823, for example, George Canning was the first politician to tour the country, giving speeches on government policy. While familiar today, it was attacked by his colleagues as 'a new system among us and excites great indignation'. The King disapproved of what he saw as blatant demagoguery. Canning was also a prolific note-sender; in 1826 he was criticized for sending a dozen notes on government business to the Duke of Wellington in a day. But his colleagues tolerated this as he was the most talented politician and finest speaker of the day.

However, the twin demands of Catholic Emancipation and the reform of Parliament continued to dog politics. In 1821 Parliament agreed to strip the rotten borough of Grampound of its MPs after a particularly corrupt election in which bribery was rife. There were proposals to award the Grampound seats to the growing town of Leeds – though this was rejected in favour of adding them to the rural county seats of Yorkshire. Nevertheless, the anomaly of many small boroughs electing MPs when large cities did not was increasingly apparent. But the Tories, who had held power since 1812, saw no reason to change the franchise or redistribute seats more widely.

The issue of granting the right to political representation to Catholics was so fraught that the government stuck to a policy of neutrality on the issue. To many people, though, laws passed during the religiously fraught days of the seventeenth century seemed to have little function in the 1820s. Lord Liverpool was willing to accept Catholics as voters but not to give them the right to be MPs. However, when Canning, Robinson and Huskisson joined the Cabinet, a majority were in favour of Catholic Emancipation. The real problem with Catholic Emancipation was that it would destabilize an already-volatile Irish political scene. In Ireland, the Catholic Association, an alliance of Irish gentry and tenant farmers under the lawyer Daniel O'Connell (1775–1847), was campaigning for Catholic Emancipation. On a number of occasions in the 1820s there were attempts to admit Catholics to the House of Lords, but these were rejected.

It was left to the Duke of Wellington, who succeeded Liverpool as prime minister in 1828, to concede Catholic Emancipation – although not the case for parliamentary reform. In some respects the change of policy reflected Wellington's skill as a tactician rather than as a politician. From 1778 onwards, the religious settlement of 1689 had been gradually eroded. A Catholic Relief Act allowed Roman Catholics to own property, inherit land and join the army, as long as they swore an oath against Stuart and papal claims in Britain – this had been the cause of the Gordon Riots in 1780. The Roman Catholic Relief Act of 1791 gave the vote to Roman Catholics who owned or rented land with an annual value of £2. It also permitted Catholic admission to many middle-class professions such as the law and judiciary. But at the time of Union with Ireland, despite the promise of reform, George III refused to consider repeal of the laws outlawing Catholicism. Since then, many English boroughs had petitioned Parliament that they did not want any grant of Catholic Emancipation. The shadow of Ireland continued to loom over British politics.

Ireland remained the focus of demand for repeal of the penal laws because it contained so many Catholics. In 1823, Daniel O'Connell campaigned for repeal of the Union, and used Catholic Emancipation as his main argument; to do this, he formed the Catholic Association. In 1828 O'Connell stood for election in County Clare and was elected, but as a Catholic was barred from taking his seat in the House of Commons. He was elected again in 1829. The serious threat of widespread unrest in Ireland led Wellington and the Home Secretary, Sir Robert Peel, to reverse their previous judgements. Peel was especially influential, his period as chief secretary of Ireland giving him an insight into how explosive the Irish situation could be.

The government conceded and introduced the Catholic Relief Act, which removed the remaining restrictions on Roman Catholics. O'Connell himself asked, 'who would have expected such a Bill from Peel and Wellington?' On 4 May 1829 Daniel O'Connell took his seat, the first Catholic to sit in the Commons since the Reformation. At the same time, as a concession to Ultra-Tories, who were shocked by Wellington's change of policy, the property qualification for voters was tightened, rising from a rental value of £2 to £10 a year. This restricted the vote to more affluent people. The Catholic middle classes benefited from these measures, but few of

O'Connell's supporters did. The only remaining impediment to Catholics remains the bar to their succession to the throne under the Act of Succession of 1701.

Parliamentary Reform

The Ultra-Tories, those who were most uncompromising in their opposition to reform, were appalled by what they saw as Wellington's betrayal over Catholic Emancipation, and the Duke even fought a duel with Lord Winchelsea over the issue. In the election following the death of George IV in 1830, Wellington lost power to the Whigs. A conservative recognition of the need for some change was as much a factor in Wellington's concession of Catholic Emancipation as was an aversion to social conflict – just as Liverpool's economic compromises had been earlier in the 1820s. But the Tories' grudging concessions were in stark contrast to the Whigs' embrace of reform, and especially of parliamentary reform.

Excluded from power for more than two decades, the Whigs had had a long time to consider their policies and how to obtain power. Besides their own growing commitment to reform, the Whigs saw reform as a key electoral asset. The Whigs' predominant concern was the need to grant the middle class representation in Parliament. A report issued by the Society of the Friends of the People indicated that 154 landowners who owned or controlled rotten boroughs were able to choose about half the members of the Commons. The report pointed out that the boroughs of Gatton and Old Sarum had only two and seven electors respectively. Such rotten boroughs and the over-representation of rural counties meant that the borough and county seats in Cornwall, Wiltshire and Yorkshire elected more MPs than all the new industrial cities of the Midlands and north of England. Moreover the right to vote varied from borough to borough. In Preston, for example, the right to vote was lodged in any male who had spent the night before the election in the town, whereas in other towns the vote was restricted to members of the town council.

The new Whig government under Lord Grey (1764–1845) that succeeded Wellington in 1830 was remarkable because its members were committed to reform of both Church and State. Foremost among them was the Lord Chancellor, Henry Brougham (1778–1868), who had been committed to every radical cause since he had espoused the abolition of slavery in 1810. Grey, however, was a modest reformer with a commitment to rule by the aristocracy, which he saw as the class that could alone guarantee the security of the state. Nevertheless, with Lord John Russell (1792–1878), Brougham persuaded Grey that reform of Parliament was a necessity.

Just as Wellington and Peel had felt forced to compromise on the issue of Catholic relief in 1829, revolutions in 1830 in France, Austria, Prussia and Russia added a sense that governments were in danger if they did not make concessions. At home there were the Swing Riots in the agricultural counties of the south of England. A combination of low wages, high unemployment and the mechanization of farming turned starving farm workers to violence. Already by 1830 there were large numbers of unemployed farm workers; in Kent and Suffolk this rose to a third of the male population. Poverty led to desperate measures. In Norfolk between 1800 and 1830 the number of committals to gaol trebled and many of these were for arson and poaching.

Starting in Kent, and often accompanied by intimidating letters to magistrates and landowners from the fictitious 'Captain Swing', the Swing Riots spread. They reached Surrey, Sussex, Middlesex and Hampshire and then the midland counties. Unrest grew more severe as the winter of 1830 drew on. The riots seemed to be organized and followed a pattern of protest. Typically, farm labourers, in groups of 200 or more, would threaten landowners if they did not concede their demands. Often there were calls for free trade to reduce the price of corn. Threshing machines were destroyed. The workhouses, tithe barns and buildings that were the object of popular protest were also attacked and the burning of hayricks often took place. It was claimed that not a single individual was killed during these disturbances – suggesting they were principally property riots, but there were other factors too. Swing disturbances were especially vehement in areas where Nonconformity was also strong. The Swing Riots have been seen as an early example of a sophisticated working-class protest movement.

The Home Secretary, Lord Melbourne (1779–1848), responded with tough measures. A special commission, necessitated by the intimidation of magistrates, put rioters on trial. Nineteen were hanged and nearly five hundred transported. Gradually the riots declined, but the government had been shaken by the events of 1830–31. Swing Riot areas were prone to intermittent disturbances for some years. In later protest movements, such as that against the Poor Law, the pattern of disturbance was often also marked by rick burning and intimidation. For farmers, the growth of farm insurance was one of the consequences of the riots.

It was not only agricultural workers who were agitating for change. In 1830 Thomas Attwood, an economist, established the Birmingham Political Union (BPU). The union argued for extension of the right to vote and redistribution of seats in Parliament to the industrial cities. What was significant about the BPU was that it mobilized the middle classes. BPU meetings brought huge attendances, including 200,000 in May 1832. The BPU was a non-violent organization and had a strong influence on the Whig government as a consequence.

Determined to make judicious concessions in order to prevent demands for greater reform, Lord Grey proposed the Great Reform Bill in 1831. Despite Grey's limited objectives, some were shocked by what they saw as the abandonment of aristocratic control of elections. Grey proposed that sixty boroughs, each with populations below 2000, should be completely disenfranchised and forty-seven boroughs would lose one of their two MPs; fifty-five seats were to be redistributed to English counties and forty-two to the unrepresented industrial towns such as Manchester, Birmingham and some London boroughs. The right to vote was also to be standardized to a £10 household value in boroughs and in counties the 40-shilling freeholders were joined by £10 copyholders and £50 leaseholders. Altogether this raised the electorate from 5 per cent to 7 per cent of the male population, to just a little over 700,000. In Scotland, however, the electorate would rise from 4,579 to 64,447 – an enormous increase.

During the debate on the Reform Bill in April 1831, after a marathon all-night session, the bill passed the Commons by a single vote. Lord Macaulay (1800–59) said that witnessing the vote was a great historic moment, like watching Caesar being stabbed or Cromwell taking the mace from the Commons table. Lord John Russell, one of the bill's supporters and a long-standing advocate of Parliamentary reform, famously claimed, 'for the institutions of the country to be stable, they must be founded on the general regard'. But the bill was rejected by the Lords in October, sparking riots across the country. The Archbishop of Canterbury and twenty other bishops had voted against the bill, and this added a strong anti-clerical flavour to the unrest. In Derby, the army had to be called out to stop rioters; in Nottingham, the castle was burnt down; and in Bristol, three days of riots saw the Bishop of Bristol's palace attacked.

By April 1832, the bill had passed the Commons again but it was unlikely to get a majority in the Lords, so Grey asked the King to make sufficient new peers to vote the bill through the Lords. William IV initially refused, but when Wellington could not form a government he conceded and promised to make sufficient peers if necessary. The use of the royal prerogative to create peers to form a majority in the Lords had been used by Queen Anne, and was to be used again in 1911. Meanwhile, the attention of the country was fixed on Parliament; in Abingdon the stagecoach bringing news of the vote on the bill was mobbed by people wanting to hear the result. Rather than lose the Tory majority in the Lords through the creation of large numbers of new Whig peers, Wellington led over 100 peers out of the Lords to abstain in the vote and the bill finally passed. In delight, the Birmingham Political Union disbanded.

The Whigs were not committed to further reform. In fact, a petition to permit women to vote was flatly rejected by Parliament in August 1832. Lord John Russell, who had strongly supported reform, was nicknamed 'Finality Jack' in 1837 when he said that the Reform Act was sufficient and that no further changes were needed in the voting system. At the time, Peel said that, far from being final, the Reform Act would open doors that it would be impossible to shut. He was right: further parliamentary reform bills were passed in 1858, 1867, 1872, 1883 and 1884.

The claim that the Reform Act was a great step on the way to British democracy is difficult to sustain. Increasingly, the Act is seen as little more than an attempt to let off steam from an overheating political system. Not much was changed by 1832. Perhaps the main significance of the Act was that the Whig government had shown its flexible response to the political circumstances of the day, and even the King and the Tories had accepted the need to do so. In contrast, European monarchies had been badly damaged by their refusal to concede change during the revolutions of 1830.

The Reform Act did not signal a general liberalization of society, as shown in the treatment of the Tolpuddle Martyrs. In 1834 a group of six farm workers who had joined a friendly society that protested at low wages refused to work for less than 10 shillings a week. They were prosecuted because they went through an initiation ritual to join the society that made them open to accusation of treason. In the ritual the workers were bound by the eyes, led into a room and read a paper that, it was said, some did not understand. They were read passages from the Bible and told to kiss the book. Some of the members wore white sheets and called each other 'brother'. The local farmer prosecuted the workers using an obscure 1797 law that prohibited the use of oaths. All six were found guilty and sentenced to transportation to Australia for seven years. Within two years they were reprieved, but they became a *cause célèbre* and were an inspiration for early trades unionism.

Factories, Mines and the Poor

In the first two decades of the nineteenth century, a number of members of the House of Commons had become concerned by the working conditions of people in factories and elsewhere. Evidence given to a select committee in 1817 investigating climbing boys recorded that smaller boys were more valuable to employers because they could get into chimney crevices. When asked about the hygiene of the children, one chimney sweep replied, 'I wash mine regularly; but some boys of the lower classes are not washed for six months.' The hard skin that working boys developed on their knees and elbows was built up over months of hard work; some employers helped the process by rubbing brine into the boys' skin. The boys were frequently kicked and physically abused by their employers. The concern at the treatment of such workers was shared by some Tories, such as Michael Sadler, the MP for Leeds. In 1830, a Commons select committee investigated the conditions in factories and heard horrifying evidence. Children's limbs and shoulders were deformed from having to carry heavy weights; they sometimes fell into machinery and received terrible injuries. Some children were beaten, most were paid at starvation levels and parents reported the demoralization of family and religious life.

Richard Oastler (1789–1861), a campaigner for factory reform, contrasted the relatively benign system of children working alongside parents in cottage industries with the exhaustion of children of 5 or 6 years of age who could not stay awake over their work in factories. The report of the Commons committee in 1831–2 revealed that girls sometimes worked from 3 a.m. to 10 p.m. They had just fifteen minutes for breakfast, thirty minutes for lunch and fifteen minutes to drink water. Often the children fell asleep when eating. Factory

Acts in 1802 and 1819 had sought to improve the lot of workers, but the penalties were derisory, and there were no means of enforcing these laws.

Besides the evidence of the select committee on factory conditions, the Whig government of the 1830s was strongly influenced by evangelicals. Among these were William Wilberforce and junior ministers Lords Howick, Milton and Morpeth, who accepted the moral case for factory reform. Wilberforce, when accused of being a fanatic, replied: 'if to be feelingly alive to the sufferings of my fellow creatures is to be a fanatic, I am one of the most incurable fanatics ever permitted to be at large'. Other Whigs were persuaded by the Utilitarian argument that factory reform would contribute to the peace of society and support the productivity of businesses.

The success of the Ten Hours Movement – led by Anthony Ashley Cooper, later Lord Shaftesbury – as a pressure group that argued for reform of factory working hours, was also seen in the government's decision that factories could not be permitted to continue without reform. In 1831 the government outlawed night working for those under the age of 21. Two years later a Factory Act outlawed work by those under the age of 9 and imposed a maximum length of the working day with breaks for lunch and for education of those between 9 and 14 years. More important, the Act brought in a system of factory inspections to enforce the law. This was a major step forward and forced factory owners to comply with this and existing laws. In the following years, inspectors managed to achieve an 80–90 per cent success rate in their prosecutions of factory owners who ignored the law.

From this date 'shifts' of workers replaced the system of long working hours. As Robert Owen had already discovered from his enlightened factory system, productivity went up when workers were not exhausted and were treated relatively more generously. There remained less enlightened attitudes to adults in factories: in 1833 it was reported that Glasgow had 12,000 factory workers each earning less than 11 shillings a week, but most people seemed unconcerned about the level of pay and exploitation of adults in factories.

In the 1840s attention turned to the mines. The 1842 *Report on the Physical and Moral Condition of the Children and Young Persons Engaged in Mines and Manufactures* recorded that a 7-year-old boy in Ilkeston was not permitted to sleep at work and had only energy to eat before sleeping at home. One collier reported that children often needed to be carried home from the mines by their fathers. There were also accounts of young girls working next to naked men in the mines. Lord Londonderry, however, claimed that it was physically rewarding for children to work in his mines. Following the report, in 1842 a Mining Act outlawed work in mines by women, and children below the age of 10. Mining inspectors were appointed to ensure that the Act was enforced. The inspection of mines was strengthened in 1850 when inspectors were empowered to enter the mines themselves to check on conditions.

Poverty was much less easily regulated than factories or mines. The Poor Law Amendment Act of 1834 was the result of a royal commission that investigated the working of the old system of poor relief. The commission made two main recommendations. First it proposed a system known as 'less eligibility' – that people had to be deterred from entering workhouses by making conditions in them worse than those outside. In this way, only the most needy and desperate would consider entering a workhouse. Workhouses would take on the flavour of prisons and places of punishment. Secondly, the old system of outdoor relief was to be reduced and poor relief should only be available in the workhouse. The old system had been discredited by employers reducing wages in the knowledge that the poor rates would make up wages to a living level. It had also been affected by migration of workers to towns in search of work, which made urban ratepayers bear a disproportionate cost of the poor.

The 1834 Act established the Poor Law Commission to oversee the organization of small parishes into Poor Law

Unions. These unions could pool resources to build their own workhouses. Outdoor relief, while not abolished, was 'discouraged'. When the implications of the law were recognized, the workhouse became an object of fierce hatred among the poor; even *The Times* objected to its brutality. Scandals, such as that revealed at Andover in 1846, showed the people were brutalized by the system and the poor were effectively criminalized. In the Andover workhouse, the master starved the inmates until they had to eat pig swill and bone marrow to survive; he also sexually abused the women. Although there was some reform of the system, a similar scandal in Huddersfield in 1848 indicated that little had changed. Charles Dickens (1812–70) wrote *Oliver Twist* in 1838 partly to point out the horrors of the Poor Law system for a boy born into a workhouse.

A Reforming Agenda?

Grey's and Melbourne's ministries in the 1830s can be regarded as the first governments to undertake a planned series of reforms. The pattern of a commission or committee to investigate an issue before legislation was proposed was established in the Poor Law, factory, mining and other reforms. The Whig aristocrats who dominated these governments regarded reform as a noble obligation, and many were influenced by religious or Utilitarian views, but they were careful to avoid radical or extreme measures. The reforms they proposed were practical rather than ideological, and responded to the circumstances of the time and to pressure from outside Parliament. For example, the law of 1836 that all births, marriages and deaths were to be registered by the State rather than only in churches was one that facilitated the political use of census data held by the registrar general in London.

Similarly, in 1837 Rowland Hill (1795–1879) proposed a uniform penny post, which would enable all postal items to use the simple and cheap penny post system established by Charles II. Beginning in 1840, the penny post ushered in the use of postage stamps and was also credited with further promoting literacy among the working classes. Postage costs were problematic even then: the penny post scheme was ruinous to the post office; it took until 1870 for postal revenues to recover from the losses it caused.

In 1835 the Municipal Corporations Act reformed elections to local government in towns along the lines of the parliamentary Reform Act. An Act in 1833 had already reformed the Scottish boroughs. The 1835 law gave the vote in 178 urban corporations to ratepayers, granting representation to 10% of the adult males. Each corporation was to have a mayor, aldermen and councillors. They were also permitted – without being required – to make provision for street paving and lighting, sewers, water supplies and police. Perhaps more significant was that a third of each council was elected each year, giving ratepayers much more experience of regular elections.

Other reforms adopted by the Whig government were motivated by some moral principles rather than simple expediency. In 1833 slavery was abolished, forbidding the ownership of slaves throughout the British Empire. It was the product of a new campaign by the Anti-Slavery Society. Former slave owners were compensated with £20 million for the loss of their slaves, and most slaves became apprentices employed by their former owners.

The Church of England was also the subject of reform, although the reformers' aim was to preserve the Church rather than undermine it. In 1835 an ecclesiastical commission was established by Peel, who briefly served as prime minister, to report on the condition of the Church in England and Wales. The commission paid particular attention to the revenues of the Church and cathedrals and the unequal size of dioceses. A year later, when the Whigs were back in power, the Ecclesiastical Commissioners Act established a permanent commission, which would receive all Church revenue and redistribute the incomes of the dioceses and cathedrals. The Act also extensively rearranged the dioceses and equalized bishops' income, and, four years later, another law also reorganized cathedrals. The government saw these measures as supporting the Church, but for some they emphasized that the Church of England had not been well organized in the past and was losing ground to Nonconformist churches. In 1836 the Tithe Commutation Act removed the payment of tithes in kind and commuted them to cash payment.

A major religious issue in this period was the provision of schools. The Church had previously been the principal provider of education through parish schools and its dominance of the universities. In the turbulent sphere of religious politics the Anglicans and Nonconformists were strong enough to see off any threat from radicals who wanted a wholly secular education system free of religious control or affiliation. Equally, the Nonconformists and radicals were able to prevent an Anglican monopoly over education. Accordingly, the Whig government made grants to support schools that both Anglicans and Nonconformist denominations could receive. Consequently the faith schools of today had their roots in the 1830s.

Moral issues extended to the lot of animals. The Royal Society for the Protection of Cruelty to Animals (RSPCA) was founded in 1824, originally as the Society for the Prevention of Cruelty to Animals, and was granted a royal charter in 1840. It was established by reformers including Richard Martin MP and William Wilberforce as a consequence of a new law to prevent cruelty to cattle. The law had excluded bulls to allow the continuation of bull-baiting, which seemed intolerable to Martin and Wilberforce. The society was strongly influenced by religious ideals – a number of its leading members were clergymen – and by emerging philanthropic attitudes to society.

Initially the society formed a committee that monitored markets and slaughterhouses. It also reported on the conduct of coachmen towards their horses. These were the forerunners of RSPCA inspectors. In its first year the society prosecuted sixty-three offenders, and by 1841 it employed a number of inspectors who toured the country to prevent cruelty. In 1835 the society persuaded the government to pass an Act that outlawed bull-baiting and was the first of a series of laws that clamped down on various forms of cruelty towards animals. It also marked the growing sentimentality of Victorian society towards animals – and perhaps more humane and refined attitudes to them. It was a long time since seventeenth-century towns had had their own bull-baiting collar and ring.

Popular Protest Movements

The Ten Hours and factory reform movements, the RSPCA and other popular campaigns that had led to changes in the law existed alongside two other major important reform movements in the 1830s and 1840s. These were the Chartists and the Anti-Corn Law League. The Chartist movement was a multi-faceted form of protest with many roots. Some Chartists inherited a radical tradition that went back beyond the eighteenth century, and saw themselves in a line of descent from Magna Carta and the Levellers of the seventeenth century in defending 'old English liberties'. Others resented the criminalization of the poor by the new workhouses, were early trades unionists or were disappointed that the Reform Act of 1832 had achieved so little. As the movement developed it also attracted those who aimed at deindustrialization and wanted a 'return to the land'.

The short-lived Chartist Land Company sought to buy smallholdings for workers to farm their own land. What marked the Chartists out was their focus on constitutional change. They hoped that further reform of Parliament would give equity and justice to the poor. The charter, from which they took their name, was formed in 1838 and sought six changes: universal male suffrage, annual elections, secret ballot, equal-sized constituencies, abolition of the property qualification for MPs and the payment of MPs. There were some Chartists who embraced violence as well as moral force to support their case.

When, in July 1839, a Chartist petition with more than a million signatures calling for the six points of the charter was presented to Parliament, the Commons refused to receive it. In reaction, Chartism became more sympathetic to those who advocated the use of violence. In November 1839 there was a Chartist uprising at Newport, South Wales, led by John Frost (1784–1877). The uprising caused twenty deaths and had to be put down by the army. In the depression of 1840–41 Chartists organized strikes and industrial unrest in Scotland, Yorkshire, Lancashire and the Midlands. In parts of Yorkshire, Chartists also attacked workhouses. The last attempt by the Chartists to persuade Parliament of their cause was the great petition of 1848.

The 1848 petition was organized by Feargus O'Connor (1795–1855). O'Connor was a former MP who had founded the *Northern Star*, a campaigning newspaper, and organized the London Working Men's Association, which sought to engage skilled workers in the demand for reform. O'Connor planned a mass meeting held on Kennington Common as a rally to receive the petition. There was concern among the police at how large and peaceful the meeting would be, and in fact, O'Connor was relieved when the police arrived at Kennington as his watch had been stolen by a pickpocket. Then a procession went to Westminster to present the petition to Parliament. O'Connor said there were 500,000 at the Kennington meeting, while the government claimed there were only 15,000. From their spies and informants, ministers knew there was no intention of unrest but there were fears of a spontaneous rising. Just in case, the royal family had left London for the safety of the Isle of Wight. The government used 8,000 troops and 150,000 special constables – among them Gladstone and Louis Napoleon, the future Emperor Napoleon III of France – to control the procession, which was not permitted to cross the Thames. When presented to Parliament, the petition of 1.9 million names was found to include false signatures claiming to be those of Queen Victoria and Mr Punch! Given the revolutions convulsing the rest of Europe in

1848, Gladstone thought that the avoidance of political violence during the Kennington protest was remarkable. Although the Chartist movement was a failure in the 1840s, it laid out a clear agenda for reform, and five of the six demands of the charter were achieved by 1918. Chartism also gave a boost to the development of trades unions and to working-class self-help movements.

If the Chartists were the epitome of a working-class 'outsider' movement, the Anti-Corn Law League was a strong contrast. Formed in 1838 in Manchester and led by the MPs John Bright (1811–89) and Richard Cobden (1804–65), the league counted professional people among its members and employed its own solicitor to deal with legal issues. The aim of the league was to help boost industry by removing the Corn Laws, which kept prices artificially high. The league argued that if food was cheaper, wages could fall. It promoted the cause of free trade for clear economic reasons, but also because it would promote good relations between the countries of the world. The league combined pressure on Parliament – including annual motions against the Corn Laws – with speaking tours of Scotland and England to promote the cause of free trade. It also formed deputations to argue the case for the repeal of the Corn Laws to ministers and influential people. Among these was the Tory Prime Minister, Sir Robert Peel, an industrialist who understood the argument for cheaper food. Five times in 1845 Peel wrote memoranda to the Cabinet, proposing the repeal of the Corn Laws and each time he withdrew them.

In the autumn of 1845, when John Bright began a speaking tour of England, he complained of the worst rains he had ever experienced. It was one of the wettest autumns on record, and the incessant rain caused the potato blight that ruined the Irish potato crop. Bright later said that the rains washed away the Corn Laws.

In Ireland the subdivision of land into tiny smallholdings led to the adoption of the potato as the staple crop for the poor –

farms were too small to sustain cattle or other crops. Between 1816 and 1842, the Irish potato crop failed fourteen seasons out of twenty-seven, while agricultural labourers' wages fell to just eight pence a day. Although there had already been crop failure in the 1830s, and especially 1839, the failure of 1845–6 was much more serious. In 1845 a third, and a year later two-thirds, of the crop failed. Despite calls for help, and public works programmes, about a quarter of the population of Ireland emigrated or starved. The potato blight that affected the Irish crop in 1846–9 meant that by 1848 there were not enough seed potatoes left. One million people died in the following famine, 1.5 million emigrated and the population of Ireland by the end of the century had halved to 4.4 million.

Already, in 1845, Peel had adopted a cautious free trade policy, but the Irish crisis persuaded him to repeal the Corn Laws. It was a great disaster for the Tory Party as more than half of Peel's MPs refused to support him. The repeal was only achieved by a coalition of Peelites and Whigs, which split the Tory Party for years. Disraeli, who had been refused a job in government by Peel, was one of the Tories who refused to follow him. He described Peel's oratory as poor, and his attempt to convey pathos was 'like that of a woman who wants to cry but cannot succeed'. Peel resigned four days after the repeal of the Corn Laws. In his resignation speech he said that he knew he would be execrated by the farmers, but they attacked him from self-interest. Peel said he hoped that he would be remembered by the labourers, who would now eat untaxed bread.

The lesson of the Anti-Corn Law League was that a combination of circumstance, influence with ministers and persuasion in Parliament could make a popular campaign successful. It was to form a model for pressure groups in the future. If 1828 saw the end of the religious settlement of 1688, and the Reform Act of 1832 eroded the constitutional settlement, the repeal of the Corn Laws in 1846 can also be seen as the beginning of the end of landed dominance of politics.

The repeal of the Corn Laws did not bring a large influx of foreign corn, though by the 1860s, when North American corn was exported, Britain was able to import it.

Ireland, Scotland and Wales

The Duke of Wellington, himself from Anglo-Irish stock, claimed that there was no poverty as bad as in Ireland. The Anglo-Irish ascendancy, established long before the Act of Union of 1801, was strengthened after it. Ireland was governed by the king's representative, the lord lieutenant, and a chief secretary for Ireland, who was the senior minister in Ireland. The seat of government in Ireland was Dublin Castle, which quickly became the symbol of English dominance. The Union had been sold to many Irish with the promise of the removal of the penal laws against the Catholics, but it took until 1828 for this to be wrung from the British government. Daniel O' Connell, who had successfully fought for Catholic relief, began agitating for repeal of the Act of Union and the restoration of Irish self-government. All that the government was prepared to concede was Irish control of local government and the Poor Law in Ireland.

With the achievement of Catholic Emancipation, the Protestants in Ulster feared that they would be swamped by the Catholic majority in Ireland, and this sparked sectarian violence. The Protestant supporters of the heritage of William of Orange, known as Orangemen, attacked Catholics and especially the Catholic Society of Ribbonmen. In 1823 an Unlawful Oaths Act banned all oaths in organizations in Ireland, including the Orange Order, which had to be dissolved. After 1829 the Orange Order was reformed as an illegal society intent on combating Catholic influence in Ireland.

At the same time, poverty and agricultural depression led to violence inspired by the grinding poverty and exploitation of the landed classes. Gangs of Whiteboys sought to extract better treatment of tenants from landowners with threats of violence and attacks on property and livestock. A further cause of violence was the 'Tithe War' of the 1830s, in which Catholics sought to evade payment of tithes to the Protestant Church of Ireland. A result of these campaigns of civil disobedience was the formation of the Royal Irish Constabulary to try to crack down on the use of violence.

By the 1840s Ireland had become a country in which anger and resentment entered the bones of its people. There seemed to be no section of the community without a bitter and deep-seated grievance. The famines and starvation of the 1840s entrenched the memory of a brutally negligent English regime in the minds and folklore of most Irishmen. The middle-class Irish turned to the Irish Confederation and the Young Ireland movements, which tried to launch a revolt against British rule in 1848. It was only contained by military action. But the Irish 'Land War' was to dog British politics late into the nineteenth century and spawned terrorism that lasted for most of the twentieth century.

Scotland was similarly troubled in the early nineteenth century. In the second half of the eighteenth century landlords made 'improvements' to their land, which included adopting sheep farming. The problem was that, to accommodate large flocks of grazing sheep, the local population had to be forced off the land. Landowners also sought to use the land for mining, salt extraction and brick making. In 1792, known as the 'year of sheep', large numbers of crofters and small farmers were evicted from their land. Some crofters were squeezed into the coastal regions and took up fishing, but most were forcibly emigrated to Canada and the United States. These Highland Clearances also had a religious dimension: many crofters were Catholic and were displaced by Protestant landowners. In some cases landlords did not want to evict the crofters and tenants; they wanted to convert them into wage labourers, which the crofters resisted. Elsewhere Scottish landlords burnt their tenants out or set dogs on them and forcibly evicted them.

The economic case for clearance intensified during the first decades of the nineteenth century; between 1801 and 1818, the price for Highland wool rose from 15 to 40 shillings a stone (6.5 kg). With such an economic incentive, the Duke of Sutherland cleared 15,000 people from his land. In this case clearances happened very quickly; in Strathnaver, Sutherland, in May 1814, 430 people were evicted in just two weeks. In a malicious divisive tactic, some tenants were forced by the terms of their leases to clear a number of other families from the land they rented. A second wave of clearances began in the mid-nineteenth century, which further destroyed the Highland Scottish culture and further depopulated the Highlands. It also had a dramatic impact on the Gaelic language. Altogether the clearances stripped Scotland of half a million people.

By the end of the eighteenth century the Scottish economy was increasingly dominated by industry. Glasgow's deepwater dock had become an important port for trade with America, especially in tobacco, cotton and sugar. It was said that half the tobacco imports to Britain came up the river Clyde. A third of the city was employed in cotton manufacture. But there were also dyeing, brewing and glassmaking. A network of canals that opened during the 1790s connected Glasgow with the iron and coalmines of Lanakshire. The access to these resources boosted the creation of textile, steel and shipbuilding industries. Like many industrial cities, the population of Glasgow rocketed, and by the mid-nineteenth century half of British shipping and a quarter of the world's steam locomotives were built on the Clyde.

The character of Scotland's industrial cities was influenced by large volumes of Irish immigrants during the 1840s. Many of these were Catholics, especially from the west of Ireland, and this gave Glasgow, in particular, a religiously divided population, which made housing, industries and even sport highly sectarian. Glasgow's industries also drew people displaced by Highland clearances, as well as attracting Jews, East Europeans and Italians. Glasgow was not an industrial city like Manchester or Liverpool: it had many parks and soon adopted municipal water and gas supplies. In places it was beautiful, and Nathaniel Hawthorne wrote in 1857: 'I am inclined to think that Glasgow is the stateliest city I ever beheld.'

Although Edinburgh experienced a similar industrial boom at its port of Leith, it also remained a cultural centre. The *Edinburgh Review* was revived in 1802 as a Whig journal dedicated to moderate reform. Its objects were 'to erect a higher standard of merit, and secure a bolder and purer taste in literature, and to apply philosophical principles and the maxims of truth and humanity to politics'. By 1815 it routinely sold 14,000 copies throughout Britain. Sydney Smith (1771–1845) claimed that the slave trade and many other 'evils' were combated by authors in the *Edinburgh Review*.

In 1822 George IV visited Edinburgh, encouraged to do so by the romantic writing of Sir Walter Scott, who orchestrated the royal progress. The King appeared in Edinburgh in over £1,300 worth of Royal Stuart tartan kilt, chains, jewels, dirk, sword and pistols. The occasion was a carefully choreographed pageant in which Highland chieftains were marshalled in their invented tartans and over 450 gentlewomen were kissed at the King's official levee in Edinburgh. While the event had more than an element of pantomime, and George was mercilessly caricatured for his ludicrously ornate dress, it led to a further revival of romantic ideas of Scotland.

The royal visit granted fashionability to the clans, which had hitherto been regarded as sources of Jacobite treason. At all official events on the visit the King decreed that the formal dress was to be the Highland costume, and kilts became genteel. This was in sharp contrast to their lowly origin as the dress of mountain peasants. The visit was seen as the ending of antagonism between Highland and Lowland Scots. George IV's niece, Queen Victoria, was to further popularize Scotland in her published Highland journals and in buying Balmoral as a Scottish home.

There had been a similar cultural revival in Wales in the eighteenth century. Some of it imagined an ancient culture that had not existed, and institutions were formed to promote Welsh culture. The Honourable Society of Cymmrodorion, for example, was founded in 1751 to encourage the literature, science and arts connected with Wales. The Gorsedd Beirdd Ynys Prydain (or Gorsedd of Bards of the British Isles) was founded in 1792 by Iolo Morganwg (1747–1826) (the bardic name of Edward Williams). Morganwg specialized in the invention of Welsh cultural history that linked Wales to Arthurian and romantic accounts of its history. His inventive antiquarianism focused on the recovery of the advanced and civilized roots of Wales, and he is often claimed to be an architect of modern Welsh culture.

By the early nineteenth century, the discovery of deposits of iron, coal and limestone in south-east Wales led to the development of coal mining and huge ironworks at Cyfarthfa and Dowlais near Merthyr Tydfil. There had been copper smelting near Swansea for some decades, but the growth in mining and smelting was astonishing. Between 1796 and 1811, the number of iron furnaces in Wales grew from 20 to 148. By 1810 the Ynys Fach furnace at Merthyr produced a record 105 tons of iron a week. Welsh coal also proved to be of high quality and consequently was sought to fuel engines, particularly in steamships. Industrialization spread up the valleys of South Wales as more coalmines opened. By the 1840s, mining reached Aberdare and the Rhondda valley. The ports of Neath and Swansea became centres of iron working and for the export of coal, iron and steel all over the world. By 1840 Wales produced 525,000 tons of pig iron a year, 36 per cent of British production.

The character of South Wales was completely altered by industrialization. Roads up the valleys and along the coast of South Wales grew significantly. In 1793–4 the Glamorgan Canal was built to transport heavy goods from Merthyr to ports such as that developed by Lord Bute in Cardiff. By the 1840s, railways were built across Wales, reaching Aberystwyth by 1864. North Wales, though less industrialized, had slate, alkalis and some coal mines, and communications here also improved. In 1826 the Menai Straits Bridge was built by Telford to link Anglesey to the mainland as part of the improvement to the route from London to Holyhead. By 1844 the railway linked Chester to Holyhead, which made passage to Ireland much easier.

Wales was also dominated by the growth of Nonconformity. In the eighteenth century it became a centre for Methodism and especially of Calvinistic Methodism led by Daniel Rowland, Howell Harris (1714–73) and William Williams Pantycelyn (1717–91). In Wales, unlike England where Methodism split from Anglicanism, Methodism remained closely connected to the Church of England, and as late as the 1820s bishops were exhorting clergy to choose whether they were Anglican or Methodist. By the middle of the nineteenth century, Nonconformity in Wales, of various denominations, had overtaken Anglicanism. In 1851, for example, there were 34 Anglican churches in Merioneth and 273 Nonconformist chapels. This had considerable cultural implications because Welsh was the main language of the Nonconformist churches. Sunday schools, which played an important role in Welsh religion, made much of the population literate in Welsh. This was important for the survival of the language as it was not taught in Anglican parish schools.

The position of the Welsh language was badly affected by a report on Welsh education of 1847. This arose from a public inquiry into the state of education in Wales, led by Englishmen and without a Welsh speaker on the inquiry board. The commissioners often quoted the views of English landowners and English speakers uncritically. The report claimed that Welsh education was poor, and highlighted the Welsh language as a cause. The report made shocking moral judgments about what it claimed were the ignorance and laziness of the Welsh people; the report was called in Welsh *Brad y Llyfrau Gleision* ('the Treason of the Blue Books') from the three blue books of evidence published with it. In the wake of the report attempts were made to stamp out the Welsh language. In schools children were forcibly prevented from speaking in Welsh, and a wooden spoon was used to punish those who spoke Welsh in classrooms.

Cities and Railways

The first decades of the nineteenth century were marked by two other important developments. The first was the continuing growth of the industrial towns and cities that had emerged in the eighteenth century; the second was the coming of the railways. In 1750 about 15 per cent of the population of Britain lived in towns, by 1850 it had risen to around 50 per cent, and in the next thirty years it rose to 80 per cent. In 1801 two-fifths of Britain's population worked in manufacturing; by 1850 this was had grown to over a half of the ballooning population. Many workers who moved to the towns in huge numbers in the early nineteenth century lived in cramped, overcrowded and unsanitary dwellings. Charles Dickens' novel *Hard Times*, published in 1854, was set in the fictional town of Coketown, whose name suggested its dirty, blackened atmosphere. In the centre of most towns and cities were the decaying remains of the original buildings. In London and Southampton these were known as 'the rookeries' and elsewhere the 'stews' – networks of alleys and tenement buildings riddled with crime and prostitution. In Merthyr Tydfil this was called 'China'; in Scottish towns they were the 'lands'.

In 1850 Thomas Beames published *The Rookeries of London*, in which he described the rookery near the site of today's Oxford Street:

The Rookery was like an honeycomb, perforated by a number of courts and blind alleys, *culs de sac*, without any outlet other than the entrance. Here were the lowest lodging houses in London, inhabited by the various classes of thieves ... the tramp and vagrant, whose assumed occupation was a cloak for roguery; the labourer who came to London to look for work; the hordes of Irish who annually seem to come in and go out with the flies and the fruit, were here banded together: driven by their various necessities to these dens, they were content to take shelter there, till the thief had opportunity to repair his fortune, and the labourer means to provide better lodging. The streets were narrow; the windows stuffed up with rags, or patched with paper; strings hung across from house to house, on which clothes were put out to dry; the gutters stagnant, choked up with filth; the pavement strewed with decayed cabbage stalks and other vegetables; the walls of the houses mouldy, discoloured, the whitewash peeling off from damp; the walls in parts bulging, in parts receding, the floor covered with a coating of dirt. In the centre of this hive was the famous thieves' public house, called Rat's Castle; this den of iniquity was the common rendezvous of outcasts. The frequenters of this place were bound together by a common tie, and they spoke openly of incidents which they had long ceased to blush at, but which hardened habits of crime alone could teach them to avow.

Health in these slums could be poor, especially when diseases came from abroad through ports. In the 1832 cholera epidemic in London, which is thought to have arrived from China, 7,000 people died. Influenza, as today, was a source of concern for young and old. In such towns and cities the average life expectancy was poor, in part due to child mortality. In 1842, of 350,000 deaths, a quarter was of children under a year of age. This infant mortality brought average life expectancy in Liverpool to just 28.1 years and in Manchester to 26.6 years. The only solution was to take public health seriously. In 1847 Liverpool appointed the first medical officer of health to supervise public health. Within seven years a law required all cities to appoint such officials. Pollution remained a serious problem for many years. Rivers in major towns and cities became badly contaminated with industrial and domestic waste; the last salmon to be netted in the Thames was caught in 1820 and sold to George IV.

The various industrial towns served different economic sectors. Manchester, for example, was nicknamed 'Cottonopolis' because it contained over a hundred cotton mills by 1850. It was Manchester's manufacturing and its workers that inspired Friedrich Engels to write *The Condition of the Working Class in England* in 1844. This described the conditions in the town and indicated that its workers were four times more likely to suffer common illnesses and diseases. Liverpool, in contrast, was built on trade and commerce, with 40 per cent of British goods passing through it in 1800. As the docks developed, between 1801 and 1841, the population of Liverpool grew from 92,000 to 286,000. In 1801 there was no direct stagecoach to Liverpool from London and only four wagon trains a week, but 125 sailings crossed to Ireland each week and 106 a month to North America, 48 to Africa and 28 to Europe.

By 1830 the economic platform of iron and coal enabled an engineering sector to emerge in which Britain produced engines, machines, tools and even bridges for itself and the world. Engineers, who formed a whole new profession, became heroic figures. Robert Stephenson had already achieved some celebrity in the 1830s from his invention of the steam engine *Rocket* in 1829, but Isambard Kingdom Brunel (1806–59) eclipsed him.

Brunel's achievements were truly monumental: the Thames Tunnel (1825–43), the Great Western Railway's (GWR) lines, bridges and tunnels, the iron-hulled SS *Great Britain* (1843) and the SS *Great Eastern* (1858). The *Great Eastern*, with its eight engines and ten boilers, was big enough to reach India without recoaling and remained the largest ship afloat until 1901. In the 1860s the *Great Eastern* was big enough to lay the first transatlantic cable. Smoking forty cigars a day and needing only four hours' sleep, Brunel was boundlessly prodigious and his talents were extraordinary. His work for the GWR included the building of Paddington and Bristol Temple Meads stations, the construction of the line between them and the longest railway tunnel in the world at the time, Box Tunnel in Gloucestershire. Brunel even designed hotels and invented the bar, for customers to stand at to be served in cafes and pubs.

Railways grew up to serve the passenger and freight traffic generated by the industrial and urban growth of London and the north of England. In 1830 the 31-mile (50 km) Liverpool to Manchester railway opened at a cost of £637,000. It quickly demonstrated the value of railways, becoming widely used by passengers as well as goods. By the middle of the 1840s, as bank rates were declining, railways seemed a good investment as the returns were strong. This fuelled a 'railway mania', during which large numbers of railways were built. These railways were often based on flimsy business cases, but they seemed to be a sure-fire investment opportunity – the 'dotcom' boom of its day.

Although, in theory, each new railway needed an Act of Parliament, the process did not check the viability of either the company or the proposed railway line. MPs themselves were often investors and therefore happy to sponsor bills, and almost all the proposed bills passed. In some cases the railway companies proposed lines that were impossible to build, let alone for engines to run along. Whatever the doubtful business behind some of them, in twenty years Britain was transformed by the building of a network of railways. By 1849, £224 million had been invested in railways.

One of the factors that had fuelled the railway boom of the 1840s was the 1844 Railway Regulation Act, which forced railway companies to provide at least one train each day (known as the 'parliamentary train') with third-class accommodation at not more than one penny per mile and a speed of at least 12 mph (19 km per hour). This made cheap railway travel accessible to the masses. Moreover, railways also became important employers – by 1870, 250,000 men worked for the railway companies.

The end of the railway boom came in 1846, when speculators realized that the bubble could not last. When the bank interest rates rose, and the share prices of railway companies dropped, the bubble burst. Some larger companies, such as the Great Western, bought up smaller ailing companies, but many investors lost heavily in the more fanciful schemes. George Hudson (1800–71), the 'railway king' who had sponsored over a thousand miles of railways, was exposed as a fraud when the Eastern Railway was investigated. It was also discovered that Hudson had bribed some MPs to get bills passed in the Commons.

Despite the bursting of the bubble, railways became part of the experience of nineteenth-century British life. Fanny Kemble (1809–93) wrote in 1830 of a railway journey:

> you can't imagine how strange it seemed to be journeying on thus, without an visible cause of progress other than the magical machine, with its flying white breath and rhythmical, unvarying pace.

Railways also brought standardized time to Britain. Railway timetabling made it impossible for towns to continue to use their own calculation of time. In the west of England this might be as much as 15 minutes ahead of Greenwich Mean Time. So time became standard across Britain.

People used the railways to take advantage of the growth of leisure time. In July 1841 Thomas Cook (1808–92), a member of the Temperance Association, organized the first rail excursion from Leicester to a temperance rally in Loughborough. The excursion carried 570 passengers, each of whom paid a shilling for a ticket, which included a sandwich and a bottle of soda. In 1851 he organized huge rail excursions to the Great Exhibition. In time, Cook was to create the package holiday, putting together railway fares and hotel costs. People flocked to the railways: in the twenty-five years after 1850 the number of GWR passenger journeys rose from 2 million to 36 million; in the same period its freight movements rose from 350,000 tons to 16 million tons.

Not all people welcomed the arrival of railways and the opportunities they presented. In 1831 the Lord's Day Observance Society was founded, in part, to oppose the growth of Sunday travel that the railways invited. In Oxford the railway station was built well to the west of the city because the university authorities did not want students to have easy access to the delights of London.

Britain in the first half of the nineteenth century had seen the collapse of an *ancien régime*. Britain's constitution no longer gave a monopoly on public office to members of the Church of England, its system of elections permitted more middle-class voters to participate, its economy no longer favoured the landed over the industrial economy, and the exploitation of workers in factories and mines was eroded. New forces such as railways and popular protest movements gave ordinary people new opportunities. Most significantly, governments had to respond to what was perceived as the public mood much more than they had previously. Democracy in Britain had not yet been born, but its birth pangs were starting.

9

MID-VICTORIAN CONFIDENCE

A New Monarchy

On 20 June 1837 Dr William Howley (1766–1848), the Archbishop of Canterbury, and Lord Conyngham (1766–1832), the Lord Chamberlain, were present at Windsor Castle at the death of William IV, the last of the sons of George III. The two then ordered a carriage and drove to Kensington Palace, arriving at 5 a.m., and asked for the heir to the throne to be woken. When the 18-year-old Victoria entered the room, the two men knelt at her feet and told her she was now the queen.

Victoria's coronation, a year later, was not auspicious; indeed it was a scene of disarray. Archbishop Howley tried to ram the coronation ring on to the wrong finger, causing the Queen considerable pain. It was a mistake he repeated three years later when, at her marriage, he put her wedding ring on the wrong finger too. Dr Law, the Bishop of Bath and Wells, accidentally turned over two pages in the coronation service and thereby omitted a whole section. During a break in the ceremony the Queen retired to a side chapel and, to her dismay, found the altar piled with sandwiches for refreshments. And throughout the proceedings, the Bishop of Durham stumbled around, unsure what he had to do. After the coronation, Archbishop Howley admitted that they should have had a rehearsal.

By the middle of the nineteenth century, when Queen Victoria had married Prince Albert of Saxe-Coburg and Gotha (1819–61) and established a large family, the monarchy had been transformed. Gone were the Hanoverian problems of inter-generational feuding and feckless royal dukes who wenched and frittered their way into debt and dissipation. Gone also was the military model of monarchy that had seen James II, William III, George I and George II as active military commanders in the field. Victoria's new model royal family was the epitome of decorum and virtue.

From their depiction in the *Illustrated London News* in December 1848, standing around their Christmas tree, to Franz Winterhalter's (1805–73) group portrait of the couple with five of their children in 1846, the image of the royal family was transformed. No longer was the royal family a troubling and unpopular feature of public life; it was widely admired, and symbolized qualities of decency, restraint, respectability and morality. The use of the images of the Queen and her family in newspapers and in advertising was widespread. It gave the royal family a currency that enabled people to identify their country closely with their monarch.

Victoria's longevity – in 1850 she had a further fifty-one years to reign – meant that by the end of the century most people had not lived under any other monarch. This confirmed the permanence and unchanging qualities that the monarchy brought to national identity.

The Confidence of Religion

Victorian England also saw religion transformed from a troubling feature of British political and public life to one that did not occasion civil strife. After 1829 Catholic Emancipation did not usher in the worst fears of those who opposed it, neither did the reforms of the Church of England's financial and diocesan structure in the 1830s. By Victoria's coronation, the detachment of politics from religion was almost complete. In 1833 it was conceded that Quakers could take the oath of allegiance for MPs by affirmation, and from 1858 the oath was amended to permit Jews to become MPs. Religion was becoming a matter of personal preference and not a cause for public concern.

In the same way that Victorian taste in architecture tended towards the elaborately decorated medieval neo-Gothic buildings, so some Anglicans developed a similar theological preference. The Oxford Movement grew out of the opposition of a number of Oxford clergy to the ecclesiastical reforms of the 1830s. The movement emphasized the medieval High Church liturgy and rituals of the Church. It was led by John Keble (1792–1866), who attacked the reforms of the Church as 'national apostasy' in his 1833 Oxford Assize Sermon. Keble was professor of poetry at Oxford and author of *The Christian Year*, a popular cycle of readings and poems, published in 1827. The leaders of the Oxford Movement attacked liberal theology. Their emphasis on historical Christianity led some supporters to incline towards the Roman Catholic Church. Opponents of the Tractarians, as followers of the Oxford Movement were sometimes called, regarded their 'Roman' outlook as dangerous, and their worst suspicions were confirmed when John Henry Newman (1801–90), a leading Tractarian, converted to Roman Catholicism in 1845. He was followed by other important Tractarians, including Henry Manning (1808–92) and later Gerald Manley Hopkins (1844–89).

Tractarians believed that priests were the descendants of the apostles and that the Church of England should rediscover the elaborate ritual and ceremonial of its past. Many Tractarian clergy were 'slum priests' who brought the mysterious and colourful nature of Christianity to the working poor. They did this through processions, incense and ancient-styled vestments. Tractarians also built large numbers of neo-Gothic churches across Britain; buildings that are prevalent in the countryside and towns today. This Anglo-Catholic wing of the Church was one of three Church parties that emerged in the 1830s and 1840s, the others being the Evangelicals and the Broad Church movement.

Broad Churchmen sought to avoid partisanship and gradually focused their efforts on biblical criticism. This tended to the view that the Bible could not be taken literally and had to be interpreted by Christians. Evangelicals in the Church of England (as well as in Methodism) grew in importance in the nineteenth century, advocating a highly personal religious experience and a belief in a spiritual conversion that motivated a renewed faith. At Cambridge, the leading Evangelical Charles Simeon trained numerous undergraduates and his followers sought to buy up advowsons – the right to appoint clergy to parishes – so that they could increase the numbers of Evangelical clergymen in parishes. In politics, Evangelicals, following William Wilberforce, regarded their personal commitment to faith as a source of a moral call to social actions. They embraced humanitarian causes and often supported the reforming agenda of the Whigs. Evangelicals heartily disliked Tractarian 'ritualism'. One High Church clergymen was said to have issued brass knuckle-dusters to his congregation so that they were ready to defend themselves against Evangelical adversaries.

Anxiety about Catholicism remained after Catholic Emancipation and came to a head in 1850 when the Pope restored the Catholic hierarchy of bishops to England and Wales. The country was divided up into dioceses, led by an Archbishop of Westminster, Nicholas Wiseman (1802–65). Wiseman sought to reassure Protestants that Catholics were not unpatriotic, and that allegiance to Rome in spiritual matters did not threaten the allegiance to the Crown in politics. Another factor that made Britain more at ease with Catholics was that numerous Catholic convents had fled France in the wake of the

French Revolution, and so nuns and monks were now seen in Britain again for the first time since the Reformation. Thus Catholicism became more familiar and less threatening to Protestants; in time, Catholicism became widely accepted, but initially anti-Catholic feeling died only slowly. The government was sufficiently concerned at what was called 'papal aggression' to outlaw the adoption of the titles of English dioceses by the Catholic Church in the Ecclesiastical Titles Act of 1852. The numbers of Catholic priests grew significantly: in 1771 there were 392 Catholic priests in England; by the end of Queen Victoria's reign there were over 3,000.

Among those who feared the restoration of the Catholic hierarchy was Charles Kingsley (1819–75), a Cambridge professor of history as well as a poet and author. He accused Newman of deception in his conversion to Catholicism, which prompted Newman to publish a defence *Apologia Pro Vita Sua* in 1864. Kingsley was also influenced by the social problems of the 'hungry forties' and embraced Chartism and Christian socialism, for which he was banned from preaching in the diocese of London. He advocated a form of 'muscular Christianity' that stressed the determination and vigour which faith injected into everyday life. In 1857 Kingsley wrote that his ideal Englishman was a man who feared God and could walk a thousand miles in a thousand hours. To Kingsley, Catholics did not seem very muscular.

Outside the Church of England and Catholicism, Christianity was both growing and fragmenting. John Wesley's Methodists numbered 57,000 at the time of his death, and by 1830 represented only 2 per cent of the population. Methodism was initially an Anglican enterprise, but grew steadily into a separate denomination. Wesley's Methodism was Arminian, rejecting the Calvinist idea of an 'elect' few who could be saved. After his death Wesleyanism grew significantly, but it fragmented into Primitive Methodists, Bible Christians, Independent Methodists and New Connexion Methodists, all of which had organizational, class and doctrinal differences.

Methodism did not have a monopoly on schisms. The Baptist Union, formed in 1812, was similarly divided between General (Arminian) and Particular (Calvinist) Baptists. The Presbyterian Church of Scotland also experienced a series of splits, the most serious being in 1843 when a third of the ministers left the General Assembly of the Church because they could not accept central control of ministerial appointments. These divisions also reflected increasing enquiries into the nature of belief and doctrine. They demonstrated the empowerment of believers who wanted their beliefs and church organization to be aligned even if it excluded others. Whilst schism in the seventeenth century was regarded with some horror and considerable anxiety, by the nineteenth century it was a consequence of diverse tastes and fashions in belief. Few thought that separation from other believers threatened their salvation.

In 1851 a religious census took a snapshot of religious affiliation in England and Wales. It identified thirty-five different religious organizations in which people worshipped. Of a population of 18 million, about 7.25 million people attended Sunday worship on 20 March 1851, and it was estimated that 30 per cent of the population could not attend for reasons of illness, infirmity, age or youth. The evidence suggested that 47.4 per cent of the population was Anglican; 25.7 per cent was Methodist; 11.4 per cent was Congregationalist; 8.7% per cent Baptist and 3.5 per cent was Catholic. Of course, such national figures disguised huge regional variations. In Cornwall, for example, Anglicans comprised just 27.2 per cent of worshippers, compared with the Methodist 64.5 per cent; in Essex Anglicans made up 57.5 per cent of worshippers and Methodist just 8.5 per cent, with Congregationalists as high as 23 per cent. Large towns often had the biggest variations. In Liverpool, for example, Roman Catholics made up 32.5 per cent of the population, which reflected the size of the Irish community in the city, due to mass immigration.

These figures confirmed that the Church of England could claim to be only one, albeit the largest, of a number of religious denominations. On the other hand, the divisions of the Methodist, Congregational and Baptist Churches suggested that regarding them as single entities was a mistake. There was also the question of what were the beliefs of the 5.25 million people who did not attend church. It was for this group in 1864 that the word 'agnostic' was coined. While different denominations took heart from the figures, together they supported the case for removal of religious qualifications. In the thirty years after 1851, church rates, religious tests for entry to Oxford and Cambridge and restrictions on burials were removed in successive Acts of Parliament.

Religion was also a key element in British identity overseas. By 1843 the Oxford University Bampton Lecturer, Anthony Grant, argued that Britain had a duty to bring Christianity to the inhabitants of the colonies. This 'duty' became one that attracted large numbers of missionaries of all denominations to India, Africa and beyond in the nineteenth century. Sometimes, as in India, Anglicans cooperated with Baptist and other denominations in a way that they would not contemplate at home.

Missionaries built churches but also hospitals, dispensaries, schools and colleges across the empire. In addition to their urge to carry out God's work and spread the Bible, missionaries also reinforced British cultural and power structures across the empire. Naturally, missionaries sought converts to Christianity and therefore endorsed the idea of the superiority of the Europeans. This was especially so in India where, by the 1820s, dioceses were formed and a bishop appointed to Calcutta. Some of the most celebrated explorers and travellers, such as David Livingstone (1813–73), were missionaries. By the middle of the nineteenth century there were more than 5,000 British missionaries, and the collections to support them and societies to maintain them were becoming important financial organizations.

The Reassurance of Land
An element in Victorian confidence was the strength of agriculture and the sense that rural life was a foundation of British

identity. This was partly behind the Chartist Land Company's aim to return industrial workers to the land. By 1851, however, agriculture employed just one-fifth of the employed population and was to drop further in the coming years. Rural life was not the natural idyll that many saw it to be: organic farming was eroded in the mid-nineteenth century. By 1842 the first industrially made sulpho-phosphate fertilizers were manufactured in Deptford. As important in fertilizing land were the large quantities of bird guano that were imported from South America. By 1858, Britain imported 300,000 tons of guano from Peru a year – Britain's dominance of the South American guano trade was such that the United States became concerned. Other new techniques in farming were demonstrated at a series of fairs held by the Royal Agricultural Society, which was formed in 1839.

Rural Britain was becoming a place of industry. In England alone there were 30,000 wheelwrights and 112,000 blacksmiths, and in areas such as Buckinghamshire, Bedfordshire and Northamptonshire there were 16,000 lace makers in 1851. Among others, glove making, quarrying, tile making, glazing, sail making and brewing were also important rural industries. Much of rural life was grindingly poor and built on the back of labour as sweated and crushing as that in factories in towns and cities. But for the Victorians, from the middle of the nineteenth century, the countryside and country life was a source of reassurance and stability that it had not been in the years of enclosures and the Swing Riots.

The sharp division between the rural and urban was not as strong in reality as some believed, but the romantic idea of land and farming remained strong. For large numbers of nineteenth-century industrialists success was represented by the purchase of landed estate, just as it had been for merchants in the eighteenth century. Lever, Lipton, Armstrong, Wills and Boot were all household names built on the industrial manufacture and sale of soap, tea, arms, cigarettes and pharmaceuticals whose founders bought landed estates with their fortunes. For prime ministers who were not from landed families, a country estate was a necessity, hence the Duke of Wellington received Stratfield Saye from the nation and Disraeli bought Hughenden Manor. Land, not money, continued to represent the pinnacle of social achievement.

The acquisition of land was not just a social ideal for the wealthy. From the 1730s people in Sheffield could lease garden plots of 150 square yards (150 square metres) for 3 pence a square yard. In Birmingham the 'guinea garden' scheme leased 300 square yards to residents for 21 shillings. In 1829 there were fifty-four allotments schemes in Britain, such as the St Anne's Allotments in Nottingham, set up in the 1830s. Over the next forty years the numbers of individual allotments grew to 242,542. Allotments enabled the urban poor to grow food to supplement their wages, and they also enabled people to maintain a connection with rural life even when they moved to the towns.

The same impulse, together with the desire to provide for the emergence of leisure and the middle classes, lay behind the public parks movement. In London, Regent's Park was completed in the 1830s and Hyde Park, Kensington Gardens, Green Park and St James' Park were also developed in this decade. Public parks were advocated for different reasons. Philanthropists felt that parks could commemorate their names and munificence in the minds of the masses, clergy recommended them as wholesome alternatives to drunkenness and public houses, and the radical Francis Place claimed they brought calm and peace to people.

There was also an early desire to provide clean air for workers, as proposed in 1829 in J.C. Loudon's *Hints on Breathing Places for the Metropolis, and for Country Towns and Villages*. Loudon argued that Hampstead Heath should be formed as the first of a series of open parkland circles around the capital to give people places to breathe clean air. He also advocated that the government should buy this land and provide under-street sewers and services. In the 1848 Public

Health Act, local councils were empowered to create 'public walks' as a means of promoting exercise among the middle and working classes.

Victorian confidence was partly built on the sense that even the land was subject to 'progress'. As Thomas Carlyle wrote in 'Signs of the Times', an article in the *Edinburgh Review* in 1829:

> We remove mountains, and make seas our smooth highway; nothing can resist us. We war with rude Nature; and, by our resistless engines, come off always victorious, and loaded with spoils.

The Mid-Victorian Boom

The 1850s was a high point in the growth of Britain's economy; Britain still lacked serious industrial rivals and therefore could justifiably be called the workshop of the world. The banking system supported investment in industry and Britain had a growing transport network and a developing domestic market. The railway boom had given Britain the most advanced public transport system in the world. The repeal of the Corn Laws in 1846 did not have the disastrous impact that farmers had feared because rising demand for foods began a period of agricultural prosperity. Population growth and the expansion of the empire ensured that both at home and abroad there was burgeoning demand for food and industrial products. For industrial workers, real increases in wages were the result of a high demand for labour, and this enabled them to buy more. Free trade allowed Britain's industrial goods to be sold across the world and to bring profits back home. The British economy grew, on average, by 3 per cent annually. The value of British exports tripled, and overseas capital investments quadrupled. For the first time stockbroking emerged as a profession in this period as surplus wealth needed to find opportunities to invest.

Technology also seemed to favour Britain's economy. The invention of the telegraph provided a means of instant communication for nations and customers. And, thanks to

Henry Bessemer's process of 1856, inexpensive steel became as important as iron. Some sectors of the economy experienced revolutionary changes, as textiles had in the eighteenth century. Brewing, for example, grew to be a major element in the economy from the 1850s. From this period many of the household names in brewing emerged: John Smith of Tadcaster, Joshua Tetley of Leeds, Henry Boddington of Manchester, the Meux family of London, Samuel Brain in Cardiff and the Tennents in Glasgow. Beer consumption had fallen in the early nineteenth century, but revived in this period to a peak of 42 gallons (190 litres) per head a year in England and Wales. Deducting volumes for women and children, this suggests that some men drank up to 16 pints (9 litres) a week. Unsurprisingly, a temperance movement followed the growth in beer sales.

House building also became an important element in the construction industry as both the urban working classes and the suburban middle classes needed more accommodation; terraced and semi-detached houses were built in huge quantities. Stonemasons also benefited from the boom in town halls, the fashion for civic statuary and clock towers, and the proliferation of museums and schools.

The mid-Victorian economic boom probably blunted the edge of radical demands for widespread reform. By the 1870s the boom had largely run its course, but in the 1850s Britain could look forward with confidence. Nevertheless, for some workers, poverty, unemployment and hardship persisted through the mid-Victorian boom.

Education

We are now only too familiar with the experience of written examinations, but in Britain, before 1800, they were unknown. The first written examination was introduced in Cambridge in the 1790s as a way to speed up the process of examining students. Before this, examinations were oral and very time consuming; thereafter written exams were widely adopted in universities, schools and other organizations. The first printed exam papers were used in the sixth form at Harrow School in July 1830. W.E. Gladstone (1809–98) called the period 'the age of examinations', reflecting the movement to an industrial economy that needed to recruit and appoint people on the basis of merit. In the eighteenth century the numbers of people entering the professions was relatively small. The networks of patronage and recommendation of people for jobs had worked effectively and endorsed the idea that the patron and client enjoyed a natural relationship in society. But in an industrial economy the main social relationship was that of employer and employee, and it was important to be able to identify those whose skills stood out. This is what examinations aimed to do.

Schools also exemplified the need to educate children for an industrial and imperial economy. Many schools began as charities that sought to provide free education for a few, sometimes poor, students. During the seventeenth and eighteenth centuries these schools grew and included fee-paying pupils too. In the eighteenth century it became fashionable for the wealthy to abandon private education by tutors at home in favour of sending boys to schools to be educated publicly.

In the early nineteenth century a number of headmasters began to reform schools. Samuel Butler (1774–1839), for example, the headmaster of Shrewsbury School from 1798, introduced the study of mathematics and history. At Rugby School from 1828, Thomas Arnold (1795–1842) introduced classes in geography, modern history and foreign languages. Arnold's reputation as a reforming head was underscored by his appearance in Thomas Hughes' novel *Tom Brown's Schooldays*, published in 1857 (depicting Rugby under Arnold in the 1830s). Although best known today for its depiction of bullying and mistreatment, *Tom Brown's Schooldays* showed Arnold to have been compassionate and determined to shed the corrupt traditions of the school's past.

The reforms of schools, often modelled on Arnold's work, was also part of the process of recognizing new domains of knowledge. New subjects emerged and were taught in schools, including modern languages, chemistry and geography, much of which was regarded as important knowledge for Britain's imperial economy. The best example of the commercial need for such schools was the East India Company College, founded in 1809 as a place for the education of clerks and other agents for India (later refounded as Haileybury College). Although nomination to the college was in the hands of directors of the Company, it taught subjects that were designed to be of use to its students, including oriental languages, law, economics and mathematics.

It was not just in schools that education changed. Once, entry to the civil service had been on the basis of patronage and influence. To know a minister meant that one might secure a junior clerk's post in government. But, as government expanded, so did the civil service. By 1850 the civil service cost the taxpayers £7 million a year and employed 16,000 people. Consequently, in 1854 the Northcote–Trevelyan report introduced competitive exams for entry to the service and further promotion on the basis of merit. The Civil Service Commission was established to ensure that the reforms were carried out in a politically neutral way and founded on the belief that the impartiality of the civil service was essential to government. So began the tradition of a permanent and impartial civil service, which marks Britain's government as different from that of, for example, the US.

In the universities there were advances. It was soon clear that England needed more than two universities, and there was a rash of foundations of new institutions. In 1822 St David's College, Lampeter, was founded to educate clergy in Wales. In 1826 University College London (UCL) was founded as a secular alternative ('godless' was Thomas Arnold's word) to Oxford and Cambridge. Unlike Oxford and Cambridge, it was open to Jews, Unitarians and atheists. Its foundation was inspired by the Utilitarianism of Jeremy Bentham, who believed that university education should be more widely available, and should not require conformity to the Church of England. Bentham left his body to UCL, where its remains are still on display in a wooden cabinet. Three years later King's College London was founded as an Anglican college by opponents of UCL. Unlike UCL, it was arranged around a chapel, although it also admitted Nonconformists. Besides theology, it also taught new subjects such as chemistry, commerce and geography. In 1832 Durham University was established by Act of Parliament in Durham Castle and endowed with some of the diocese's income from coalmining.

While these new foundations increased the numbers of graduates and the range of subjects studied, they did not significantly widen participation in higher education; women were still excluded from most colleges, as were non-Anglicans at Oxford and Cambridge until the 1870s. Education remained a privilege for the sons of the wealthy. Slowly Oxford and Cambridge changed: in 1848 and 1850 respectively Cambridge and then Oxford expanded the courses on offer to include sciences. They also established the systems to classify the award of degrees with honours. In 1850 a royal commission was established to reform Oxford and Cambridge, and subsequent legislation widened the system of government of the universities, enlarged the numbers of professors and opened scholarships, fellowships and prizes from their previously closed and privileged status. Within twenty years all universities were opened to all men, regardless of religion.

In Ireland, the sort of secular education embodied in UCL was introduced in 1849 by the foundation of Queen's Colleges at Belfast, Cork and Galway. In 1850 they were incorporated as a single university. Catholics in Ireland established a Catholic university in Dublin in 1854 and appointed John Henry Newman – the Tractarian convert to Catholicism – as its rector. In Scotland, though no new universities were founded, a number of colleges were established that were the foundations of later universities. In 1821 the School of Arts in Edinburgh (later Herriot–Watt University) was established for 'the education of mechanics in such branches of physical science as are of practical application in their several trades'. A similar college in Dundee was the origin of the University of Dundee.

These new institutions began the process of developing a much larger higher education sector and enabled the teaching of new subjects that better served the economy of Britain. Knowledge became divided into the subjects that we recognize today, and the classical subjects of Greek and Latin, which had previously dominated elite education, diminished in importance. 'Modern' knowledge formed the basis of growing skills in a wide range of disciplines, including engineering, with branches of civil, mechanical and electrical engineering, each of which obtained a chartered society during the nineteenth century. Mechanics institutes for technical training were established in London and Glasgow in 1823, and the *Mechanics' Magazine* was founded in the same year. New professions of veterinary surgery, dentistry, pharmacy, accountancy and architecture were formed, with regulatory bodies and, in some cases, legal status and standards.

Empire and Foreign Policy
Britain's empire emerged in the early nineteenth century from its foundation as an economic and commercial force into one that endorsed Britain's national confidence and identity. By the end of the Napoleonic wars, Britain had few global rivals, other than Russia in Asia and the US in Latin America. Throughout the century, Britain added to its overseas territories, including Java, Singapore, Malacca and Burma before 1830. Trade remained at the centre of the empire and Britain's foreign secretaries saw their role as partly to defend merchants' interests. Free trade became a means by which the empire could develop new markets for British goods. Even before the repeal of the Corn Laws at home, the British were asserting free trade as financially beneficial overseas.

In seeking to force China to trade freely with the European powers, the British tried to eliminate the customs duties the

Chinese forced them to pay. The Chinese authorities, however, were keen to stop the growing trade in opium. Opium had originally been used to treat diarrhoea, but it was quickly realized that it was highly addictive. Most opium was grown in India, and in 1800 the Chinese government outlawed its importation, fearing that the Western countries wanted to exploit opium to erode Chinese society and destroy the balance of trade. Despite the ban, the opium trade continued to flourish. Private merchants from the US, Britain and France made substantial profits from the sale of opium to Chinese addicts.

In the late 1830s, 4.5 million pounds (2 million kg) of opium were being illegally traded in China by various foreign powers. But in spring 1839 the government of China outlawed the sale of opium and confiscated and burnt an opium consignment at Canton. In response, the British, using steam-powered gunships, occupied land in the area with 2,000 marines. In the ensuing war China could not match the military superiority of the British, and by 1842 was forced to accept the Treaty of Nanking: Hong Kong was ceded to Great Britain, and other ports, including Canton, were forced to be opened to British trade, including opium. Two years later France and the US forced the same trade concessions from China. A second opium war broke out in 1856, and the Chinese were forced at the Treaty of Tientsin (1858) to open further ports and to allow foreigners and Christian missionaries to travel inside China to trade and convert the Chinese. Drugs were a means to enforce free trade in China.

Few ministers realized the huge popularity of the empire in the minds of the British public more than Lord Palmerston (1784–1865). As foreign secretary, Palmerston fuelled imperial ambitions with episodes of 'gunboat diplomacy'. Among these was the Don Pacifico affair in 1850. In this, a Jewish Portuguese trader was defended against the Greek government because he claimed to have been born in Gibraltar. Palmerston's claim that every Briton abroad ought to be protected by the claim '*civis Britannicus sum*' (I am a British citizen) – as the Ancient Romans were by their citizenship – was extremely popular. His speech proclaiming the doctrine was a five-hour triumph in the Commons.

The empire became a popular icon for people. Packaging and advertising used the empire and imperial images of lions, elephants, Britannia, Union Jacks and scenes of India, the navy and royalty on every imaginable product. Some, such as Rippingille's stoves, which depicted Queen Victoria giving stoves to all varieties of colonial subjects, claimed that their products exemplified the advantages of empire to colonial subjects – Rippingille's advertisement claimed, 'England's gift, a blessing to all nations'. Popular magazines, like *Punch*, used the empire as a backdrop to news and stories. British imperial superiority was born.

In many fields the empire was used as a source of inspiration, and artists increasingly depicted imperial subjects. Fashionable clothes adopted styles from the colonies, notably Indian and Chinese forms. Food from the empire, such as mulligatawny soup, kedgeree and curries grew in popularity. The English language adopted words such as bazaar, bungalow, cushy, dinghy, guru, thug and veranda from India. Writers such as Wilkie Collins (1824–89) were inspired by the empire and wove its cultures into their books. Collins' *The Moonstone* (1868) presented a sentimental and sympathetic view of Hindus and humanized the people who had been demonized in the wake of the Indian Mutiny of 1857. Collins' heroes and heroines crossed racial boundaries that were often sternly maintained by Victorians.

Architecture also began to feature empire as a theme. Between 1815 and 1822 John Nash (1752–1835) had designed Brighton Pavilion for George IV in ornate Indian style and with exotic Mughal and Chinese interiors. London also developed as an imperial as well as a national capital. When the Palace of Westminster burnt down in 1834 it was rebuilt, following a design competition, in grand Gothic style befitting an imperial parliament; Indian architecture strongly influenced other buildings in Britain. In 1851 half a billion bricks each year were being made in London brickyards within a 5-mile radius of London Bridge. Many were used in permanent structures that celebrated national and imperial identity. Marble Arch, for example, which was moved from outside Buckingham Palace to its present location in 1851 (having been originally built in 1828), contained images of *Naval Warrior with Justice* and *Peace and Plenty* by E.H. Baily.

The zenith of Victorian imperial architecture was the India and Foreign Office. In 1858 George Gilbert Scott (1811–78) was appointed to design a new India Office building, but Lord Palmerston disliked his Gothic design and insisted on a Palladian style instead, which was completed in 1867. The centrepiece of the India Office was the Durbar Court, three storeys of elaborate Indian-inspired architecture decorated with busts of great figures in Anglo-Indian history and images of Indian provinces and cities. In 1858 the art critic John Ruskin compared the artistic and architectural vitality of India with that of Scotland, claiming that Indians were a 'race rejoicing in art, and eminently and universally endowed with the gift of it'. From the 1840s few public buildings, whether prisons, post offices, palaces or parliament lacked some echo of empire in their design. Bungalow was not just a word transplanted from India, it was also a style, like that of the neo-colonial villa. In return, the British built in European style in India. St Andrew's Church and St George's Cathedral in Madras and St James' Church in Delhi look as if they could have been transplanted from Britain. In this way colony and colonizers were brought closer together in a shared visual experience of empire.

The empire was, however, changing during the early nineteenth century. Britain had learned the lessons of the crisis of the 1770s in America and did not seek to shackle its emigrant colonies to Westminster in the way ministers had tried to with America. In 1839 the Durham Report proposed to unify and grant self-government to the two provinces of Upper and Lower Canada, as way of reducing political unrest there. The principle that a 'dominion' (though the word was not used until some time later) such as Canada could rule itself, without control from Westminster, was an important precedent for the development of the empire. By the end of the century, Australia and New Zealand had also obtained self-government.

The Reassurance of Culture

The mid-Victorian period saw the growth of a number of great national cultural institutions. The eighteenth-century private collections of connoisseurs gave way to public museums and galleries, inspired by those in France – where the aristocratic collections had been broken up during the Revolution. In Britain at the turn of the nineteenth century the British Museum was open to the public, as was the Ashmolean Museum in Oxford, but in practice only small numbers of anti-quarians and scholars used them. There were some small museums that relied on sensational items such as shrunken heads to attract members of the public. The best known of these was the London Missionary Society museum, which displayed items brought back from missions to far-flung places. Even these museums had low attendance.

What changed all this was the display of the Elgin Marbles in 1817. The exhibition, at the British Museum, of marbles from the Parthenon in Athens bought by Lord Elgin (1766–1841) from the Turkish Empire, attracted huge numbers of the public. Over 1,000 people attended on the first day, and the whole exhibition was seen by more visitors than the total number the museum had received since it opened in 1759.

In 1838 the National Gallery was opened in Trafalgar Square; it had been in existence since 1824 and had started with just thirty-eight pictures. It quickly became an important cultural experience for Londoners, and the elite were surprised by the quiet and respectful behaviour of the people who visited the gallery. Above all, the National Gallery promoted an interest in British art, and began a period in which Constable, Turner and other British artists became more popular than continental artists. The other principal artistic institution, the Royal Academy of Arts, chartered in 1768, held summer exhibitions that were so popular that it had moved to new premises in the Strand in 1780.

The proceeds from the Great Exhibition were used to establish a museum that would treat industrial and manufactured materials as 'art'. In time this became the Victoria and Albert Museum, a radically different museum that presented collections not by chronological period but by their manufacture or design: ceramic, metalwork, glass, jewellery, textiles, furniture, and so on. It also began the practice of selling postcards or replicas of some objects so that people could buy souvenirs of the items they had seen. Most radically, the museum opened in the evenings, so that working people could visit it.

The cultural confidence of Britain was also seen in the development of a powerful literary culture. The religious census of 1851 showed that of a population of 11.5 million, perhaps 6 or 7 million could read. Reading became a voracious passion for the British people – some of the figures for the appetite of the reading public are astonishing. The publishing sensation of the mid-nineteenth century was *Uncle Tom's Cabin*, an anti-slavery novel by Harriet Beecher Stowe (1811–96), published in 1852. Stowe claimed that she did not write the novel, it had been dictated to her by God. In October 1852 in two weeks it was published in ten different editions and Routledge was selling 10,000 copies a day. Before long, eighteen publishers were issuing the book and by the end of the year 150,000 copies had been sold. Total sales in Britain and the colonies reached about 1,500,000 copies. *Uncle Tom's Cabin* may have been exceptional, but the reading public appreciated a wide range of literary forms – small wonder that in 1852 the *Edinburgh Review* claimed that the demand for books had increased ten-fold in seventy years.

Cheaper publications were also popular. Charles Dickens' *Bleak House*, published in serial form in shilling editions in 1852–3, sold 40,000 copies. Weekly or monthly publications such as the *Penny Magazine* reached sales of 200,000 in the 1830s. Popular reading was supported by an Act, known as Ewart's Act, that permitted local corporations to levy a small tax for public libraries, and Manchester was the first city to establish a free library.

The success of the book trade led to attempts to establish a cartel, preventing books from being sold below the publishers' prices and threatening to boycott shops which sold them below the set price. The novelist Wilkie Collins claimed that there were four sorts of readers: those who sought religious books, those seeking information, those seeking amusement (who were especially catered for by the new W.H. Smith (1792–1865) bookstands at railway stations) and newspaper readers. In 1851, when a committee of the House of Commons investigated the tax on newspapers, it was clear that wholesale newsagents were a key factor in the success of the newspaper market, supplying local newsagents with not only newspapers but also with mass-circulation periodicals. In Manchester one wholesale newsagent sold 3,400 sensational 'penny dreadfuls' (often full of crime stories), but even penny editions of Shakespeare's plays sold 150 a week to Mancunians.

Besides novels and poetry, an important publication in the mid-Victorian period was Thomas Babbington Macaulay's *History of England*, first published in 1848. Macaulay was an MP, colonial administrator and author who claimed that British history was a story of progress and advance leading to the sunlit upland of the Victorian age. His *History of England* was hugely successful: 3,000 copies of the first two volumes were sold in two weeks, and 13,000 in a few months; the following volumes doubled these sales (2,400 copies alone were bought for Mudie's library to lend out). Macaulay sold more than 140,000 copies of the complete four volumes in twenty-five years. His view of history was one that endorsed the supreme self-confidence of the

Victorian age. He wrote: 'the history of our country during the last hundred and sixty years is eminently the history of physical, of moral, and of intellectual improvement'. The Glorious Revolution of 1688, for example, was treated as the foundation of the modern State with an almost democratic motivation. Industrialization had made Britain rich, but also the 'most highly civilised' nation on earth. Writing of the history leading up to the Victorian era, Macaulay argued:

> While revolutions have taken place all around us, our government has never once been subverted by violence. During more than a hundred years there has been in our island no tumult of sufficient importance to be called an insurrection; nor has the law been once borne down either by public fury or by regal tyranny: public credit has been held credit: the administration of justice has been pure: even in times which might by Englishmen be justly called evil times, we have enjoyed what almost every other nation in the world would have considered as an ample measure of civil and religious freedom ... Under the benignant influence of peace and liberty, science has flourished, and has been applied to practical purposes on a scale never before known.

Britain, claimed Macaulay, had 'no parallel' in history. How could Victorians not be confident and proud of this account of the past and optimistic for the future? His work was enormously popular among ordinary people: in May 1849 Macaulay received a letter of thanks from the working men of Dukinfield, near Manchester, for the book. They had spent their Wednesday evenings having the book read aloud to them. The power of Macaulay's view of Britain's history was such that two years after the publication of the complete four-volume set he was granted a peerage and, when he died in 1859, he was granted a funeral in Poets' Corner in Westminster Abbey.

The optimism and self-confidence of Macaulay's work was echoed in much of the other literature of the period. Alfred, Lord Tennyson (1809–92), poet laureate from 1850, was similarly fashionable and admired. Tennyson's great poem *In Memoriam A.H.H.* (1850) – a testimonial to a friend, which Queen Victoria thought one of the greatest English poems and which foreshadowed ideas of evolution – sold 60,000 copies. It exuded confidence, as did his patriotic poems *The Charge of the Light Brigade* (1854) and *Idylls of the King* (1859).

The Great Exhibition of 1851

The peak of mid-Victorian confidence was the Great Exhibition of 1851. It had been organized as a self-financing exhibition by Prince Albert and members of the RSA. It aimed to be a showcase for British industrial technology and design. It was also a response to the French Industrial Exposition of 1844 and the 1849 exposition in Birmingham. The government had been persuaded to support the exhibition by a royal commission.

The exhibition was held in a special building, nicknamed 'the Crystal Palace', which was designed by Joseph Paxton (1803–65), the Duke of Devonshire's head gardener at Chatsworth House, Derbyshire – who had previously designed greenhouses there – and constructed by Brunel. It was 1,848 feet (563 m) long and 454 feet (138 m) wide, and was designed and built in just nine months. The frame of the Crystal Palace was constructed from cast iron and glass, most of which had been made in Birmingham. Many of the builders were former railway navvies who were skilled in working with wrought iron.

The palace was enormously popular with the public and with Queen Victoria, who opened the exhibition on 1 May 1851, and visited it three times. After three weeks of exclusive viewing, the exhibition was thrown open to members of the public who could afford the 1-shilling entry fee. In all, 6 million people, a third of the population of Britain at the time, visited the exhibition. Fortunately it included one of the first public lavatories in the country, which could be used for a penny. Thomas Cook alone brought 165,000 visitors to it on his excursion trains from the Midlands. To direct visitors, signs were used, which became widely adopted as the model for street signs. Some people feared that the sheer volume of visitors might be dangerous, but 200 policemen were organized to patrol the exhibition. Radicals, including Karl Marx, regarded the exhibition as an example of capitalist focus on consumption and commodities; snobs regarded it as a cathedral of vulgar utilitarianism.

The 13,000 exhibits were drawn from all over the world. Size seemed to awe the public: there were huge blocks of coal and the largest steam engines and steam hammers in the world. There were also miniatures, including a scale model of Liverpool docks containing over 1,000 tiny ships and craft. Ingenuity was to the fore. New inventions such as sewing machines, ice makers, cigarette-rolling machines, a vote-counting machine and cameras were shown to the public. There were also displays of new consumer goods such as toothpaste and bars of soap; brochures enabled visitors to buy items they had seen. Among the visitors to the exhibition was William Whiteley, who owned a shop in Yorkshire. In the 1860s he moved his shop to London and, basing it on the exhibition, opened London's first department store.

The exhibition also brought empire into people's minds more clearly. The Crystal Palace included an Indian Court that displayed many products, principally textiles and metal goods from Britain's Indian possession. It also displayed the images of empire: elephants, a howdah and jewels that were the presents of Indian princes to Queen Victoria. The 6 million people who saw these items marvelled at the supremacy Britain claimed over its colonies.

The Great Exhibition made a profit of £186,000, of which £55,000 had come from Messrs Schweppes for the right to supply refreshments to visitors. The surplus was used to found the Victoria and Albert Museum, the Science Museum and the Natural History Museum in South Kensington.

In 1850 William Thackeray (1811–63) described Britain as 'a Gothic society, with its rank and hierarchies, its cumbrous ceremonies, its glittering and antique paraphernalia'. These were not necessarily criticisms. Mid-Victorian confidence may have been a fantasy built on illusions and myths about Britain and its history, but it was a powerful fantasy. The economic boom of the mid-Victorian period masked the start of a slow industrial decline; wages were rising, but the quality of life for many workers was low; empire clouded the fact that Britain carried little weight in Europe; politics was fiercely divided between Peel and Russell, and would remain so under Gladstone and Disraeli; Parliament was still largely unrepresentative of the majority, and the middle classes were as effective as the aristocracy in excluding others from the professions. None of these seemed to matter to the mid-Victorian man or woman on the Clapham omnibus. For them the sexual prudery of the era, the growth of the numbers of domestic servants and the sentimentality of Victorian painting and poetry promoted a comforting respectability.

'Victorian' might today be associated with hypocrisy, now that we know that Queen Victoria enjoyed a healthy sex life, and many a respectable Victorian gentleman indulged himself with the large numbers of prostitutes in towns. It was estimated that in 1850 there were 80,000 prostitutes in London – including housemaids, servants and other women who 'dabbled' in it. But to contemporaries such matters were outshone by values such as strength, certainty, progress and a degree of liberalism that were sources of reassurance and confidence. At the core of Victorian society was a sense that Britain was both benevolent and destined for global dominance. To a society that had not abandoned faith, there seemed to be some providential design to such supreme economic, technological and imperial dominance. It was a world view that was shared by the aristocrats, the bourgeois and the poor.

SELECT BIBLIOGRAPHY

The following section suggests some further reading. However, for the period as a whole there are some books that will complement this work. Such a list is not intended to be comprehensive; in fact it is quite the opposite: a selection of books and articles that I think are stimulating. For an excellent selection of facts and figures about the eighteenth century, see J. Gregory and J. Stevenson (eds), *The Longman Companion to Britain in the Eighteenth Century*, London, 1999. Easily the best work on the eighteenth century is Jeremy Black's *Eighteenth-Century Britain*, 2nd edn, Basingstoke, 2009. A thoroughly stimulating and important work is J.C.D. Clark, *English Society 1660–1832*, 2nd edn, Cambridge, 2000.

Allen, R.C., *Enclosure and the Yeoman: The Agricultural Development of the South Midlands, 1450–1850*, Oxford, 1992.

Arnold, A.J. and S.M. McCartney, *George Hudson: The Rise and Fall of the Railway King*, London, 2004.

Ashton, J., *Chap-Books of the Eighteenth Century*, London, 1969.

Bennett, A., *Shops, Shambles and Street Market: Retailing in Georgian Hull, 1770–1810*, Hull, 2005.

Black, J., *A New History of Wales*, Stroud, 2000.

— *The English Press, 1621–1861*, Stroud, 2001

— *Walpole in Power*, Stroud, 2001.

— *Europe and the Wider World, 1650–1830*, London, 2002.

— *The Slave Trade*, London, 2007.

Bradley, J.E., *Popular Politics and the American Revolution in England: Petitions, the Crown, and Public Opinion*, Macon, GA, 1986.

Burchardt, J., *The Allotment Movement in England 1793–1873*, London, 2002.

Cash, A., *John Wilkes: The Scandalous Father of Civil Liberty*, New Haven, CT, and London, 2006.

Colley, L., *Britons*, New Haven, CT, 1992.

Davies, A., *The Gangs of Manchester: The Story of the Scuttlers, Britain's First Youth Cult*, Preston, 2008.

Gerhould, D., 'The Growth of the London Carrying Trade 1681–1838', *Economic History Review*, 41 (1988).

Gibson, W., *Church, State and Society, 1760–1850*, London, 1994.

— *Religion and Society in England and Wales, 1689–1800*, London, 1998.

— *The Church of England, 1688–1832: Unity and Accord*, London, 2001.

Gregory, J., *Restoration, Reformation and Reform, 1660–1828: Archbishops of Canterbury and the Diocese*, Oxford, 2000.

Hair, P., *Before the Bawdy Court*, London, 1972.

Harding, V., *The Dead and the Living in Paris and London, 1500–1670*, Cambridge, 2002.

Harris, T., *Restoration: Charles II and his Kingdoms*, London, 2006.

— *Revolution: The Great Crisis of the British Monarchy, 1685–1720*, London, 2006.

Hay, D., P. Linebaugh, J.G. Rule, E.P. Thompson and C. Winslow, *Albion's Fatal Tree: Crime and Society in Eighteenth-Century England*, London, 1975.

Henderson, A., *Disorderly Women in Eighteenth-Century London: Prostitution and the Metropolis, 1730–1830*, London, 1999.

Himmelfarb, G., *The Roads to Modernity: the British, French and American Enlightenments*, New York, 2005.

Hitchcock, T., *English Sexualities, 1700–1800*, Basingstoke, 1997.

Holderness, B.A., *Pre-Industrial England, Economy and Society from 1500 to 1800*, London, 1976.

Jackson, C., *Restoration Scotland, 1660–1690: Royalist Politics, Religion and Ideas*, Woodbridge, 2003.

Jacob, W.M., *The Clerical Profession in the Long Eighteenth Century, 1680–1840*, Oxford, 2007.

Landes, David S., *The Unbound Prometheus: Technological Change and Industrial Development in Western Europe from 1750 to the Present*, Cambridge, 1969.

Langford, P., *A Polite and Commercial People: England 1727–1783*, Oxford, 1989.

Marshall, P., *The First Industrial Nation: An Economic History of Britain, 1700–1914*, London, 1969.

Mavor, E., *The Ladies of Llangollen*, London, 1974.

Miles, D., *The Tribes of Britain*, London, 2006.

Morrah, P., *1660 the Year of Restoration*, London, 1960.

Mui, Hoh-cheung and Lorna H. Mui, *Shops and Shopping in Eighteenth Century England*, London, 1989.

Neeson, J.M., *Common Right, Enclosure and Social Change in England, 1700–1820*, Cambridge, 1996.

The Old Bailey proceedings online: www.hrionline.ac.uk/oldbailey/

Overton, M., *Agricultural Revolution in England: The Transformation of the Agrarian Economy, 1500–1850*, London, 1996.

—, 'Re-Establishing the English Agricultural Revolution', *Agricultural History Review*, 43 (1996).

Owen, D.M. (ed.), *The Minute-Books of the Spalding Gentleman's Society 1712–1755*, Lincon Record Society, vol. 73, 1981.

Pearce, E., *Reform! The Fight for the 1832 Reform Act*, London, 2003.

Picard, L., *Restoration London*, London, 2006.

Porter, R. and M. M. Roberts (eds), *Pleasure in the Eighteenth Century*, London, 1996.

Presto, W., *Albion Ascendant 1660–1815*, Oxford, 2001.

Priestley, U. and A. Fenner, *Shops and Shopkeeping in Norwich 1660–1730*, Norwich, 1985.

Richardson, B., *Longitude and Empire: How Captain Cook's Voyages Changed the World*, Vancouver, 2006.

Richardson, D., S. Schwartz and A. Tibbles (eds), *Liverpool and Transatlantic Slavery*, Liverpool, 2007.

Robb, P., *A History of India*, Basingstoke, 2002.

Rogers, N., *Crowds, Culture and Politics in Georgian Britain*, Oxford, 1998.

Sher, R.B., *The Enlightenment and the Book: Scottish Authors and Their Publishers in Eighteenth Century Britain, Ireland and America*, Chicago, 2007.

Sloan, K. (ed.), *Enlightenment: Discovering the World in the Eighteenth Century*, Washington, DC, 2003.

Smith, E.A., *Reform or Revolution? A Diary of Reform in England, 1830–2*, Stroud, 1992.

Smith, M., *Religion in Industrial Society: Oldham and Saddleworth, 1740–1865*, Oxford, 1994

Smyth, J., *The Making of the United Kingdom, 1660–1800*, London, 2001.

Snape, M., *The Church of England in Industrialising Society: The Lancashire Parish of Whalley in the Eighteenth Century*, Woodbridge, 2003.

Spurr, J., *The Post-Reformation, 1603–1714*, London, 2006.

Strong, R., *Coronation*, London, 2005.

Taylor, G., *The Problem of Poverty*, London, 1969.

Thirsk, J. (ed.), *The Agrarian History of England and Wales, V, 1640–1750*, Cambridge, 1985.

Thompson, E.P., *Whigs and Hunters: The Origins of the Black Act*, New York, 1975.

Uglow, J., *Hogarth*, London, 1998.

Vickery, A., 'Women and the World of Goods: A Lancashire Consumer and her Possessions, 1751–81', in J. Brewer and R. Porter (eds), *Consumption and the World of Goods*, London, 1993.

Wahrman, D., *The Making of the Modern Self: Identity and Culture in Eighteenth Century England*, New Haven, CT, and London, 2006.

Warham, D., *Imagining the Middle Class: The Political Representation of Class in Britain, c. 1780–1840*, Cambridge, 1995.

Wicks, E., *The Evolution of a Constitution: Eight Key Moments in British Constitutional History*, Oxford, 2006.

Wrigley, E.A. and R.S. Schofield, *The Population History of England, 1541–1871: A Reconstruction*, Cambridge, 1989.

Yates, N., *Eighteenth-Century Britain: Religion and Society*, London, 2007.

INDEX